The Theatre of Socìetas Raffaello Sanzio

'It burns you and you don't want to burn, but you are burned anyway, it burns you inside. A drama is in operation, the drama of the spectator.'

The Theatre of Socìetas Raffaello Sanzio chronicles four years in the life of an extraordinary Italian theatre company whose work is widely recognised as some of the most exciting theatre currently being made in Europe.

'Among the most conceptually interesting, visually compelling and provocative theatres working today.'

Ted Shank, *University of California, San Diego*

In the first English-language book to document their work, company founders, Claudia Castellucci, Romeo Castellucci and Chiara Guidi, discuss their approach to theatre making with Joe Kelleher and Nicholas Ridout.

At the centre of the book is a detailed exploration of the company's eleven-episode cycle of tragic theatre, *Tragedia Endogonidia* (2002–4), including

- production notes and extensive correspondence giving insights into the creative process;
- essays by and conversations with company members alongside critical responses by their two co-authors;
- seventy-two photographs of the company's work.

This is a significant collection of theoretical and practical reflections on the subject of theatre in the twenty-first century and an indispensable written and visual document of the company's work.

'an exemplary study wrought from within Europe's most audacious theatre company. Lucidly rendered, intellectually felt and passionately argued, the imperative "required reading" barely does it justice.'

Alan Read, *Professor of Theatre, King's College London*

Claudia Castellucci, **Romeo Castellucci** and **Chiara Guidi** are founding members of Socìetas Raffaello Sanzio. **Joe Kelleher** teaches in the School of Arts at Roehampton University, London. **Nicholas Ridout** teaches in the Department of Drama at Queen Mary, University of London. Joe and Nicholas are joint editors of *Contemporary Theatres in Europe* (2006).

The Theatre of Socìetas Raffaello Sanzio

CLAUDIA CASTELLUCCI, ROMEO CASTELLUCCI,
CHIARA GUIDI, JOE KELLEHER AND NICHOLAS RIDOUT

PHOTOGRAPHS BY LUCA DEL PIA

LONDON AND NEW YORK

First published 2007
by Routledge
2 Park Square, Milton Park, Abingdon, Oxon OX14 4RN

Simultaneously published in the USA and Canada
by Routledge
270 Madison Ave, New York, NY 10016

Routledge is an imprint of the Taylor & Francis Group, an informa business

Reprinted 2009

© 2007 Claudia Castellucci, Romeo Castellucci, Chiara Guidi, Joe Kelleher and Nicholas Ridout

Typeset and designed in Stone Sans by
Keystroke, 28 High Street, Tettenhall, Wolverhampton

Printed and bound in Great Britain by
The Cromwell Press Group, Trowbridge, Wiltshire

All rights reserved. No part of this book may be reprinted or reproduced or utilised in any form or by any electronic, mechanical, or other means, now known or hereafter invented, including photocopying and recording, or in any information storage or retrieval system, without permission in writing from the publishers.

British Library Cataloguing in Publication Data
A catalogue record for this book is available from the British Library

Library of Congress Cataloging in Publication Data

    The theatre of Socìetas Raffaello Sanzio / Claudia Castellucci . . . [et al.].
       p. cm.
    Includes bibliographical references and index.
    1. Societas Raffaello Sanzio (Theatrical company) 2. Theater–Italy–
    Cesena–History–20th century. I. Castellucci, Claudia, 1958–
    PN2686.C46T54 2007
    792.0945′48–dc22
                                                                      2007013952

ISBN10: 0–415–35430–7 (hbk)
ISBN10: 0–415–35431–5 (pbk)
ISBN10: 0–203–00097–8 (ebk)

ISBN13: 978–0–415–35430–1 (hbk)
ISBN13: 978–0–415–35431–8 (pbk)
ISBN13: 978–0–203–00097–7 (ebk)

Contents

Acknowledgements ix

Introduction: the spectators and the archive
(Joe Kelleher and Nicholas Ridout) 1

PART ONE
Makers and spectators, *Tragedia Endogonidia* 2002-4 **23**

Laboratory, 2001 25
Letters to Scott Gibbons (Chiara Guidi) 25
Making space (Claudia Castellucci) 27
System, functions and workings for a tragedy of gold (Romeo Castellucci) 30
On the Earth's stage (Romeo Castellucci) 32

C.#01, Cesena 34
Letters to Scott 36
An organism on the run (Joe Kelleher) 39

A.#02, Avignon	46
A letter about the goat that gave its name to tragedy (Romeo Castellucci)	47
First grammatical exercise with twenty amino acids (Chiara Guidi)	48
Letter to Scott	53
From the final script of *A.#02*	53
Night, writing, gesture (Joe Kelleher)	57
The form of a blot (Claudia Castellucci)	61
B.#03, Berlin	71
Letters to Scott	72
From the final script of *B.#03*	75
A play of grief (Joe Kelleher)	76
From the final script of *B.#03*	81
On being there (in the beginning) (Nicholas Ridout)	84
On not being there (Berlin) (Nicholas Ridout)	87
BR.#04, Brussels	90
Letter to Scott	92
Storytime (Joe Kelleher)	95
Out in the open (Nicholas Ridout)	103
BN.#05, Bergen	112
Fluid earth	112
P.#06, Paris and R.#07, Rome	118
Letters to Scott and Marco	119
Modern acting (Nicholas Ridout)	124
Somebody, anybody (Joe Kelleher)	127
Letter to Scott	132
From the final script of *R.#07*	132
Monkey business (Nicholas Ridout)	135
From a conversation about dramaturgy	137
The Italian comedy (Joe Kelleher)	139
S.#08, Strasbourg	148
Letters to Scott	149
Earth and glass (Joe Kelleher and Nicholas Ridout)	150
A conversation about dramaturgy, contd.	156

L.#09, London	159
A conversation about dramaturgy, contd.	159
From the final script of *L.#09*	161
On the idea of *crescita* (Romeo Castellucci)	161
Francesca and the machines: on *Crescita XIV Prato* (Joe Kelleher)	164
From the final script of *L.#09*	166
A theatre dream (Joe Kelleher)	169
M.#10, Marseille	171
From Marseille sketch	171
Letter to Lavinia	172
Asking for it (Nicholas Ridout)	173
From the final script of *M.#10*	177
Beware what you wish for (Nicholas Ridout)	178
The picture, the place, the drama, us (Claudia Castellucci)	181
To live episodically (Claudia Castellucci)	182
C.#11, Cesena	187
From the technical script for *C.#11*	188
On make-believe (Nicholas Ridout)	188
From the final script of *C.#11*	190
The enchantment (Joe Kelleher)	192

PART TWO
Conversations **201**

'The theatre is not our home': a conversation about space, stage and audience	203
A conversation about dramaturgy, contd.	213
A conversation about pretence and illusion	220
A conversation about composition	227
A conversation about rehearsal	235
A conversation about gesture	244
A conversation about the future	252

PART THREE
Disjecta Membra   **261**

    Entries from a notebook of Romeo Castellucci   263

    Theatography   270
    Bibliography   272

Acknowledgements

Joe and Nick's thanks are due to everyone at the Comandini in Cesena, in particular Gilda Biasini and Cosetta Nicolini, who have made everything possible; to Talia Rodgers and Minh Ha Duong at Routledge, who have supported this project with care and imagination from the get-go; to the ever-resourceful Alan Read, who first brought us together with the Castelluccis at the day-long symposium 'Voice, Ruin, Play' in 2001; to Lucy Neal and Rose Fenton at the London International Festival of Theatre, who brought Socìetas Raffaello Sanzio to London in the first place; to our friends in Italy who helped with transcriptions when help was sorely needed, namely Lucia Amara, Tihana Maravić and Enrico Pitozzi; to our fellow spectators at the *Tragedia* (we might mention Céline Astrié, Rebecca Groves, Sophie Nield, Alan Read again and others, but you know who you are) who shared conversations and insights throughout the journey; to the Arts and Humanities Research Board, for research leave support for Joe; to our colleagues and students at Queen Mary, University of London and Roehampton University, for invaluable provocation and debate, as well to the universities themselves for invaluable research support (including funds); and, above all, to Scott Gibbons and our fellow authors, Chiara, Claudia and Romeo, for their wisdom and generosity of spirit. We have learned a lot and are still learning.

Introduction

The spectators and the archive

JOE KELLEHER AND NICHOLAS RIDOUT

A fall into representation

In an essay that appears later in this book ('Making space', p. 27) Claudia Castellucci asks what the theatrical arts of mime can amount to in a contemporary world that is in thrall to the technologies of spectacle. Theatre-makers, Claudia would remind us, hang out in the worst sort of places; they occupy the same realms of human expression as advertising, television and fashion. Just like these, theatre-makers communicate – and, it may be, seek to persuade – by arranging the appearances of 'surfaces', and any claim on theatre's part of a moral or aesthetic superiority to these other media amounts to little more than the posturings of 'a small maestro with a baton, and there are so many of those'. Rather than wasting time on such claims, she suggests, theatre-makers might acknowledge their complicity and then get on with looking forward, 'into the future', through a form of flight that is not so much a reaction to the present times, nor an attempt to escape from them, but an act of foundation, the foundation of the new. This flight, this foundation, she writes, is one of theatre's most pressing 'political tasks' and involves for the theatre-maker, first and foremost, a thorough examination of theatre's 'own specific language.'

During another text that appears here ('A conversation about dramaturgy', p. 213) the three core members of Socìetas Raffaello Sanzio, Claudia and Romeo Castellucci and Chiara Guidi, discuss the implications of this task. Again, the discussion turns around the possibilities of a specifically theatrical communication in a situation where the mediatised 'spectacle' has become 'the principal vehicle for political consensus', a spectacle whose untruth, so to speak, appears to have 'got the better of' the work that theatre-makers do. There is a suggestion that theatre-makers might deploy a certain exposure of the 'reality of representation', working both with and against the spectacle at the same time, 'moving one way as your horse moves another', using the language while at the same time showing how it is put together. Immediately, though, and insistently at this point of the conversation, there is a refusal of the sort of assumptions that might attach to a 'Brechtian technique' of theatrical self-reflection. Instead, something more disconcerting is proposed, which has to do with the ways that an exposure of the realities of representation might work on the emotions of a spectator. An example is given from their own work, from the Brussels episode (*BR.#04*) of *Tragedia Endogonidia*, where a police beating is acted out, excruciatingly and at length but with the explicit use of fake blood poured onto the stage from a props bottle. The peculiar thing is that even with the exposure of the bottle – the 'reality of the representation' in that sense – 'the scene proceeded', as Romeo says, 'to become very violent all the same and leap up against the reality of the blood'.

Of course, there is more than the visibility of a props bottle at work here. There are, for example, also the gestures of the actor, a certain articulate surface that communicates information to the audience, and also the complex of montage, dramaturgy and rhythm – the arrangement of the elements in the stage space, the amplification of the truncheon, the monotonous 'beat' and drawn-out duration of the scene – whereby the theatre, rather than being undone by the exposure of its devices, appears somehow to be feeding, ravenously, upon its own manifest fictionality. The spectator knows what's going on alright, we know that it is pretend. We understand this language too, however dimly, and somehow that is what really hurts (and, it may be, really excites). Against our better judgement, perhaps, we have fallen into representation. As Chiara puts it,

> my body, my mind has not been able to react to this image with the same cool and lucidity with which I said look, let us open the bottle, let's empty it on the floor. I am sliding, I've fallen into representation, but not by a logical route which was the

logic of opening the bottle. I have crashed emotionally into a representation that has neither narrative nor logical context.

Except one doesn't just fall into representation. Representations are things which are made, constructed, set forth, considered and so on (although something may be 'born' from what is made, constructed . . .). It could be said that the construction of the fall into representation, the making of the thing, along with the articulation of the spaces of thought and feeling through which this fall might be reflected upon, challenged and transformed – even as one falls – is what this book is about. In short, this is a book about theatre-making. It has things to say about composition, about dramaturgy, about scenography and light and sound design, about rehearsal and working with actors and objects and animals and machines, about negotiating different theatrical spaces and how to work with the dimensions and volumes of the space, how to work with the curtain, the audience seating, the texture of the stage floor, how to use the walls and windows that separate (or connect) the theatre and the city outside. It has things to say about how to give a body to ideas, and how to relate that body to a form that might stake its claim to a right to exist – however momentarily – upon the stage. It speaks about the making of theatrical texts, texts that are fashioned, sculpted almost, from the basic raw materials of language: words, phonemes, living speech and dead letters, cries and whispers (human and non-human) and speaks too about fashioning a voice (a human voice, or perhaps a machine) that can give these texts the 'life' they deserve. It is a book about collaboration, history, location, economics, about courage and fear, commitment and uncertainty. It is about the creative act in the theatre, how to conceive that act and follow it through, and how to live in its specific language. It is, in short again, a book about practice, and, as such, it is inevitably a book about theory, if we think of theory as having to do with a way of seeing and taking responsibility for speaking to what one sees, how one sees, in the sort of ways in which one might hope to think through, and take responsibility for, how one lives.

In particular, this is a book about the theory and practice of a group of theatre-makers who have been producing work out of their home base in Cesena in the Romagna region of northern Italy for twenty-five years, work which over that quarter of a century has been seen around the world, from Tokyo to Seoul, in Australia, Mexico and the USA, as well as at leading venues across Europe. To that extent, the book is a gathering of understandings, discoveries and arguments that have accumulated over that time and that feed the company's current and future work. What this book attempts to do, however, is to situate these understandings within the contingencies of the theatre-making process, a process which is made out of collaboration and dispute, out of the friction between ideas and plans and the material *stuff* (living stuff) through which ideas will be put to the test. This is a process which may well – as any professional theatre must – describe an horizon for itself, but which finds its 'destiny', as Claudia puts it in another text ('The picture, the place, the drama, us', p. 181) in the unforeseeable, unimaginable gaze of other people, the spectators: those alien and intimate presences who, at the same time, seem to constitute the fundamental ground of the work from the moment it is conceived, who are its insuperable motivation.

This last point is important, to the extent that throughout these pages it might seem that it is the spectator, not the author or director or actor, who is the first subject of the theatrical realm. Everyone here will have something to say about spectatorship (and not just the two professional spectators, the authors of this introduction, whose responses to the work are scattered throughout the book). As Romeo writes in one of many texts we had, regretfully, to leave out of this volume: 'I believe that today theatrical experience is founded on the intimate experience of each spectator [. . .] contemporary theatre has become an experience of sensitive awareness. Awareness in the sense of an opening, awareness of what opens up.'[1] It is also with a view to this opening up and the situating of a discussion of practice within an immediate and ongoing process that this book focuses primarily on the work that was being made as the volume was being put together: work that has occupied the major part so far of the company's third decade, the three-year sequence of the eleven episodes of *Tragedia Endogonidia*, made for ten European cities in the first years of the twenty-first century (2002–4). The exchange of texts and conversations assembled here follows this work from inception to completion, and then a little further – aiming to imitate really, as far as the medium of a book will allow, the theatre-making process as it attempts to give a necessary existence to what flees before it and seeks out its proper future in that flight.

Forms of life

It remains a question, however, for a book of this sort, especially as this is the first English-language volume on Socìetas Raffaello Sanzio, how to do some sort of justice to twenty-five years of work beyond this focus on the company's most recent projects. You will find in an appendix at the back of this book a selected list of theatre productions, projects, publications and other output. Such lists are usually supplemented by a brief biographical note that would tell us that the company was formed in 1981 by Claudia Castellucci

---

1 Romeo Castellucci, 'Il sipario si alzerà su un incendio', *Art'O*, 18, autumn 2005, pp. 4–6.

(born 1958), Romeo Castellucci (19   ) (1960) and, as the biographical note in the 2001 collection of texts and dramaturgies in Italian *Epopea della polvere* (*Epic of Dust*) has it, 'other young companions who share an interest in theatre and the plastic arts', including for the first decade Chiara's brother Paolo Guidi. The *Epopea* note continues:

> The conception of theatrical art as the sum of all the arts and as a single rhythm of vision and sound, has brought all of them to occupy themselves deeply and in detail with every aspect of the mise-en-scène, beyond their various specific jobs. Romeo takes care of the direction, the staging, the lights, the sound, the costumes and the graphic design of the books. Chiara prepares the voice and speech, and writes musical scores; she has also created an experimental theatre school for infants. Claudia at times takes care of movement and writes some of the dramatic text; she has also founded a school for young people interested in the problem of representation. Since 1992 the Socìetas Raffaello Sanzio have been working in Cesena, at the Theatre Comandini, an old professional school for lathe-turners in iron.[2]

Such lists and notes, not least in their transferability from book to book, and from book to press release to website to theatre programme and so on, have something of the 'sufficient' about them. As information, this suffices, although it is also a little terse: terse, perhaps, in relation to the biographical *as such*, which is never at any level the point of the work, except as a sort of minimal frame upon which the work itself – or rather the remains of the work, the titles, the credits, the dates and places – can be marked up as a chronicle of what was made and done, on those occasions, in the company of those people. Not that the chronicles themselves are terse. The company's previous books – in particular the Italian-language *Il teatro della Socìetas Raffaello Sanzio: dal teatro iconoclasta alla super-icon* (*The Theatre of Socìetas Raffaello Sanzio: From the Iconoclastic Theatre to the Super-Icon*) which documents the work from 1986 to 1990 with dramatic scripts, commentaries and theoretical texts; *Epopea della polvere*, which does the same job for the work from 1992 to 1999; and *Epitaph*, a documentation in colour photography of this entire period – are fulsome and, in the case of *Epitaph*, lush. Add to these a series of carefully designed special publications in a range of formats that accompanied the major touring shows by which the company's international reputation was made, as well as other forms of documentation such as Cristiano Carloni and Stefano Franceschetti's

---

2   Claudia and Romeo Castellucci, Chiara Guidi, *Epopea della polvere: Il teatro della Societas Raffaello Sanzio 1992–1999*, Milan: Ubulibri, 2001, p. 319.

sophisticated 'video memory' of the *Tragedia Endogonidia* sequence, and it is clear that the company have not been reticent in gathering the remains of their work and making these available for retrospective reflection. Even so, there is something in the titles of those books, *Epic of Dust, Epitaph*, or in the title of a French collection of theoretical texts by Claudia and Romeo, *Les Pèlerins de la matière* (*The Pilgrims of Material*), which might suggest an equivocal relation to the monumentality of such documentation. At least, the present writer has never been sure to what extent those titles record the (epic) labours of the theatre-makers and to what extent they speak, as it were in a voice of ash, to the reader or scholar who encounters the remains of those labours as funerary images, as tracks in the sand, as so many mounds of dust. If it's a case of a theatre biography (though be it a biography of the life of the work) that might do justice to twenty-five years of theatre-making, such a biography might also seek to do justice to this same equivocation.

Something of the equivocation – which, again, has nothing to do with reticence: it's more like a sort of vivid certainty, a sort of arrogant obedience to the facts – comes out in a comment by one of the company in a 1986 interview, before there were any books to speak of:

> The idea of a lasting existence is part of our work . . . just as marble stands the test of time over the years, we create a show which can defend itself against any contingency, constructed like something already dead which can resist over the years, which overcomes Time, cancels it . . . Each time, it's like manufacturing a corpse . . .[3]

The comment suggests too that the afterlife of the work, figured here as a larval, deathly quality, is already to be built in, as it were, to the life of the work. But then to call it a life, and to conceive this life as a life that remains, is also to conceive a mutation, beyond the will or craft of the maker. We spoke earlier of a specific theatre 'language'. In a recent commentary upon Ovid's tale of the nymph Io, who gets transformed into a cow and who can only identify herself to her astonished father by printing out the two letters of her name with a hoof in the sand, philosopher Daniel Heller-Roazen remarks that what remains of the nymph, i.e., a minimal alphabet, the letters of her name, functioning (barely) as language, 'first emerges, so to speak, in the process of remaining, and it

---

3 Frederico Tiezzi, 'Società Raffaello Sanzio: L'anima mentale e l'anima passionale' ('The Mental Soul and the Passionate Soul'), *Westuff: Quarterly Magazine of Art, Fashion and Music*, **5**, September–November 1986, p. 69. The company's name had not yet been changed to Socìetas.

remains, for this reason, utterly unlike that to which it bears witness'. He goes on to suggest that if a language can persist in the eventual absence of its speakers, it is 'because it has always already changed itself by means of them, being by nature "more capable of mutation" than those who would use it. [. . .] It lasts, but only as another.'[4] The biographical – or here, autobiographical – 'io' (which also happens to be the Italian word for 'I') is, whether or not one credits the biographical as worthy of attention or seeks it solely in the 'body of work', an epitaph for one who is no more, who is survived by the remains of language, an alien speech, that has 'always already changed'.

Maybe it had to do with the difficulty of trying to read texts in a foreign language that I was barely familiar with one very hot summer two years ago, working through the company's archive in the roof of the Teatro Comandini; or maybe it was the unsettling feeling attached to going through the documentation of work that was made many years before I first encountered Socìetas Raffaello Sanzio and found myself struck, for good, by the livid rhetoricality of their deployment of the languages of theatre (for both of the present authors, the first encounter was *Giulio Cesare* in London in 1999), but the documents of the 1980s work that I was leafing through seemed to have something of that peculiar quality about them that Heller-Roazen suggests attaches to all speech, 'of letters traced in the sand by the hoof of the nymph who no longer was'. Something remains, perhaps, of the dead letter in even the most vivid speech. I'm reminded now of a gag in an early Situationist text that shows a photograph of graffiti on a wall in a Paris street in 1968, and then captions the image, as if this were some sort of ethnographic relic: 'remnant of a form of life that tried to assert itself in these parts'. None of our marks will be immune to this comment.

Here, then, is one graffito from the Comandini archive (which even so does register a certain form of life), from a theatre critic in 1984 describing one of the early *Oratorios*, a series of text-based pieces inspired by the techniques of classical oratory, through which the company sought to address aspects of their immediate historical and political context. The review comments upon the weave of theorisation and physicality in the work, and goes on:

> connected to this is the ample space granted in *Oratoria no. 2* to the word, which will be brought into play not as an actor might speak it, but rather as someone at a political meeting might say it, proclaimed, rhythmically beaten out, recited, hurled into the microphone: at one and the same time a clear indication of a phonemic and gestural route or series, and also logorrhoea: a sort of 'free verse' fabulation of

---

4 Daniel Heller-Roazen, *Echolalias: On the Forgetting of Language*, New York: Zone Books, 2005, pp. 126–7.

contents and 'tales' which seems to be a transparent, vitreous, impassive parodying of the traditional sales pitch or the bullying, authoritarian instructor, like 'admonishments' fallen from on high. The fixed installation is dominated by a background on which stands out a large ear of wheat and in front of which is situated a long table with the word 'ozone' on it, around which is assembled the presidency of some sort of late-libertarian and neo-ecological clique.[5]

And here is another from the same year:

Primitives, but true primitives (not for fashion's sake), the Raffaello Sanzios bring onto the stage – discharging them like volleys of cultural garbage – the delirious gestures and theories of a 'savage thought'. Their theatre is less about dramatic construction and more about provoking sensuous disturbance. Everything is coarse (unrefined, without any formal elegance) on their stage; the materials: bins, mud, crude sculptures made out of foam rubber, big plastic sheets covered with graffiti like the walls of the South Bronx, and then the movements of their bodies: schizoid and disarticulated, like psychotics devastated by continual electric shocks.[6]

Here are the company themselves, again around the same time, in a group interview-cum-statement, ever so young, but already putting on and casting off whatever names and labels they have been given, staking a claim, devouring what comes to hand and turning it into their own invention, carving their names on the wall:

Firstly we threw out some ideas which other people gathered up under the term *Savage*. [. . .] You could see in the work a *psychedelic iconography*, which was a new sense of the *comic*. [. . .] We've also been defined as *neo-expressionists*. This is true in terms of our total adhesion to certain typical manifestations [. . .]. I believe that we have conquered the world of *clarity* [. . .]. They've also called us *neo-mannerist* [. . .]. Our use of the particular is not a contradiction of another of our important inventions: the practice of *impersonality*.[7]

As Chiara says in the same text, in another animalistic characterisation of the working process as voracious, self-forgetting, even as it marks out its territory: 'overall the direction

---

5 Marco Palladini, 'Cultura metroplitana e civiltà contadina', *L'Umanità*, 28 February 1984.
6 Carlo Infante, in *Frigidaire*, n.d. (c. 1984).
7 Società Raffaello Sanzio, 'Questioni raffaellesche', *Patalogo 5 & 6* (1983 Theatre Annual), pp. 181–3.

of our work is not a progression. This is because we have the mentality of dogs. The dog eats everything because it assumes that everything is a priori good. Even if a lot gets rejected, the choice is rigorously successive [. . .].' So it is that the work mutates, not so much through a settled process of transformation but more like a series of radical metamorphoses, while the dog, the unevolving dog, remains dog (however transformed in shape), sniffing out what's good, leaving its traces in the dirt.

It seems, though, to be another time and place. The 1980s. The place, Romagna and the surrounding regions, is still a location for significant and diverse reinventions (rediscoveries) of the language of theatre, even if several of the groups forging this language have been up against it recently with the arts-funding policies of the Berlusconi years (for more on this see Claudia's text, 'To live episodically', written for the programme of the 2004 Santarcangelo Theatre Festival). But then again, where was 'Romagna', in those days, for them and their compatriots? A text written by the company for the 1986 *Patalogo* theatre annual (a sort of New Year's letter from the insistently 'non-aligned' Raffaello Sanzios) gives us some directions. The letter is quoted here pretty much in its entirety:

> Puglia opens to Albania. Ravenna opens to Turkey. In this sense ourselves and Puglia represent the Italy of the East, we make up the Italian part of non-aligned Eastern Europe, together with Yugoslavia, the always heroic and glorious Albania and certain Greek and Turkish fringes [. . .]. The role of international co-ordination is taken care of by Radio Tirana, audible in Cesena at 8pm sharp on 1000 kHz MW. It is thanks to Radio Tirana that we receive more clandestine news that is un-involved with the western war and hear things we would never be able to hear. This is no joke. This news is food for us, upon which we are continually fattened by things that enter the brain by force.
>
> With three hours of navigation, and thanks to the complacency of a few coastguards, we can reach the coast of Yugoslavia, where friends are waiting to discuss politics with us.
>
> At any moment we can get visas to enter Albania (via Yugoslavia), and in Puglia we have a group of friends of the Orthodox religion, with whom we discuss the terrible future that awaits us if together we have been unable to formulate a new calendar that employs a way of reasoning completely detached from tradition.
>
> The Romagnola base is in Ravenna. It is in '. . .' that the International European Congress of the non-aligned takes place. At these meetings there's certainly no talk of trivial things: here the partitioning of the theatre is considered unacceptable, redeemable only if one is able to bear the practical consequences. In this fight, we are the underground. For decades Romagna has supported the nuclear suppositories

which NATO has placed in Rimini pointing at Prague. How is it possible to live here without suffering? Without being cowards? It is only possible in the conspiracy of the non-aligned, be they resistance fighters or Hesychasts;[8] and so you who are reading this and who share the same anti-traditional ideals as us, join us, but don't ask us to give you an address because this is news media. The way here must be other, on pain of death.[9]

They say it was no joke, and we have no reason not to believe them, a point that was made at the time by the last critic we shall cite for the moment, Franco Quadri, someone who has followed and supported the group's work since the earliest days. In a review of the 1986 theatre piece *Santa Sofia: Teatro Khmer*, Quadri writes about the seeming violence of that work: a violence at the level of the text and the action but also a certain violence of thought and imagination, a violence at the level of the representational means, and which seems wrapped up in the ways that Chiara, Claudia, Paolo and Romeo, as actors in the show, don't so much '"represent" their invention in the way performers might, but live it like an acquired reality', like adepts or like practitioners of a religion. Quadri continues:

> Naturally however the true object of all this violence is the theatre, to cancel it out as a language and as an object of fascination. But the great strength of this unusual proposal is really born from the capacity to develop a language and a fascination, advancing through blows to the stomach, deploying a humour that the members of the group don't acknowledge, given the total seriousness with which they are engaged. As for the rest, the truth of their showing themselves on stage, beyond the fictions, is but a consequence and a continuation of how they represent themselves in life.[10]

Quadri's comments of twenty years ago bring us back again to the question with which we started out, of a lived relation to practice and the politics of practice, which amounts to a question of how to live one's relation to the times and places in which one is situated, a theme that Claudia will develop – of course, always with humour, but a humour that is deadly serious – in the essay cited earlier, 'Making space', which opens with the sentence 'I live my craft as a duty'. Thinking from this point back to the 1980s,

---

8 Hesychast: one of a mystical sect of the fourteenth-century Greek church; a quietist.
9 *Patalogo* 7 (1986 Theatre Annual), pp. 236–7.
10 Franco Quadri, 'Pol Pot e l'imperatore', *Panorama*, 29 June 1986.

and in particular to *Santa Sofia*, since this is the work under discussion, I find myself now looking at the double spread of photographs from this show that open the book *Epitaph*. On the one side is an image of Chiara Guidi as Pol Pot; on the other page, Claudia Castellucci in the role of the eighth-century Byzantine iconoclast emperor Leo III the Isaurian, making obeisance before a massive Orthodox icon of the face of Christ that covers the back of the stage. The show, directed by Romeo and based upon a dramatic text by Claudia, fantasised an encounter between these two 'great' iconoclasts, destroyers of images and, in the case of the leader of the Cambodian Khmer Rouge, destroyer of the things, the flesh, the forms of life – ('I hate . . . I hate the power of things. I hate . . . I hate the things of the world')[11] – that give body to the images, and which the images themselves recall. *Santa Sofia* (the title refers to the great church, later a mosque and now a museum, in Istanbul, the former Byzantium), through the transhistorical convolutions of its action and the radical starkness of its staging, would appear to have been rehearsing a complex, seemingly paradoxical argument, whereby the iconoclastic drive *against* the spectacle, *against* the images – and by extension against the theatre – can only be pursued *through* the language of the spectacle. The argument is, then, as a note in the 1992 book has it, pursued to the extent that 'the actors are brought to curse their own presence, living the stage as an horrendous place'; even if at the same time 'from this phase of burning, from this stigmatising experience, the true image is sought out [. . .] the remains of its supporting pillars, the more intimate roots of the image'.[12]

So much for the argument. I have read Claudia's text and Romeo's notes, and I have seen a grainy single-camera video of the show, but I feel I can't speak of these things, beyond attempting to reproduce these texts in a language that approximates (even as it mutates) the language in which they already speak of themselves. I am, though, still drawn to those two photographs. I am, I think, drawn to that which seems to remain in the images, like a stain; or better, something that remains of a form of life that has already withdrawn from the scene, and perhaps been 'transformed utterly', to borrow a phrase from the poet Yeats. You'd think, though, that the Christ icon has not transformed at all. It still appears to stare out of the image, the 'irreal' gaze of the icon an 'opening of a world', as the philosopher Jean-Luc Marion would put it, an 'aim addressed to the spectator' that potentially liberates the visible from the status of spectacle, but an opening 'born from a black hole, which, in the dialogue I look for or flee from, I want to capture or avoid, precisely because its irreal space fascinates me, as the source of the invisible, at

---

11 Claudia Castellucci, *Santa Sofia: Teatro khmer*, in *Il teatro della Societas Raffaello Sanzio*, p. 13.
12 *Il teatro della Societas Raffaello Sanzio*, p. 182.

the centre of the visible'.[13] The appearances of the actors in these images, however, tell a slightly different story. The gaze of Chiara as a young, idealist Pol Pot looks up and out of the image, drawing attention to the way that the gaze of the Christ icon on the facing page is turned, just slightly, in the same direction, up and out of the picture, beyond the representation. There is, after all, nothing here that directly meets our gaze. I'm reminded of a line from a text by Romeo written at the end of the decade, for a symposium that the company convened 'On the Nature of Theatre' at a time when they were completing a series of works based upon the myths of ancient, pre-tragic, pre-theatrical cultures (as far as the Western theatrical tradition goes). Romeo speaks of the 'extremism' of the actor's 'beauty' as having to do with 'a lack of historical substance (that which, mysteriously, is given to be seen, is barely the tail of the animal, ". . .", as it hides itself)'.[14] Maybe, after all, nothing of the animal, nothing of the actor, is transformed. The actor turns and hides, already in flight, 'into the future', into the new, and it is us, the spectators, who find ourselves touched by the imprint that this flight makes upon us, the imprint of an image which we make for ourselves, as we are drawn into a language where thought and feeling are – as it were – brought to life, but with an emotion devoid of pathos.

Enter the spectators

Might it be any different had we been there? Perhaps the imprint left upon the spectators is as fleeting when the performance has touched us live, and in person? Here too the memory reaches out only to glimpse the tail of the fleeing animal moving out of sight. The spectator is already in the archive, reexamining the state of the imprints.

One of the tasks, or rather, duties of this introduction is to offer a kind of biography (for 'the horror of biography' see Romeo Castellucci's *Disjecta Membra*, Part III of this book). Another is to attempt to account for the experience of the work, an experience of spectatorship. The five authors of this book came amongst themselves, and very early, to the conclusion that there was little to be gained – in terms either of pleasure or of interest – from talking about the past, when what interested us all was the dynamics of the present situation, the project in hand, the ideas that animated the work now. The

---

13 Jean-Luc Marion, *The Crossing of the Visible*, trans. James K. A. Smith, Stanford, Calif.: Stanford University Press, 2004, pp. 21–2.
14 Romeo Castellucci, 'Per una riconquista della visione' ('Towards a Reconquest of Vision'), in Socìetas Raffaello Sanzio, *Atti della disputa sulla natura del teatro* (*Proceedings of the Dispute on the Nature of Theatre*), Cesena: Edizioni casa del Bello Estremo, 1989, p. 22.

company's past, therefore, has come to the writers of this introduction only in the various forms of the archive: forms such as the press clipping, the photo, the programme, the interview and the anecdote. We do what we can with this material. As for our second task, for which we, the writers of this introduction, alone among the five, are not disqualified, the task of trying to tell you how it was, for us, is already becoming just as complicated. As we have already revealed, our own experience of the work of Socìetas Raffaello Sanzio began with the company's production of *Giulio Cesare*, seen in June 1999 at the Queen Elizabeth Hall in London, as part of the London International Festival of Theatre. Here, then, from the spectator-archive, is an earlier attempt to account for how it was:

> it felt like an encounter with something absolutely alien, unlike any theatre I had ever witnessed before. The obvious explanation for this might be offered in terms of the real, live horse, the emaciated bodies of the two women playing Brutus and Cassius, the visceral impact of an actor playing Mark Anthony without a larynx, the sheer volume of the wrestler in the role of Cicero, not to mention the extraordinary experience of being shown another person's vocal cords. The overwhelming sense of an encounter with something strange and powerful would be attributed to the impact of all this 'real' stuff. But, as I've already suggested, it wasn't real at all. An image of vocal cords was displayed, not the cords themselves. The horse was caught up in a complex system of representations (involving the skeleton of a horse and a model of a sea-horse), so that its value as real, live horse was subsumed by its position as one of several signs for the idea of 'horse'. The actor without a larynx spoke 'viscerally', but as part of a rhetorical strategy in which the character Anthony claims not to be speaking rhetorically, a subterfuge clearly articulated and amplified by the way the actor pointed out to the audience the Latin word 'Ars' (art), inscribed upon the pedestal from which he stepped down to speak. The strange and alien thing that I had encountered here was theatre. The tendency in critical responses to the work to emphasise the 'real' as opposed to the pretend is testimony to the success of the pretending. The theatre is working: it is making us take its make-believe for real. The intensity of the encounter was produced by the fact that I had never seen anyone else taking the imitation game so seriously. It was as though no other theatre had considered that it might be possible to make representations that might be taken for the real thing; as though no one else believed that the theatre might be a kind of magic.[15]

---

15 Nicholas Ridout, 'Make-Believe: Socìetas Raffaello Sanzio Do Theatre' in Joe Kelleher and Nicholas Ridout (eds) *Contemporary Theatres in Europe: A Critical Companion*, London and New York: Routledge, 2006.

The production had been touring as part of the company's repertoire for over a year at this point. The existence of this repertoire, and the company's ability (born partly of economic necessity) to support and distribute the various productions across a network of mainly European theatres, allowed a certain amount of retrospective reckoning with the company's work of the 1990s. It was during the 1990s that the company's work first entered the network of European theatres in which it was regularly playing at the end of the decade, and which, eventually, would make possible the multi-agent co-production that would become *Tragedia Endogonidia*. Thus, it was possible, in the years immediately after the *Giulio Cesare* event, to see, among others, performances of the company's concert on Céline's *Voyage au bout de la nuit*; a staging of Monteverdi's *Il Combattimento di Tancredi e Clorinda* which marked their first collaboration with Scott Gibbons, produced, as *Il Combattimento*, as one of a series of commissions from Brussels' Kunstenfestivaldesarts, which invited contemporary theatre artists to engage with the musical repertoire; a new production, *Genesi: From the Museum of Sleep*, which toured extensively, in Europe, Australia, Korea and the USA, and which included three performances in London, at the Sadler's Wells Theatre, again as part of the London International Festival of Theatre in the summer of 2001.

If we were to continue the attempt to construct some kind of biography of the company and seek to put some flesh upon the bones of the terse and portable collection of dates, places and productions and, specifically, give them some kind of narrative shape, we might find ourselves tempted to take up the language of the marketplace and to look for some kind of 'breakthrough', a decisive moment at which a hitherto-unknown group of young artists struggling in their own corner of the theatrical world suddenly secured the acclaim of a wider public, garnering prizes and invitations to tour their work to the leading festivals and theatres of their day, just as a band might move from the obscurity of its local cult following to the blaze of a deal with a major label. We might look, then, for the moment at which this group of theatre-makers established for themselves the 'canonicity' necessary for their work to have become the subject of a book such as this in the first place. In the case of Socìetas Raffaello Sanzio, then, we would almost certainly be drawn to a consideration of *Amleto, la veemente esteriorità della morte di un mollusco*, a version of Shakespeare's *Hamlet*, with additional material from Saxo Grammaticus, first presented at the Wiener Festwochen in 1992. The production was still presented occasionally as late as 2000, when it could, for instance, have been experienced in the particularly alarming location of the disused football stadium in Bari, where it was played in a bare concrete room underneath the stand, and where its action and *mise en scène* seemed suited to a space in which it was not hard to imagine a history of anonymous acts of torture and brutality.

A more canonical point of departure for theatrical production could scarcely be imagined, and, given the company's complex attitude to iconicity in works like *Santa Sofia*, it would be reasonable to assume that the issue of canonicity, as such, would be at play in their engagement with *Hamlet*. Indeed, what seems to establish itself, by way of *Hamlet*, is a rigorous practical and theoretical engagement with theatre itself, as a cultural form, as a system of representation and as a mode of thought. The framing of *Amleto* is the presentation of Hamlet's story, as requested in his dying breath, by Horatio. Thus, the dramatic figure who appears in the piece is both Horatio and Hamlet, although there is nothing in the performance itself – by Paolo Tonti – that distinguishes between these two 'characters'. This device emphasises what we might identify as a key feature of the company's engagement with canonicity, or rather, with the history of theatre. It involves a movement that always begins 'after the event' but which always seeks to go back to a moment that preceded it. Thus *Amleto* comes 'after the event' of Shakespeare's play and starts, as it were, at the end of the play, with Horatio taking up the burden of Hamlet's narrative and thus taking us back to before the beginning of the play, exposing the relationships that set its story in motion, but doing so by, in effect, repeating the play. This movement towards the moment before the theatre, before the beginning, seems to have been repeated in various inflections in subsequent work, with both *Orestea* and *Genesi* involving direct engagements with 'original' material: the first trilogy of the tragic theatre and the first book of the Bible, respectively. Writing about the company's work on tragedy, Romeo articulates his interest in the recuperation of the pre-tragic:

> For me, theatre always involves a theological problem. It has been this way from the beginning, from the very foundation of the theatre. The theatre is shot through with this problem, the problem of the presence of God, because for us westerners, the theatre is born when God dies. It is clear that the animal plays a fundamental role in this relationship between the theatre and the death of God. In the moment when the animal vanishes from the stage, tragedy is born. The polemical gesture which we are making as regards Attic tragedy is to take a step backwards by returning the animal to the stage. To turn the plough back along its own path, to see an animal on stage, means to move towards the theological and critical roots of the theatre.[16]

This movement of going back to before is repeated, of course, in *Tragedia Endogonidia*, as we shall see, where an interest in natality expresses itself through a sustained consideration of conception rather than birth. In this instance, by asking the question 'How might

---

16 Romeo Castellucci, 'Il Pellegrino della materia', in Claudia and Romeo Castellucci, Chiara Guidi, *Epopea delle Polvere: Il teatro della Societas Raffaello Sanzio 1992–1999*, Milan: Ubulibri, 2001, p. 271.

it be possible to make tragedy today?' the company once again seem to be avowing an interest in understanding what might recur, persist and endure in a human civilisation.

It is with the moment of this question that this book has its own origins, initially in conversations between the five of us, in Cesena, in September 2001, shortly after the company's visit to London with *Genesi*, and at a time when the work towards *Tragedia Endogonidia* documented here, was in its early stages. It was in these conversations that an orientation towards the future and towards the development of *Tragedia Endogonidia* took shape, and it was in the wake of these conversations that the specific obligation to write in response to the making of theatre was conferred upon the two spectators, later to be discharged through the writing of essays originally printed in a large format, small-print black quaderno, entitled *Idioma Clima Crono*, distributed by the company at the successive points of the flight of the *Tragedia* across Europe. This book is thus, in part, an attempt to render public the consequences of that obligation and to open those conversations, which have continued ever since, to a wider audience, as a way of understanding the theatre-making of the company, through the medium of their interaction with two of their spectators.

Those conversations, that theatre-making and, indeed, the archive upon which we have built some of this introduction, are all located at the Teatro Comandini, where the company have based their work since 1992 (*Amleto* will have been the first production to have been created here, and traces of it remain on the walls of the building). It is just a short walk from the centre of the small town of Cesena, 'an insignificant town in north Italy' as the company administrator, Gilda Biasini, announced on the occasion of our first arrival. The former iron-workers' factory has been occupied partly by Socìetas Raffaello Sanzio, partly by people responsible for screening films in its courtyard during the summer and partly, it seems, by a blood-donor agency. It is clear which door leads to the part of the building occupied by Socìetas Raffaello Sanzio, as it is marked with a simple marble plaque on which, in capital letters, the word 'teatro' has been inscribed. Inside this door, a passageway along the front of the building leads to a costume room and two toilets to the right and, on the left, into the main body of the Raffaello Sanzio operation. A foyer, in which the public tends to gather on performance nights, gives access to rooms on all sides. To one's left on entering the foyer, a large rehearsal/performance space, with wooden floors and bare walls, to the right a longer space, more often, it seems, used for performances, at the very far end of which there is a small office. Also accessed from the central foyer are two small offices, in one of which company administrators Gilda Biasini and Cosetta Nicolini are often to be found. Across the foyer, a larger office accommodates other administrative staff and gives access, via a spiral iron staircase, to the archive in the roof space. The point is that, while any space of creative labour can be presented in a romanticising manner, there is nothing particularly unusual about the conditions in which the company make their work. The company seem to be constantly struggling – in minor but always practical ways – with these given circumstances: with spaces that are too small for the work to be rehearsed properly, with the conflicts between noisy work on machines and the need for quiet when working in detail on sound material. Cesena is where they live and work. It is not a choice, let alone an aesthetic one. It is a situation in which the work of theatre takes place.

In a closing effort to offer a sense of the scope of the company's work, both past and present, we pay a brief visit to the company's website, where details of current and future activities may be read. This visit takes place on 18 February 2007, towards the very end of the period in which this book was composed. From 13 February to 25 February 2007, the company are presenting *Buchettino* in Japan (in Kuchi and Yamaguchi). This will be the Japanese version of their very popular version of the fairy tale Tom Thumb, adapted by Claudia Castellucci and directed by Chiara Guidi. Spectators – mainly, but not exclusively, children – are invited to take their places in beds, climbing under scratchy blankets in a specially constructed wooden house. A woman opens a book and starts to tell the story of the little boy and the terrible giant. Frightening sound effects are performed outside the house, above and around it, an entire universe of sound whipped up alongside the sometimes alarming amplification of the storyteller's own voice. *Buchettino* is the most widely seen aspect of the company's substantial body of work with and for children, which has ranged from the *Scuola sperimentale per un teatro infantile*, led for three years by Chiara Guidi at the Teatro Comandini (1995–7), to large-scale immersive adventures, such as *La prova di un altro mondo* (1998). The Japanese *Buchettino* will not, we imagine, be performed by the show's most regular storyteller, Monica Demuru, who despite successful performances in English, German, French as well as Italian, has chosen not to continue with the show in its Japanese incarnation. There must be at least two versions of the wooden house, since the performances in Yamaguchi are happening simultaneously with a run of performances at the Teatro delle Bricole in Parma (21–4 February), in which Monica Demuru is taking her regular role.

Before those members of the company currently in Italy can get to Parma, though, they have engagements in nearby Reggio Emilia, where they are presenting four performances of *BR.#04*, the Brussels episode of *Tragedia Endogonidia*. The cast for this production includes Claudia Castellucci, as well as Sonia Beltran Napoles, who also appears in the company's most recent production, *Hey Girl!*, which will be seen in a single performance in Parma a few days after the end of the short run of *Buchettino*. Romeo Castellucci, who, we imagine, will be at the lighting or sound controls for both *Hey Girl!* and *BR.#04*, is also taking part in a public discussion in Reggio Emilia on 16 February. One day after the single performance of *Hey Girl!* in Parma, Romeo will be in Paris, taking part in a conference at the Opéra National de Paris. The same day Claudia will be back in Parma for an event entitled *Il movimento di tempo,* in which she will read and comment upon some pages from the work of Henri Bergson. This, we may imagine, is part of the presentation of the work of the *Stoa,* taking place the same day at the Teatro delle Bricole, under the title *Ballo individuale in circostanze costrette.* The *Stoa,* or *scuola sul movimento ritmico di Cesena,* is an ongoing project led by Claudia, in which children, and, most recently, adolescents, participate in a regular programme that combines the reading and discussion of philosophy (Plato, Heidegger) with the development of a collective dance. This presentation will be the outcome of a previous programme of work. Another pair of presentations, which we encountered in Florence at the end of 2005, involved a public seminar on Heidegger, followed by another collective dance – *Ballo eccezionale degli incontri e delle esclusioni.* This will be seen again over two days at the Teatro Petrella in Longiano in April. A new programme of the *Stoa* has just begun, on 19 February. It will last three years (running nine months a year), with a weekly session lasting four hours.

Meanwhile, back at the Teatro Comandini in Cesena, a second season of international theatre and other performance forms is opening on 13 February, with the Italian première of work by a young Belgian company, Abbatoir Fermé. This season, now titled *Incunabula,* follows a similar experiment in curation in spring 2006 at the Comandini, at which the company mainly presented work previously seen as part of the 2005 Venice Biennale Theatre Festival, for which Romeo was the director. The Venice event brought together a mixture of well-known and less well-known experimental artists, many of whom Romeo invited to engaged with the form and practice of theatre for the first time (these included sound artists Chris Watson and Carl-Michael von Hausswolff). Artists more familiar with theatrical form seen as part of the festival included the Americans Richard Maxwell and Goat Island, the British collaboration of Bock & Vincenzi, some emergent Italian groups (Habillé d'Eau and Orthographe) and the Slovenian company Via Negativa. *Incunabula* will include performances at the Comandini from mid-February through to the beginning of April, with music and computer art as well as theatre and dance featuring in the programme. The idea of using the Comandini as a resource for supporting and developing other people's work is clearly an important one for the company, even as they continue to develop their own work on several fronts. The inclusive nature of the event, like the Venice Biennale, reflects the way in which a variety of non-theatrical art practices continue to appeal to and influence the work and imagination of the company.

During March, *BR.#04* will play for two nights at the Teatre Liure in Barcelona, and another episode, *M.#10* (Marseille) will be seen at Créteil and Mons in France. *BR.#04* will be performed at the Teatro Bonci in Cesena at the close of *Incunabula* at the very end of the month. The Teatro Alessandro Bonci – a typical nineteenth-century

Italian theatre, with parterre and boxes – plays an interesting and important role in the life of the company. It is just around the corner from the Teatro Comandini, and the company have previewed productions there, often in order to prepare work created in the Comandini for presentation in more conventional theatre spaces. The company's productions are sometimes included in the subscription seasons of the Bonci, and this has in the past involved regular Bonci subscribers coming around the corner to see work in the Comandini, too. The Bonci is also, we imagine, where a teenage Romeo Castellucci saw a performance by the famous Italian actor and director, Carmelo Bene, apparently one of the theatrical events that contributed to his desire to try to make theatre himself. Otherwise Bene's relationship with Cesena appears to have been less happy. After receiving a hostile or unappreciative reaction from the Cesena public, Bene, we are told, got up the morning after – a Saturday morning and a market day – stepped onto the balcony overlooking Cesena's Piazza del Popolo and pissed down into the square. This is not an event at which the present authors can claim to have been present, however.

On 2 April Claudia is reading Robert Walser in Modena. Walser, a Swiss novelist, the contemporary and indeed, for his admirers, the equal of Musil and Kafka, has been involved in the company's work before. In 1995 Romeo shot a twenty-five-minute film of *Brentano*, after Walser's novel. From the middle of April the schedule appears to be dominated by performances of the new show, *Hey Girl!*, with dates in Antwerp, Florence, Ljubljana and Budapest. On 19 and 20 May there is a restaging of one of the Crescite from *Tragedia Endogonidia*. The Crescite, as you will see from an explanation offered in a short text by Romeo later in the book, are growths from the episodes of the *Tragedia* cycle. Staged in non-theatre spaces, with minimal *mise en scène*, they tend to crystallise a single image or gesture, opening out its emotional potential in an extended treatment, usually of ten to fifteen minutes. In Udine, the company will present *Crescita VII*, originally created in Rome.

At the end of May, there's a single performance of another *Tragedia* offshoot: *The Cryonic Chants, canti e poemi oggetivi, tratti di un impassibile animale*, in Chieti. This is a semi-staged concert, created by Scott Gibbons and Chiara Guidi, with video material by Romeo Castellucci, which reworks and substantially extends material developed in the context of *A.#02*, the Avignon episode. Here, as texts elsewhere in the book explain in greater detail, vocal material was derived from the recording of the movements of a goat (the poet) across a carpet printed with the symbols of its own DNA. This material, used briefly in sequences sung by Chiara Guidi and Claudia Castellucci in *A.#02* and by Chiara Guidi and Monica Demuru in *BN.#05* (the Bergen episode), is developed in *The Cryonic Chants* into a seventy-minute concert, performed by Scott Gibbons, on tympani and synthesisers, and four female singers (Chiara, Monica, Claudia and Teodora Castellucci), on a stage whose walls and floor are painted in black and white vertical stripes. In July, the company will once again appear at the Festival d'Avignon, where numerous earlier pieces have been presented (*Gilgamesh, Giulio Cesare, Voyage au bout de la nuit, Genesi*) with performances of *Hey Girl!*. In September the Brussels episode of *Tragedia Endogonidia*, *BR.#04*, plays Belgrade, Riga, Vilnius and Moscow, clearly making *BR.#04* the most widely seen of the eleven episodes. It is possible, we imagine, that by the time the lights go down in Moscow on 5 October 2007, on the uncanny image of an old man vanishing into the depths of his own bed, this book will be meeting the eyes of its own audience for the first time, and it will be your turn to experience what is to come.

By that time, perhaps nearly everything in this book, in spite of our determination to orient our thought towards a future, will already have become retrospect. But at least from the end of this introduction, which is approaching, that gaze over the shoulder that almost always fails to catch a glimpse of its own back, falls in the very recent past. The first, and longest, section of the book ('Makers and spectators') traces the development of *Tragedia Endogonidia*, from early experiments in sound between Chiara and Scott, through the creation of eleven episodes, beginning and ending in Cesena, between January 2002 and December 2004. The material in this section includes selections from e-mail correspondence between Scott in Chicago and other members of the company (mainly Chiara) in Cesena, other occasional writings (including some more e-mail letters to collaborators) by Claudia, Romeo and Chiara about the development of the project, excerpts from the scripts or scores that describe the action of each episode and essays written in response to the episodes by Joe and Nick. The section is organised more or less chronologically, by episode, and is illustrated by images from the productions. Our aim is not only to offer an insight into the particular conditions, ideas and practices that constituted *Tragedia Endogonidia* but also to offer this insight as at least partially representative of a distinctive theatre-making practice, evolved over twenty-five years and in continual development. The second section ('Conversations') is composed of edited transcripts of conversations between the five authors of this book, recorded at the Teatro Comandini in Cesena in the summers of 2004 and 2005. These conversations represent a collective attempt to think togther and out loud about the theatre-making process and about the spectatorial experience of theatre. The third section (*Disjecta Membra*) presents excerpts from Romeo's notebooks, compiled as a crucial part of the creative process, over the period of this book's composition. It includes, as Romeo explains in a conversation that appears later in this book, 'elements of reality, elements of the mind or of an imagined reality, all converging towards a point: this transcription of ideas into notes, which is work that goes on every day'. Including today.

Note on translation

All of the texts by Chiara Guidi, Claudia Castellucci and Romeo Castellucci, including citations in this Introduction and the collection of 'Conversations' towards the end of the book, have been translated from Italian for this publication by Joe Kelleher and Nicholas Ridout. We have attempted to find an English that is recognisable and enjoyable as such, while retaining something of the sometimes very particular timbre and lexical range of the Italian.

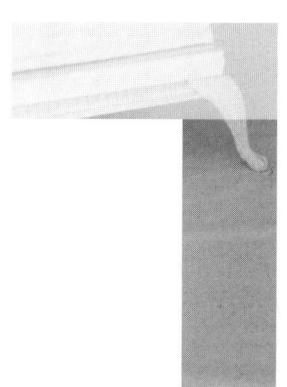

PART ONE

Makers and spectators, *Tragedia Endogonidia*, 2002-4

Dear Scott,

We are waiting for a clearer sign – a title, a drama – that can turn the thoughts that are being solidified on paper into something necessary. We are trying to catalyse each idea around a theme, but there are still many mysteries open. None of the words I'd like to use have any necessity. For me at the moment they all seem useless, and every idea that appears fascinating is devoid of urgency.

    I want anyway to create a method for working with you.

    Right now I have a question for you: What type of voice, do you think, could bring out that obscure and hidden sound that accompanies the entrance of the audience, which only later might be recognisable as belonging to a voice? Do you think a masculine or a feminine voice? Could it be a chorus? For now I will call this idea and its realisation VOICE OF SILENCE.

Chiara

Laboratory, 2001

11 MARCH 2001

Dear Scott,

Towards the end of March I'd like to do some work with a few people so I can know who to call when you get here. I want to record some cries and noises and ask these people not only to reproduce them but also to perform them before your arrival. I'm not thinking of texts but emulsions of sound, built up rhythmically and then covered with their own breath. I want to get between the folds of the specific sound that a machine makes, or get inside the cry of an animal and move it and shake it in a dramaturgical key. I'd like the cry of an animal or the screech of a machine to cause the sort of commotion that makes me want to intervene, to placate an anguish that doesn't even exist. We need to make a lot of sound-filters: I want to see if an individual voice can sound not just singular but choral, like the voices of everyone gathered in one person.

    I'm thinking more of whispers than shouts.
    I'm thinking of voices in fragments rather than a compact block.
    I'm thinking of a breathless voice and a voice made up only of breaths.
    I'm thinking of a chorus that is variegated but barely perceptible.

I'm thinking of a voice that arrives unexpectedly like a fist.

I'd like to listen to my voice from inside my stomach or else put my ears far away from my body.

The beating of the heart will be going on deep down, and left there as always.

As you can see, everything is still unformed and, although I warned you it would be like this, I can't bear it. The acoustic magma shaking up inside me awaits its dramaturgical catalysation. But it will happen.

Have you thought of any particular voices to do the voices of silence?

I'll speak to you soon, dear Scott, and don't be discouraged if I still sound somewhat vague and abstract.

Chiara

4 MAY 2001

Dearest Scott

We've realised that maybe by presenting the future show as choreography we can risk a new type of dramaturgy, unconnected to tradition. It's not easy in the theatre working outside the Western tradition; for audiences it can make things seem incomprehensible and arbitrary, a work of abstraction. With choreography, perhaps, an audience is better able to participate in an act of creation which can take account not only of theatre but also the visual arts. And this is the freedom that we need now.

Anyway it will be necessary to identify the figures, the 'characters', so as to dig out in them all of the scenographic ideas, the sound ideas, the voice and light ideas that are already starting to emerge. The problem now is the same as it always was: the Figure must be set free from representation, which has something to do with the sort of feeling that gets into the flesh and the nerves. And this setting free happens through a fall. We must struggle, then, to bring about this fall.

A lot of the sounds we've found are sounds that shift the hearing, as if the ears might turn up in the heart, or in the stomach, or outside the body, as if the ears themselves were a body, equipped with movement and gravity. Often it felt as if my body were without ears, until I found them again, here, in this part of my body, or there, or further up or further down. My ears felt like bodies detached from me, responding to the provocations of my voice. I could see them clearly, or rather I felt myself as ear. My voice was another's voice, and with my voice I could feel, for a moment, the vanishing of sounds that had barely been audible. My voice was a memory of hidden sounds. My voice was water and fire. I've been using the sound of some bones, and it sounds like the skeleton rising up against the flesh.

Always, before a fall, certain forces, that were already there, become audible. We haven't worked on reproduction and invention, but we have given a sound to forces that are not usually heard. Now I would like to give a sound to time, to pressure and gravitation, to attraction and repulsion, to dilation, contraction, cracking, stretching and straining. These will be the themes that will engage us in our second phase of research. What do you think?

Ciao, Chiara

Making space

I live my craft like a duty. It is not a moral duty. I only know that I must do it. Everything we'd done in the theatre and everything we lived outside were squeezed together in a doorway, beyond which there was the future. It was no longer anything to do with what we'd done. The future was not an empty land, even if it did have space for things that even now aren't there yet. It was very similar to the usual life, if not to say identical, except there was much more space. An enormous, disorientating space, to tell the truth, good for spinning tops a long way away from each other. Tragedy was an emptied-out space. The freedom which this space accorded us was intimidating, like a barely discovered country, where the sort of life that needs space could be established. Freedom existed in the future. And you could go into this future. It was immanent. You needed to occupy it naked. The nakedness of the flesh and the empty place are the primary conditions for the spatial occupation of tragedy. We are going deep into an art that belongs to the whole planet. Ours is a form of mime very different to African, Indian or Oriental mime; rather, it is similar to North American, South American, Euro-Asiatic and Australian mime. The ocean, the great icebergs of Greenland and the South Pole remain foreign and superior to our microbial existence.

Our Euro-Asiatic mime is not linked (any longer) to an earth to which we feel we belong. Language, cooking are nothing more than warm kennels, foundation myths, nocturnal callings of the blood. Religion is an excuse to make war. And culture is war's lackey. It is always being dragged in.

Personifications, incarnations of concepts, symbols. We are on similar ground. But ours is still a mime. What, then, does our Euro-Asiatic mime amount to, in a world in thrall to the technologies of vision and spectacle? Can we make sense of this confusion?

The theme of tragedy is violent death. Whenever destiny knocks, a chorus rises up: whose job is to orientate, to explain, to communicate . . . Nowadays it is all chorus. The chorus is continuous, pervasive, gaseous. Either it expresses me, or it forces me to express myself. In practice, it co-opts. We find ourselves stuffed with analogy; fused to the same words: death, tragedy, spectacle. The word 'surface', perhaps more than any other, bears witness to the extent to which the same word can contain opposite meanings. Surface is the part of the body that appears. It is an immediate offering of reality. It is capable of producing the maximum communicative effect with the least possible communicative means. It is a field of torture. It is the material that we are, and have. How can we not see now, in this one word – surface – the common concentration of advertising, of fashion, of televisual communication and of theatre?

As long as the theatre cannot admit that it hangs out in the same places – the worst sort of places – of human expression, it will be incapable of any greatness or understanding. As long as it claims its distinct superiority over these potent forms of human expression, it will be nothing more than a small maestro with a baton, and there are so many of those. We are aware that we find ourselves in this same place, but we cannot waste time declaring ourselves to be in the right, while everyone else meanwhile . . . This attitude is always folding things up so as to have something to unfold again, an explanation to lay out, always reacting . . . never creating, never throwing itself forward, into the future, beyond the sort of weighty inducements that crush and take over the mind, forced only ever to respond, to be moulded in this way and that, while the loss of certainty about things and the loss of judgement remains as dangerous as ever.

This is the main reason, I believe, why mime always survives in times of war. In times of war, theatre has always been a way of suspending the yoke of reflex thought. This is why performances have gone on wherever there was still a room to perform in, along with a vigorous flowering of cabarets and sketches, which is deeply significant, it seems to me, with regard to the means of resistance and the conquest of life. Every creation, however stupefying, however strange or otherworldly, that springs up in conditions that would appear to demand other kinds of thoughts, other preoccupations, other sorts of reflections altogether, shows us how the capacity to project oneself into the future can be a form of flight which is something very different from escapism; which is, rather, a founding; a creating of unconnected thoughts; a making of artefacts that serve life and that put fresh water side by side with cooked food.

> There is nothing more active than an escape. It is the opposite of the imaginary. The same goes for a forced escape, not in terms of forcing others to flee, but running something off, causing a run off in a system, like when you drill a hole in a pipe. George Jackson wrote from prison: 'I may be running, but I'm looking for a gun as

I go.' To flee means tracing a line, or lines, a whole cartography. They reveal their worlds only through a long, fractured flight. [. . .] The great error, the only error, would be that of believing that a line of flight consists in an escape from life; the flight into the imaginary or into art. On the contrary to flee means to produce the real, to create life, to find a weapon.[1]

We mime the images of tragedy. We put figures in a golden room that destroys the sense of perspective. The gold walls mirror the forms, but not exactly; they meld together in an indistinct depth which can be related to the Ionian philosophers' concept of nature as 'origin of all the species of being; reality of the possible, with the features of that *apeiron* (indeterminacy), which Anaximander saw gushing from every individuated form'.[2]

One of the political tasks of the theatre as I see it now is to get right to the bottom of its own specific language. Without fear either of incomprehension or the impossibility of communication; without translation or commentary or explanation; without anxiety about the absence of speech on stage or anxiety about speech in general; with a strategy for words and a strategy for images that is capable of organising a new reality. This, in short, is what the movement of *Tragedia Endogonidia* is all about, a cycle of eleven episodes extending over three years. It is not a finished show that is moved from city to city. Its moving around is the show; a rhythm that strikes; a transformed organism, like the different phases in the life of an animal or vegetable. The economy must change; the economy of touring must change.

Tragedy fixes death. 'Endogonidia', on the other hand, designates the perennial life of an individual that, splitting itself, continually self-generates. And so *Tragedia Endogonidia* produces the continuous fixing of those deaths that succeed each other ceaselessly. Anonymity, nocturnal darkness, the privation of words, alphabetic and microbial invasion in league with the law, these are the initial conditions of our tragedy.

Cities, places of civil history and expectation; lands which bear an idiom; lands which support a climate, these are the spatial conditions of our tragedy. The immense melancholy of a prophecy that is about to take place. The face of so many Italian Virgins holding a child in their arms that will die on the cross. The resurrection will come, but first death must pass through and break up the perfect fullness of the face with the

---

1 Gilles Deleuze, 'Un nuovo tipo di rivoluzione sta per diventare possibile', *Marka*, no. 28, 1990. For another formulation of the same ideas see Gilles Deleuze and Félix Guattari, *A Thousand Plateaus: Capitalism and Schizophrenia*, trans. Brian Massumi, London: Athlone Press, 1987, p. 204.
2 Paulo Virno, 'Moltitudine a principio di individuazione', *Derive e Approdi*, no. 21, 2002.

putrefaction of time. So as to defeat time and take flight. The silence of Andrei Rublev,[3] the weeks of darkness before the painting, these are signs, now and once more, of the intensity of life, and of the future.

CC
November 2002

System, functions and workings for a tragedy of gold

It starts from the reasonable assumption that an authentic foundation of tragedy is impossible today.

At the same time, we sense, in the core of Attic tragedy, the structure of sensations that reveal something of the human condition that does not belong to this world, to this reality.

Nevertheless, tragedy's way of presenting a dramatic situation to the spectator is still the unsurpassed model for every intimate human representation.

Our times and our lives are completely detached from any concept of the tragic. 'Redemption', 'pathos' and 'ethos' are inaccessible words that have fallen into the coldest of abstractions. Disasters and the slaughters of innocents are everywhere referred to as 'tragedies', but this is an idea of tragedy that does not know how to distinguish these things from spectacle; nor how to think of them in terms of political crisis; nor how to gather them up on behalf of a metropolitan community, amongst people who are at the same time amassed and dispersed, who lack any common ground or mother language, who lack even 'a people': who lack those foundations that are the basis for the invention of tragedy. Turning again to tragedy doesn't mean looking back; we have to break Aeschylus' thread – not follow it. The theatre I respect, now, is a theatre of commotion. This is a tragedy of the future.

In conclusion, we need to think of tragedy as the only worthy opponent. I would add that we need to have the courage to look at tragedy's true face. Because I still don't know what it is.

The plan is to put into question the very idea of theatre. The project is called 'Tragedia Endogonidia' because it invokes a mechanism of increase and autonomous genital reproduction, typical of certain simple animals.

---

3 Russian fifteenth-century icon painter. Subject of Andrei Tarkovsky's film *Andrei Rublev* (1966).

Tragedia Endogonidia

Endogonidia: the word is adapted from the vocabulary of microbiology; it refers to those simple living beings with two sets of sexual organs inside themselves that are able to reproduce continually, without need of another, according to what amounts, effectively, to a system of immortality. The price they have to pay is their continual division and separation from themselves.

The word 'endogonidia' is altogether antithetical to the word 'tragedy'; the latter presupposes the inevitable ruin of whoever comes up against the splendour of the hero's solitude, which, soon enough, has its own death for an horizon.

The dramatic structure of the cycle *Tragedia Endogonidia* follows closely the exoskeleton of Attic tragedy; the most striking dissimilarity is the absence of the chorus. But the chorus is not simply wiped out; it is, so to speak, left outside the door. Like a naughty schoolboy, it must think things over for a while outside the classroom. The job of the chorus was to explain the facts, comment upon them and judge them; it followed a moral, educative purpose. In *Tragedia Endogonidia* there are only the facts, without any chorus. The sections of the Attic tragedy that preceded the intervention of the Chorus were called 'Episodes' whereas the sections that had to do with leaving and reflecting upon the consequences of the action were called 'Exodes', as Aristotle tells us in his *Poetics*. 'Episode', therefore, is the name that will be used to distinguish the different phases of *Tragedia Endogonidia*. The basic structural idea, indeed, is a work of progressive becoming.

It will be a process of evolution. The next phase involves a series of 'bases' in which the episodes will be generated, a mechanism of growth that is to be understood in an endocrinal sense: governed by an internal logic, and determining the unique character of each episode.

The episode, by its own admission, renounces the coherence and wholeness of the work, so as to place itself outside of narrative. The episode does not carry the weight of a message to be delivered and communicates as little as possible, although that doesn't mean it should be thought of as a 'fragment' or a 'metonymy'.

Every episode puts on stage its own ontogenesis and that is all it can do. An episode is closer to a series of pure and complete acts. It is a meteor which, as it passes by, gently touches the surface of the world. It remains rootless.

So as to understand this, we need to reconsider from the beginning the mechanism of Attic tragedy. If we could imagine a tragedy without the singing of the Chorus, we might realise how every episode resides in the splendour of its entelechy, in its substantial and sidereal silence. A sculptural group. Without that will to understand which the Chorus brings, the episode represents, with its naked action, the inexplicable *I* of the spectator; whereas the Chorus explains and conjugates the it of the character according to the coordinates of a story.

What remains of an episode can only be the pseudo-biography of a hero. But it is really from the unspoken that *form* takes shape. In the most extreme synthesis, tragedy can be defined as the art of anonymity: anonymous because it contains the communal us, which it is capable of constructing instantaneously (inexplicably) around the figure on stage.

The cycle of work will involve a first base in Cesena, with the auto-generation of a chain of images (*tragoedia endo-gonidia*) from which a series of spores will be detached so as to be gathered up by other 'bases'. In turn, these spores will generate individual tragic units. These units (which will be identified by the name of the city hosting them: Avignon, *A.#02* . . . Berlin, *B.#03* . . . followed by Brussels, Bergen, Marseille, Rome, Paris, Strasbourg, London) will then fall on the successive 'bases'. The process will not be an accumulation, but rather a living transformation.

A + B will not equal AB.

A + B will equal C.

The general structure is a sequence which includes a transmigration of forms inside itself.

It will be a process of evolution. We won't have many performances, we won't have one big performance. What we will have will be an organism on the run. The form's ability to react and change quickly is a necessary strategy if we are to answer to the scope of these times.

RC

On the Earth's stage

Generation endogonidia

Conception has always been opposed to the realm of reality. It receives, without passing judgement, all material phenomena according to a new design created by a blind and endocrinal parthenogenesis (*endo-gonidia*).

Conception is a virgin in the world, but welcomes inside herself a plan for the suspension and recapitulation of all reality.

Different worlds and knowledges conjoin according to internal logics and establish rules for endocrinal lives.

To conceive means to 'receive' (*conceptus, con-captio*, to take in). Thus, the womb of

Conception becomes a place of incubation and pure invention where every contact with the real world is suspended and deferred.

Every sensible element is to be perceived and considered through the drastic mentality of the tragic: lights, voices, spaces and bodies are there, before us, and they show us all of the strangeness, all of the stupidity, all of the foreignness of the 'theatre' support.

- In the realm of Conception there is a total absence of ideas. This is not a problem: it is a guarantee.
- In the realm of Conception it is possible to see things that have never been seen and hear things that have never been heard.
- In the realm of Conception any tradition is factually reproducible.
- In the realm of Conception any language can be pronounced forwards and backwards.
- In the realm of Conception every dead language can be spoken again.
- In the realm of Conception every sentient being has the right of citizenship.
- In the realm of Conception every non-sentient being has the right of citizenship.
- In the realm of Conception every creature is born by parthenogenisis, without intercourse with an other.
- In the realm of Conception the real is produced by suspending reality.
- In the realm of Conception there is no form of political antagonism, because all forms have already emigrated.
- In the realm of Conception there is no intercourse with chronological time, with history, with the present times.
- The realm of Conception is worthy of the present times and supports it in potential.
- In the realm of Conception no irony is possible, no form of snobbery, no form of alterity.
- The realm of Conception is the orphan of poetry. Only a reproduced life can be poetry.

RC

C.#01
Cesena, Teatro Comandini
January 2002

In the first Cesena episode, in a pre-scene, a robot shakes on the floor, and later, the very living Demetrio Castellucci lies as if dead in the golden box that is the dominant scenic element of the production. Beside him lies a fire extinguisher, a machine that in its extinguishing, in its accelerated, pressurised exhalation, saves lives, but which, in this image, will always be associated with death. Demetrio's black balaclava, white T-shirt and black boots, the exact position in which his body rests on the ground, the presence of the fire extinguisher all identify him – to those who care to recall or to anyone who ever knew – as Carlo Giuliani, the young demonstrator killed by Italian police during the protests at the G8 Summit in the summer of 2001.

Downstage of Demetrio stands a young man in black formal trousers with a red stripe down the side of one leg and shoes, but stripped to the waist. He sings. He is a soprano, Radu Marian. He sings a song in a language I do not understand. Romeo Castellucci had earlier suggested that this piece might include 'a language no one understands, like Hungarian'. But it is not just the strangeness of the language, but the extraordinary and genuine male soprano voice that demands attention. And his breathing. His ribcage

The mechanical bow will only work in this space in a diagonal direction.
(Photo: Socìetas Raffaello Sanzio)

seems huge compared to his stomach. In the movement of his flesh we see the voice itself making its way out of the body; we see the breath move the flesh; and we don't know what it is that this breath articulates. Is his song a song of praise for the deeds of the fallen, or a lament over the wasted youth of the too-soon dead? We don't even know if we are witnessing a killer at the scene of a murder, or a mourner at a funeral, or both.

Tragedy, then, is where the dead live, and where, because they both breathe, it is impossible to tell the difference between them. It creates, therefore, a space in which the impossible appears as possibility, a moment, perhaps, in which we grasp what Messianic time might feel like. A promise, not just that there will be redemption, but that you and I will be there to see it, that we will be there, on the scene of history, when the moment comes, that we that are young shall live so long; a promise that the redemption in question will be ours, mine, and that we shall be witnesses to that promise made good.

NR

LATE 2001

Dear Scott,

First of all, you can stop searching for the rubber mummy since I've found out how to get it. Yes, I know it is not mass-produced. I saw the image on a German web page for fetishists, and when Gilda called to get information about the product someone replied that the person who made these artefacts was dead, and we didn't have the guts to ask about how he died. . . .
I'll try to describe a possible beginning for the show.
When the audience enters the sound will already have spread to the ticket office, and it will be so loud it will leave little room for normal communication. Probably someone will already be put off entering . . .
As the public sits down the sound continues (golden room). When everybody is seated a video-projection starts on a white screen that covers the stage space. It should be a projection capable of getting into the brain and playing with the cerebral cortex. We've been trying out a range of very fast sequences of complementary lights such as red–blue, green–red, that might provoke an induced emotion. We need something very optical, something cold, as if an experiment or a test were being carried out on the entire audience.
It's the spectator's encephalon that is interesting here, not his soul (that comes later). I've tried to introduce a few frames of letters of the alphabet, in white, into the very fast colour sequence, anticipating the appearance of the 'letters box' later. The result, though, isn't really satisfactory, it looks too simple. I don't know whether Golan might have something useful, something fast and 'bad' that might capture the spectator's eye and put his cerebral cortex to a severe test. Something like

A killer at the scene of a murder, or a mourner at a funeral, or both.

perceptive tests or brain tricks. I've tried introducing subliminal shapes, drawings of everyday things, but they look too slow (I can't get below 1/25 of a second). This first part needs to be scientifically disturbing and aggressive.

One further image that could be introduced, before the mechanical bow and right after the bombing of the colours, is an epileptic who flings himself about on the floor. I'm thinking of a mannequin, whose spasms are human at first and then become more and more frantic until they seem bestial; although the public mustn't be able to tell for sure that the mannequin is powered by compressed air. But before we get to this figure, we need to solve the problem of the projection. It should consist simply of colours and shapes, but this means it needs to be very accurate and have a sort of 'elegance'. That's why we thought of Golan.

We added another figure, and a problem came up. This is an actor who will perform in the skin of a woman. The skin will be made of rubber and needs to be obtained from a real cast of a woman. Only at the very end will the actor take this skin off and reveal their true nature. The problem is whether the actor should be male or female. With a male everything will be clear and the identity game will be evident. With an actress, however, it will convey a sense of parthenogenesis and regeneration. If we succeed in putting this scene into practice, the sounds recorded in April – the 'voices of silence' – should be very good. We will keep you informed about the development of this scene.

One last thing: we have the possibility of working with a Romanian singer who really is an incredible and impressive soprano. We still have to meet him and we will let you know. Listening to him, though, gives the idea of a voice *tout court* (but this time free of any other related image).

A big hug from Romeo and Chiara

In the realm of Conception, every creature is born by parthenogenesis, without intercourse.

LATE 2001

Dear Scott,

The construction of the golden room is still in progress and as soon as it is finished we will start rehearsing. It is very deep and not too wide, with a ceiling. Compared to the stages of our other performances, it is much more intimate and closed. At the moment, there are no openings, neither for the entrances and exits of the actors, nor for objects to be brought on stage. We're going to think about it. The mechanical bow will only work in this space in a diagonal direction. Most likely the target will be the body of a pig hanging up somewhere.

We need to add to the sound the thud of the arrow hitting the target. At the moment, there is no thud and the arrow seems lost in the void. The background sound (of the golden room), as we discussed, is going to be more complex. We were thinking this sound needs to strike the body more than the ears, but it's coming out monotonous and plain at the moment. It should sound as if there's a hidden design behind it, and there should be an emotional dynamics and also, perhaps, a metamorphosis?

Ciao, Romeo and Chiara

An organism on the run

Last week, as forty or fifty of us gathered in the Teatro Comandini in the northern Italian town of Cesena, the converted factory which is the home base of the theatre company Socìetas Raffaello Sanzio, the deep bass throb being churned out from behind the high heavy doors of the performance space seemed to image the dream and the dread of a sonic second coming. As I understand it, this inhuman noise and, indeed, most if not all of the sound and music throughout the piece have been processed by sound artist Scott Gibbons, in collaboration with the company, from the human voice. If this is dread or deliverance, it is made out of a mouthful of air. In what follows, it is as if the tremors and agitations of a range of places and moments, gathered up like bacterial scrapings from the face of the culture, are being worked through the guts of a localised machine, a theatre machine as we shall see. Here they will be recirculated, pumped back into the everyday economy of screwed rhetorics and bruised representations, as a piece of unfinished business: a piece of beauty, perhaps, to choke the system or a belligerent silence to stop up the mouth of power and make space and hearing for a new articulation. As for this sound that rolls around our chatter in the Comandini foyer, it is as if the voice as melody and tool of communication has been abstracted from itself and the remaining vacuum occupied by the voice's shadow: its timbre, its audio static, its outer frequencies; all the clicks and drippings and passages of air through the vocal cavities amplified in the manner of endogenous sonic growths upon the vocal organs.

When we take our places, instead of a curtain we are faced by a video screen, which seems almost too close to us, too immediate. The projected still image combines a repertoire of diagrammatic forms, geometric shapes, quasi-alphabetic inscriptions and male and female figures in an archetypal occidental Adam and Eve pose. I am told later that this image was a communication carried by the Voyager space probe, a typology of 'human' messaging systems. As such, it might serve as a grammar handbook for 'extraterrestrials' to jam the channels and send messages back to humanity, if we humans should survive long enough, or care enough, to keep the channels open.

The piece we are here for is an inaugural showing over two nights of *C.#01*, the first semi-public phase of a projected trans-European performance project. This is either its launching pad or its first touchdown, in Cesena (hence the 'C' in the title), where a structured sequence of theatre images has been generated, from which – as director Romeo Castellucci writes in his programme notes – 'a series of spores will depart in order to be collected by other "bases"'. These bases are other locations, city sites in Europe which the company plan to visit and work in, allowing the work to transform, as a series of stand-alone 'episodes', in response to these locations and in response too to the 'process of evolution' in the work itself. 'There will not be many performances, there will not be one large performance. The final result will be an organism which is on the run.'

The peculiar combination of locatedness and itinerancy that characterises this project is captured in the arena of performance where the images take place. The video screen is drawn up, and the performance space itself is discovered 'over there', somehow too far away for us to be intimate with it. Any communication delivered from that space will have to cross a perceptible distance, it will either have to exert a force or trust itself, like a spore or a wave, to drift and radiation. Nor is the performance space properly speaking something intimate with the Comandini building. It seems like a construction deposited or abandoned here. It is not a stage, it is not a platform, it is a box, sealed in on five sides to conceal any theatrical trickery and covered on all five sides by a yellow reflective metal. At the level of metaphor, it is a room of gold and bears at that metaphoric level something of the transhistorical aspirations of the Byzantine mosaics in nearby Ravenna, or an Emperor's treasury anywhere, wherever it was still imagined that a certain quantity of imperious, atemporal, perspectiveless reflecting surfaces could ever really anchor the fluctuating circulations of finance, the systemic pumping of fantasy and blood. However, even if gold is not altogether inimitable, it remains maybe a limit case for theatre's

He is citizen grotesque. (Photo: Socìetas Raffaello Sanzio)

circulation of mimetic representations in real economies of desire and debt. So, away from that metaphoric level, what this room 'looks like' is an index of what I take to be its actual substance: a cheaper metal, copper, and not a reflector so much as a heat-greedy conductor. This is not theatre as mirror to the world, but theatre as oven, where scraps and traces of human imagining (call these language, or legend, or idea) are cooked up until they discover themselves altered, right down to their molecular structure; where it gets so hot even the peculiar self-transforming creatures who inhabit that space will have to climb out of their own skin to survive.

Within the box, we are offered a sequence of singular appearances. There are three of them, and they may be the ghostly reflexes, beamed back at us from a distant futurity, of an antique cultural form we used to call 'tragedy': the exposition of a legendary suffering; the messenger; and the lyric lament over a hero's corpse. The first figure to appear goes through a series of respiratory and muscular exertions, of maskings and unmaskings (from the peeling of a glove or stocking to the shedding of flesh in the form of a latex body-skin), suffering transformations of species, of gender and dramaturgical status. This figure becomes, in turn, hieroglyph, actor, victim, perpetrator, 'woman', insect, parent, infant . . . each of them a fiction as far as the stage is concerned, each surprised self-encounter arising out of a sloughing off of the previous stage, the turning inside out of an apparent corporeality to display an unoccupied shell, the whole thing sustained by the briefest flashes of extreme illumination, as if something 'real' could be recuperated before it flies. Meanwhile, there is an insistent, rhythmic, amplified breathing, like a persistent forcing out of the breath in the face of all this dissolution. All these events are ghosted by the presence on stage beside this figure of an infant's buggy, a scrap of the quotidian, the chariot in which my parents abandoned me here, a token for a recognition scene which may never happen. Hooded figures in black, in red, in black which turns into white, approach the open face of the box, impassive, like a silent chorus, plague doctors perhaps, or perhaps the pilots of this time machine, or the scientists who oversee and record this experiment in endogenous reproduction, one of them entering the box at one point to 'fertilise' (or sterilise, or maybe just desecrate) the subject of the experiment with urine. In spite of this last, these figures approach with some delicacy. The sound field seems to capture and perform on their behalf their solicitations towards the unapproachable space, at a certain moment tuning in on what sounds like a child's voice, internalised, attempting to soothe – or appropriate – the inarticulate creature's sufferings by means of a secret word.

At another moment, though, the distance between the performance area and the marking of its meanings is approached with a more explicit violence, and a violence of the *mise en scène* itself. A machine towards one wall of the Comandini, motored by electricity and compressed air, jerks into action by remote control, feeding arrows into a mechanical bow which flexes and slams them, one by one with full force, across the face of the box into one of its inside walls. The actor, meanwhile, curls up in a far corner. If what is imaged here is something of the ancient tragedies' depiction of a vicious and implacable 'justice' meted out by the 'gods' or 'nature' or the 'law' or whatever, this machine is also too actual and ingenious and straightforwardly dangerous for us not to grasp that power, right here and now, is not a mystery but a mechanism, not an abstraction but a material force.

The second actor to appear is the first to address us directly with his gaze, as if he knows something about us. He is dressed strangely, in a tweed suit topped off all over with ribbons and fringes, an elaborate paper hat, a home-made ceremonial lance. His is

The problem is whether the actor should be male or female.

also the most ordinary of appearances. He is citizen grotesque. He is shaman familiar, one of us but returning from a journey beyond our ken. In another memory, this is the spear-carrier, the theatre proletarian. Palace servant. Gaoler. Shepherd who watched. Satyr. Except he appears to us from a time and place so far in the future that the names of those precursors have long been forgotten, even as they are ghosted in him. He eats one of the buttons off his suit jacket and then farts while he stares at us, the chewing and crunching miked up loud, an echo of an old 'popular' comedy – a satyric comedy – of mouth and stomach and anus but beamed back at us across unimaginable distance from the quarterdeck of some sort of golden spaceship. His messages are as enigmatic as they are insistent.

Meanwhile, a mechanical lettering device, like that of a railway-station information system, descends in front of the box. The device winds manically through its alphabet repertoire, barely freezing long enough to display in demotic English and mock Latin the phrases barked out ever faster and louder by our satyr messenger, who now dances too, a chorus of one, cranking up the frenzy with the crescendo of sound. GREETINGS FROM THE EARTH. ORACULUM EGO HOSTIUM SUM. THIS IS NOT MY TRAGEDY, DADDY. This is language crunched up, masticated, like that suit button earlier, but spat back at us. It is as if, on the one hand, there were an immediate and vital necessity to deliver something across the cavernous gap that separates that hermetic box theatre from us, the spectators, who listen and watch, in all willingness and, it may be, need, and, on the other hand, as if the only thing shared were a bitter understanding that the spectatorial 'we' is no more easy to apprehend than the performative 'I', that both of these are fictions wound up and popped out by the theatrical machinery, like two clockwork cuckoos facing each other across a gorge.

When the golden theatre box is illuminated again, a person lies there, fallen, thrown down, his face obscured, beside him an overturned fire extinguisher. The figure recalls the corpse of Carlo Giuliani, the young man killed by police during popular demonstrations against neo-liberal globalisation at the G8 summit in Genoa in summer 2001. A second young man, black trousered like a *carabiniere*, bare-chested, steps into the box, glances at us for a moment, then positions himself sideways on to our gaze and sings what may be a lullaby or a lament. Whatever the lyrical genre, the singer performs with such an undemonstrative dignity that the musical gesture does not succumb to gathering the 'victim' into the short-circuit of a sentimental appropriation. The language of his singing is unfamiliar and untranslated. His voice, too, is so high, almost like a child's soprano, and his thoracic muscles so visibly still, that the sound seems at moments to come from some other source than the singer's voice. The golden room now is an open burial chamber at the face of which, like the three Marys 2,000 years ago in Jerusalem gathering at the tomb of one crucified by the machinery of state terrorism, we are met by an angel. The angel of theatre, however, cannot – in all conscience – testify to a resurrection. He can only draw a line at the limit of the illusion and point us towards a messy and difficult inheritance, to be worked through on our side of the line, back in the world of history and politics, of ethics and economics. The singer finishes his song and, before he leaves, he stretches two wires diagonally across the face of the box. Current passes through the wires and they glow in a hot 'X'. This is the limit of the illusion, a double line, at one and the same time a mark of erasure and the identification of a pinpoint location. It says: this is where to look. It says: this is the place where looking breaks down.

The video screen descends again. The room is darkened, and the sound becomes assaultive, fixated upon the pumping beat of what might be the theatre's own respiratory system. This sound touches us too it seems, intimately, somatically, each of us in our own blood. The repetitive beat is like something knocking for entrance at the door of my sensations, insistent, unforgiving, an experience exacerbated by the projection on screen of random alphabetic inscriptions which, as the projections accelerate, speed into a strobic blur of blots and splatterings. If catharsis has a location, it is maybe here, neither in the experience of spectators nor protagonists but in the systems that hold us at the same time in common and apart: our breathing, our languages. Voyager's crib of human messaging systems is here zapped back at us, purified, translated and with the utmost urgency. But this is a language we barely know how to play with yet. The things we might articulate in such a language, the 'we' that this non-community might become through articulating and understanding such things, are still to be imagined. The video stops and the brutal, simplistic, boom boom boom of the theatre organism, this pseudo-organism, this stranger of our own making, continues a while in proper darkness. Then this too stops. Out of this silence, this wordless infancy lodged in us, we might begin, clumsily, patiently, to respond . . . Something new begins.

JK

A.#02
Avignon Festival,
Baraque Chabran
July 2002

For the language of the goat's text, we have adopted an analogical system using a combination of phonemes drawn from the actual protein sequences belonging to 'this' goat (who from now on we will call 'The Poet'), a four-year-old male. The amino sequences chosen are those responsible for:

1. cellular respiration;
2. the growth of the horns;
3. putrefaction.

The sequence of letter-symbols for each amino acid of the chosen proteins was reproduced on three white carpets; the Poet was free to graze on the diagram of the chosen letters. Its route constitutes a tracing of its surface. This tracing maps out a constellation of letters that, in turn, make up a basic writing. The Poet has made a choice and his choice is infallible.

RC

A letter about the goat that gave its name to tragedy

Dear Scott

Some words need to be heard during the show, but they must not have a literary origin. They must have a strength which is objective, definitive and altogether alien. Text is merely one thing among others, and, like all things, it is subject to the destiny of a form. There is no poetry, no vertical principle to justify its presence as there would be in the presence of an author, a poet or a writer. The text must 'come' from a goat. The word *tragos*, from which the word 'tragedy' derives, means 'the song of the goat'. The time has come for the eponymous animal to take back what belongs to it: its name. From the name derives the word and from the word a whole series of words: a text-testicle. Our idea, then, is to extract a series of words from the objective body of a real, living goat. This goat will thus become a body of writing and through its body it will 'donate' us a few words like a holy oblation (holy because unaware and indifferent, as indifferent as any other creature). The idea is to have a text literally 'written' by a living goat; to record this in Cesena; and then in Avignon to use these written words, objectively derived from the goat's body-sign.

To have a text coming from a goat in the context of a tragedy means disowning and suspending all at once the entire tragic tradition and endorsing a brutally traditional, etymological and literal significance at the same time. It means having an animal behind one's back instead of a poet. An animal leads us into the 'open', into a non-narrative dimension, into a dimension of real danger.

The technical problem that arises is the following: how to obtain a series of words from a goat? How to obtain a text from the marrow that emanates from the very core of all literatures, which is to say from the unexpressed of the body? By decoding the movements it makes upon a ground marked up with a set of coordinates? But how can the choice of phonemes not appear arbitrary? It is absolutely necessary that the system be ordered and precise. In order to decode the animal's movements, it will be necessary to apply a decoding system based on a diagram (like the late Renaissance diagrams of the *ars combinatoria*, or some mathematical structure like the Fibonacci sequence) and then plot onto this the coordinates given by the movements of the goat. Another possibility, even more objective, could be to read that which the goat has already, which all goats have already: the amino-acid sequence of a protein, something that determines some organic processes. For instance: decoding the protein responsible for the growth of the horns; or perhaps the sequence of the enzymes on which the principle of decomposition depends: putrescine, cadaverine . . . This will be the poetry of our tragedy. People will know that we have a poet writing for us, a very old but still living poet. A poet who writes at his ease.

It will be necessary, therefore, to make a video documenting the moment when the poet's 'writing' takes place, showing the principle of composition and the non-arbitrary character of the words obtained. The most urgent thing is to come up with a technical idea for obtaining an objective animal text. It will be Chiara's job then to give solidity and form to that which, otherwise, is necessarily formless. The big danger in all this is falling into a certain 'experimental' spirit whereas in fact everything must appear necessary, linear and logical. Something inflexible, something invincible, because already inside the 'thing'.

Greetings, Romeo

First grammatical exercise with twenty amino acids

ASPARTIC ACID (D)   GLUTAMINE (Q)
GLUTAMIC ACID (E)   CYSTEINE (C)
LYSINE (L)   GLYCINE (G)
ARGININE (R)   ALANINE (A)
HISTIDINE (H)   VALINE (V)
SERINE (S)   LEUCINE (L)
THREONINE (T)   ISOLEUCINE (I)
TYROSINE (Y)   PHENYLALANINE (F)
TRYPTOPHAN (W)   PROLINE (P)
ASPARAGINE (N)   METHIONINE (M)

The amino-acid writing system gives weight to a nocturnal voice existing before mankind. It is a biological code, conventionally written but unpronounceable. There are about twenty amino acids, which through almost limitless combinations produce innumerable proteins. There are about the same number of symbolic letters for the amino acids as there are letters in the alphabet. Amino acids are basic to the energy of every

[*Breathe in*] **MI NIRK _ / _ _ _TH.**

living thing. The code that designates them, therefore, is inalterable and immune to the passing of time. Amino-acid chains have neither accents nor punctuation. The letter-based codes from which they are composed are unified and consecutive: they have no distinct form. There is the base and the acid, the hydrophilic and the hydrophobic.

Giving voice to a possible 'writing' of the amino acids is like a gymnastic inhaling exercise for the throat. I notice immediately that pronouncing these abbreviations of the amino acids is a research process that neither moves nor surprises me. How to tear the proliferation of amino acids from the grip of silence? How can I consume it through repeated attempts upon a vocal timbre without falling immediately into vocal garglings? That is, without falling into the worst of dangers: vocal experimentalism? I must restore the living voice that is hidden in the depths of being. The letters of the amino acids live in the silent darkness closed up in the body. They know nothing of pitch, timbre, tone or volume. And I am looking for volume. I place some accents and make some marks, I perforate what condenses. The 'writing' comes to light by taking on a human form.

It happens like this: the first draft is like an instinctive coordination, which is followed by a meticulous architectonic construction. Every letter becomes a subject. There is no verb, rather the subject is both verb and predicate of itself at the same time. There is neither mode, nor tense nor person. The individual letters seem gigantic to me. They turn around an axle, allowing themselves to be read from the inside. They peel off and produce a dilation of my visual capacity. I see beyond. I see more than what is written. Each letter is the synthesis of a complete and emotional sound world, as solid as a glass palace. I manage to perceive images. I combine some letters with others and, as new chemical reactions are generated, fragments of a history start to appear. I trace their ramifications. I see something real, something perhaps with which I have lost contact, something that had been long buried. I nurture myself on letters, and I am moved. And finally, a surprise. Every letter is a flight, an 'escape'. Searching and not searching is the same thing. L stands for Lysine. I pronounce the body 'L'. From top to bottom there is a fall, which is followed by a brief horizontal movement, a straight turn – or tone – to the right. Q stands for glutamine. In Q, the breath closes its inspiration within a circle and hints at its expiration with a lowering of tone towards the base of the circle. The tracks that make up the single letters become arrows following a vector. There is a graphic effect as if of something abstracted from the perpetual flux. They are like neumes, those medieval notational symbols that make a song possible. A complex architectural music is born. I examine the amino acids that regulate cellular breathing. I listen to this first reading of the tracks that make up the letters. It is an uninterrupted reading. My body is dragged breathless through a state out of which emerge deeper, more originary echoes. A few of the letters clump together, grasping onto each other. Clots are formed.

The gold surface is at the same time mirror and pool.

Exemplum: 'LAMHY'

L
Vertical vector: from top to bottom, a slowing and weighted fall.

Horizontal vector: from right to left, imperceptible vocal emission capable of withholding energy.

A
Oblique vector: quick unbalancing from the bottom to top, a fast oblique fall.

M
Vertical vector: parallel surge from bottom to top.

Oblique vector: symmetrical conjunction of two thrusts towards the bottom, with a collision at the point of contact.

H
Vertical vector: symmetrical flight from bottom to top.

Horizontal vector: median tension that – after having grasped the vertical vectors – tries to join them.

Y
Oblique vector: the symmetrical flight of vertical vectors preceding H is interrupted and the fall meets a point of conjunction in the middle.

Vertical vector: final inert fall.

Timbre: the voice is pervaded by an occipital tremor. High, vibrating, heartfelt.

Intention: a violent and unexpected blow surprises and interrupts a being's energy at the moment of maximum physical power.

CG

SPRING 2002

Dear Scott

In Avignon, the space for *A.#02* is very similar to the Comandini except it is larger and the seating will be much wider and higher. It needs to seat 180 people. This gets in the way of the cloths that rose up in Cesena behind the backs of the audience; at present, the lights for the golden room are an unknown factor and a serious problem. Sometimes we think about replacing the golden room with a completely different idea, but it's indispensable for the skin woman, for the mechanical bow, for Carlo Giuliani and Radu. Anyway, the golden room can't last for long, and there will have to be other scenographic ideas later. Romeo's been thinking of covering the whole space in white, pleated curtains marked up here and there with big alphabetic letters. But the fabric is too expensive, and we'd need kilometres of it. And so it's impossible to do it! Perhaps it will be possible to whiten the walls, floor and ceiling of the entire room, but it's not the same thing. Using fabric is important because it'll remind people of a curtain and it could be interesting to get a real-time sound from the material being touched, hit, slashed or shaken [. . .]

From the final script of *A.#02*

Outside the audience receive a little sheet with the structure of the show subdivided into themes.

Exterior zone

In the black room there are two video projections on two white screens:

1. the designs traced by the goat
2. the Voyager greeting

The sound inside the room mixes with the sound coming from the other room.

A (child) actor who performs even as he is performed upon.

Interior zone

ENTRANCE OF THE AUDIENCE

The door opens while the video image of the goat's hoof is playing above, on the left and right.
The sound is of the goat's hoof.
The light inside comes from a few open windows.
The room is completely white with big lettering (like the letters on footballers' shirts) stitched onto the walls. On the left it reads OZ, and on the right UR.
A raised seating area covered with the same white PVC as the floor occupies the centre of the space.
At the back, the gold room is covered with white fabric embroidered with initials.
On the right of the stage, three epileptics.
When the audience are all seated the letters box descends. It is illuminated.

LETTERS BOX

The letters box gives out some texts.
Movement of the three epileptics (trembling with a lot of pauses).
After a period of general convulsions two of the epileptics suddenly stop, then get up and walk off.
The milk glass descends.
The letters box goes off.
The ambassadresses enter. Chiara stifles a laugh and leans her hands on the glass.

GOAT TEXT

At the sound of the letters box and the mechanical epileptic, the text begins.
After a while, the milk slowly leaks out of the cavity between the sheets of glass into a glass vase (Teodora opens the tap for the milk).
As the glass empties it reveals the two women.[1] One directs the other, occasionally striking the glass.

---

1 Teodora is Teodora Castellucci. The 'two women' at this point are Chiara Guidi and Claudia Castellucci. The 'text' that follows in this script is the goat text, the composition and vocal rehearsal of which are described in the short essays by Romeo and Chiara that open this section.

TEXT

A M M N P N F T R M G Q G T
PL NIG P P DL G G G
AP MIN PL NI FIF [*breathe out*]
NIGVIL L [*air and breathe in*]
FAT MATA F [*breath*] M
[*breathe in*] MI NIRK _ / _ _ _ TH
PL ? M ? KI ! VN ?
NA FI DL / PAP SNI'
SS WW NeFG S L
[. . .]

When the milk has run out of the glass a sound is added.
Chiara steps back and kisses Claudia's hand.
Claudia goes to the harmonium while Chiara rotates the glass.
Chiara approaches Claudia and whispers something in her ear, then leaves.
Light comes from all of the windows.

ENTRY OF THE CHILD

A young boy appears dressed as a judge. Walks angrily around the space then stands beside the tablets of the law. At a wave of his hand the mechanical epileptic is taken off.

The boy turns his back to the audience. He makes another movement with his hand and the sound is interrupted.

Extends his arms and puts one hand behind his back.

The boy steps backwards and with a kick knocks over the tablets.

After extending his arms, and a brief bow, the boy stands on the fallen tablets.

Three soldiers in white, abstract uniforms enter above: they have sistrums[2] and an elegant white flag with black Hebrew characters . . .

---

2 Sistrum (Italian *sistro*): a musical instrument with an oval frame and a set of rods that sound when the instrument is shaken. Originally peculiar to Egypt and the worship of Isis.

Night, writing, gesture

Even though the entire dialogue of the show amounts to just one word, the young Cosma Castellucci's utterance of the word 'Mama', this episode seems constituted around the practice, the materiality of writing. But this is an insomniac writing, something buried like an irritant in the very deeps of night, scratching at the overexposed surface of things like the video loop of the goat's hoof that plays behind our shoulders, not so much in order to leave a memorable mark but to work away like a stylus at the spaces of our forgetting. It is perhaps not what we remember that keeps us awake but the aftershocks, the ripples and resonances, of what we have forgotten.

As I look back on the work, I feel I can trace through it a 'way' of writing. First, there is the video in the antechamber of the goat (the 'poet'), recuperating for itself the etymology of the goat song, the *tragos*, tracing a path of its own choosing across diagrams that represent an alphabet of its animal destiny, the coding of its DNA. There is then the beautiful sequence in the white chamber where the 'ambassadresses of the poet' read from a device that I imagine being marked with the goat's choices. Already, though, those choices are something that occurred outside, in the night, they have become esoteric. The device itself has to be drained of a white liquid, a life-liquid of sorts (milk? semen?) so that this hollow tablet can function after the fashion of an Egyptian book of the dead, like texts buried in the tomb with the departed bearing prayers and spells, the speaking of which would open doors from the underworld into the afterlife. An impossible dogma. And so, the reading from this hollow tablet is already an invention, a performance of gestures and phonemes grafted upon the redundancy of the written object, as if the rigour of the performance might inaugurate a *Mysterium*, the mimed performance of a secret that our late modern unbelief can never credit. Finally, between us and the space of the performance, there is the alphabet screen and its accompanying cacophony, where writing and speaking are configured as the self-production of their base elements, already alien to us, even as these insinuate their way back into the grain of our feeling and our thought. Shall we say the pursuit of writing in this episode shadows *Tragedia's* pursuit of 'tragedy' as such, which is to say a theatrical tracing, through whatever remnants can still be touched upon, of everything theatre has long ago forgotten of itself?

This night of writing begins with three 'sleepers' – mummies, chrysalides, astronauts – laid out for the first sequence in the white chamber in Avignon, freezing to death or twitching into consciousness. Their epileptic shudder is a degree zero of gesturality, a bad dream without content, a literary anathema, perhaps, but by the same token the embodiment of a specifically theatrical intervention into the space of writing: actorly bodies jerked into movement and with nothing to say. What follows then is a series of actions that seem to bear witness to Agamben's observation that an epoch obsessed with gesture is one that has lost and forgotten its gestures, if we can understand gesture – in Agamben's terms – as 'the muteness inherent in humanity's very capacity for language, its speechless dwelling in language [. . .] the gesture [simply] of being at a loss in language'. The epoch that has forgotten its gestures is peopled by men 'from whom all authenticity has been taken', for whom life has become 'indecipherable' and gesture has become 'destiny'. An epoch suffering such a loss would be then 'ready for the massacre'.[3] I am troubled then – confused, provoked, mesmerised – by these 'soldiers of the conception' that take over the management of the stage. The precision with which they pursue the etiquette of their labours, the hyper-coding of every detail about them, their costume, their hair, their movements, every object they bring on or take from the stage, seems to speak of a secret withheld by this sect (I read them at present as a late modern nightmare of some sort of *ancien-régime* cabal). At the same time, though, it is as if the secret itself is emptied of content, as if 'the crystal of historical memory' that the gesture might represent were precisely that, a crystal, something beautiful and hard and sharp-edged but empty of any substance other than what it makes appear – refracted, reflected – in a particular light, encountered by this or that specific gaze.[4]

There may, though, be no legislating for the form gesturality will take, nor from where it will appear. At this point in the show, like the recalcitrant body of memory itself shattering the procedures of a formal and 'scientific' remembering, a *commedia*-like intruder shatters a window from outside and climbs down into the theatre. This is a startling, remarkable moment. A *coup de théâtre*. And, to put it as simply as I can, it messes everything up. Literally, there is a messing up as this malevolent clown 'cleans' the floor, not with a mop but with a bucket of what look like cows' livers. After pulling back the drape on the 'golden room', he then enters that room and pisses on the figure that is displayed there. Later, he will lie on the bed that has been occupied by the child, as if the nightmare itself had taken shape and body and displaced the body of the dreamer.

It seems that whatever takes place in the metal box gathers up, beyond the purities of the white room, the infections of our vision. As in Cesena, the box is impossible to light 'properly', so what we get next is a fractured, interrupted illumination of a figure, the skin woman, who performs at last an absolute gesturality. But even this (as the forced violent breathing indicates) must take place in a situation of emergency – the emergency of a birth – and under conditions marked by the emergence, or the invasion, of the

---

3 Giorgio Agamben, 'Kommerell, or On Gesture', in *Potentialities: Collected Essays on Philosophy*, trans. Daniel Heller-Roazen, Stanford Calif.: Stanford University Press, 1999, pp. 77–85.

4 Agamben, 'Kommerell', p. 83.

I'm thinking of a breathless voice and a voice made up only of breaths.

'historical' signifier: the violence of the automatic machine that fires missiles into the walls; the stain of what look like Nazi armbands; the anonymity of the ski-mask worn by this figure as well as by the child; the burden of responsibility to the child alluded to in the empty pushchair in the corner of the metal room; and, in the latex body-suit and the business with the gold cloth, stuffed inside the body or wrapped around it like a cocoon, the fetish of gender and the fantasy of its overcoming.

Even as the actions of the child later, making a telephone call ('Mama') to a world outside that can't reach in to him, or else entering the golden room and bringing the haemorrhage down upon himself, anticipate a difficult and maybe impossible birth, so too the unfolding of this spectacle – so far away from us, so enclosed upon itself, so entangled already in the labyrinths of its self-remembering – seems exposed to a way of remembering that has already gathered these events within the embrace of its own wiser and more elemental gesture. That way of remembering is not ours, it is something of the theatre itself, but we overhear and we glimpse its articulations. We glimpse them in the shifting play of light upon the semi-transparent draperies hung around the white chamber. We hear them in the pulsations of Scott Gibbons' soundtrack, as if what we hear there is the very switches and circulations of the theatre's nervous system. And the night lends a gesture of its own. From the high window broken earlier, a wind blows into the space from the night outside, billowing the drape drawn in front of it. In this motion, there is neither pity nor indifference – it is, after all, merely the wind – but we can seize that motion all the same as an image of acknowledgement, of the evocation in this place and time of human struggle and suffering.

However, even as such an image is seized as image, i.e., as something we can 'make something of', that contributes to the pathos of the spectacle, still as a gesture it remains alien. Simply put, we do not believe anymore in a 'natural' mimesis: the stars do not shine down upon our sorrows, the waves of the sea do not capture the rhythms of our desires, and the wind does not do our remembering for us. As if the organism were unapproachable as regards the 'life' inherent in it, we grasp it instead as a mechanism, as something that can be made to perform a function: a rhetorical function that is only performed within the arena of our hearing and seeing. So, the beast's writing is itself rewritten as a stroll along the etymology of its own destiny (as *tragos*, and as 'goat'). Even that etymology, though, does not relate to any code the goat understands, and so we can say too that the animal's destiny is not petrified in this mimetic gesture, even as it is framed and projected upon the artificial darkness and donated to our remembering. Rather, the beast's gesture – whatever that gesture is – has happened, and is still happening, somewhere else. Its life is not assimilated to the theatre being improvised upon its appearance. It 'remains', so to speak, forgotten.

The same goes for the scene of the anatomy lesson based on the Rembrandt painting, where the 'soldiers' anatomise the boy's arm. Here a well-remembered scene (or at least what remains in the memory of a famous painting) is approached as a mimetic mechanism, which is to say it is put together, wound up, assembled, mimed, framed, presented – just as the 'original' painting was itself a reconstruction of another theatre, the anatomy theatre, where certain ways of knowing were rehearsed around the rhetorical display of a more or less docile body. In the reconstruction of the scene in the Baraque Chabran, the potentiality of gesture is made available to us in the obvious fact that the 'subject' is something much more than that, he is a (child) actor who performs even as he is performed upon. He lives and breathes and remembers. And he pretends. In the uncertainty as much as in the clarity of that pretence, the 'not enough' of the theatre's rhetorical machinery might be exposed. Which is not to claim a transcendence or a recalcitrance in the child's performance but just to suggest that right there something forgotten withholds itself and prepares its gesture. Indeed, later in the piece when Cosma speaks the word 'Mama' into the telephone, the shadow of a figure appears briefly for a moment against one of the drapes, as if the theatre 'organism' were beginning to recall something it had left behind.

Meanwhile, in the 'real world', the eruption of gesture is met with the gesture of violence: a young man raises a fire extinguisher in Genoa as an act of demonstration and is shot to death by the police. A remembering of his interrupted gesture is attempted in the reconstruction of its image within the golden room. As spectators, we either remember what is captured here or we do not; the theatre does not judge us either way. What it does do is perform, to the music of John Dowland, its own gesture of remembrance – on the site, not of the event itself, but the occasion of its representation. The theatre meets the threat and promise of a radical gesturality with a gesture of its own. A commemoration, an inscription. A crystallisation of the event that mimes, let us say, its speechlessness, 'its speechless dwelling in language'. The theatre prepares a welcome for what may be born from that speechlessness, even if – for the moment – what emerges is a harsh birth, as announced in the automatic poetry of the alphabet machine: with writing looming as the first and last gesture on the nocturnal horizon.

JK

The form of a blot

Notes on the first episodes of Socìetas Raffaello Sanzio's
Tragedia Endogonidia

SPATIAL SOLITUDE

There are events in nature that have no part in the political, aesthetic or social reality of the city: orientated reality. Reality is a vision without will. The figures of *Tragedia Endogonidia* have no history. From an historical point of view they are inexplicable. They are dense, although not because they are full of significance but because they are closed like a bubble. Every dense natural form tends to be unmixed. The character lives in complete ignorance of social consequences; it acts outside of communication, neither asking nor responding. The danger it lives through is totally internalised, it is only aware of itself. These forms are not rooted in the earth but rather sunk into the sea, spreading out beyond place or pretext. In order to join with them, I have to immerse myself in the depths, where all I am able to hear is a cannulated breath, like the sound through a diver's snorkel linking the eardrums to the lungs, where the only sound in the world passes, the sound of spatial solitude. Spatial solitude is rehearsed in the stalls as we watch what happens on stage: like the thermal solitude of a liquid going down the oesophagus;

The 'black fire on white fire' of the Holy Scriptures.

Three 'sleepers': mummies, chrysalides, astronauts.

like being in one's own bed; like a small child's experience of being alone, in the presence of its mother. Here the mother is the figure.

GOLD

Gold is the first material I find in this tragedy, and I find it first inside a cube that almost entirely fills the scenic space. This room has no curtain, no wings, nor any other sort of opening. If any actors are going to enter it, they will have to do so 'in full view', that is to say, in full view of the spectators, which means the actors will be visible in those parts of the show that are not usually seen. In this simple circumstance, there is a first allusion to the condition of being a spectator, which will become ever more important during the course of *Tragedia Endogonidia*. The actors enter with their burdens (the semblance and also the weight of life). All of their exits and entrances are visible and heavy and without any tricks: as heavy, monolithic and rough as the cube that occupies – rather than decorating or theatricalising – the stage. This cube would appear to be planted there to define the optical relations within the space, were it not that its internal walls, the ceiling and floor included, are entirely covered with sheets of pseudo-gold, so that these same optical relations, according to the laws of geometry, explode in a confusion of reflections. The gold surface is at the same time mirror and pool. When the figures pass in front of the golden walls, their reflections come into contact with a background that multiplies them and coagulates them along with all the other forms that it takes in. Writing of a tension between the indifference of the common human form and the singularity of individual humans, Giorgio Agamben remarks in *The Coming Community* that 'common and proper, genus and individual are only the two slopes dropping down from either side of the watershed of whatever'.[5] This tragedy is called 'the tragedy of the gold of the I'. It is any I whatsoever.

The bodies are lit, but the sources from which the lights come are invisible: the gold confounds them. As in certain portraits by Rembrandt, where a bunch of luminous particles appears to burn through the opacities of the material, the organic marrow of these bodies is stimulated by waves that shake them from inside. In Rembrandt, the light comes from inside, and this is an invention of ontological significance, because it means considering birth to be an event of darkness. Darkness appears as a light from inside. It is the *beginning* which, as Franz Rosenzweig says, *is the only enigma in the world*.[6]

---

5 Giorgio Agamben, *The Coming Community*, trans. Michael Hardt, Minneapolis, Minn.: University of Minnesota Press, 2003, p. 20.
6 Franz Rosenzweig (1886–1929), author of *The Star of Redemption*, Notre Dame, Ind.: University of Notre Dame Press, 1985.

Now, the light that comes from itself does not have a solar psychology: rather, it is cut out of the universal darkness and is pulled towards itself by its own gravity. Gold gets in the way of geometrical perspective, it interrupts the gaze that looks forward, offering up instead a large number of moving forms, different to the life we know: just for the sake of thinking.

Gold's many-bodied background is a reality which is supported by the definitive singularity of the body. It seems as if the body might coagulate in its finitude, into a single photogram of the simultaneity of forms. Seeing this, the spectator becomes aware of a pre-individual sensation which unites her with newly born presences. This is the political dimension of a theatre that is realised without any deliberate will and is the means by which *Tragedia Endogonidia* touches upon a future. And, perhaps, the lights that attach themselves to the gold, which the theologian and mathematician Pavel Florensky, writing about icons, calls 'powers that are no longer abstractions even if they still don't have a determinate quality',[7] are, indeed, the lives that the gold rejects, invisible to the seeing eye, but not to the mind's eye which intuits new life, lives ready to be begun. In Plato's *Cratylus*, Socrates derives thought, *noesis*, from *neou esis*, 'the desire of the new'.[8] Gold is matter that imitates the pregnancy of the thought that desires the new. To think is to desire the new.

Gold is capable of capturing and multiplying a minimum quality of light. Even in the least possible light, where not even the source of light is visible, it manages to show something of it. A soft phosphorescence, along with a degeneration of the illuminating source, endows bodies with their own light, like distant stars; only their reflection on the walls reunites them with what remains, and it is indeed a fusion of remains not of actual bodies. We do not find gold among the colours that we perceive in reflected light. According to Florensky, gold and colour belong to two distinct optical spheres. Gold doesn't have a colour, even if it does have a tone; and it does not blend, it isolates.

In the episodes *C.#01* and *A.#02*, at a certain moment, coloured backgrounds were hoisted up behind the backs of the spectators, washing the internal walls of the gold cube with their own tint. Even so, the gold remained gold. It wasn't a presence that it absorbed but rather a quality. It was as if the colour raised up at the back entered a circuit of collective respiration, and only at the moment of impact with the golden background did it reveal itself. This idea of a sensuous immateriality reminds me of Yves Klein's exhi-

---

7 See Pavel Florensky, *Iconostasis*, trans. Donald Sheehan and Olga Andrejev, Crestwood, NY: St Vladimir's Seminary Press, 2000, pp. 115–16.
8 Plato, *Cratylus*, trans. Benjamin Jowett, The Internet Classics Archive, see <http://classics.mit.edu/Plato/cratylus.html>.

bition at the Iris Clert Gallery in Paris in 1958: a 'radiance' of 'pictorial sensibility' inside a gallery absolutely empty of works. And, curiously, the two colours that for Klein were closest to immateriality, blue and gold, were those that were hoisted up at the back during *C.#01* and *A.#02*.[9] The spectators are gathered in a field of reflections, wrapped up in an atmosphere of changing light that begins from behind their backs. There is no noise to draw attention to what's going on behind. It only dawns on the spectators when the immateriality of the colours finally beats against the golden walls; and then the eyes of everyone present are filled with what before was purely aleatory. It's like a gigantic eyelid sinking over every retina. But what is more important here is that the phosphorescence cuts every link with the light sources, rendering vain any return to an origin. A beginning, right here. Everything begins, here. From degeneration to degeneration.

EPILEPSY

At the beginning of the first two episodes of *Tragedia Endogonidia*, a mannequin lies on the floor, and later two actors as well, moving as if struck by an epileptic fit. If death cuts our mental connections with things, the small death (epilepsy) even disconnects the forms that remain in the mind. The body makes a sieving movement, as if through the sieve of itself might pass every terrestrial articulation. The body accepts the morphology of the world; its consciousness is intimately linked with it and would say along with St Paul: 'the world in its present form is passing away' (1 Cor. 7:31). In me, it passes. This consciousness is a form of obedience. It is a totally ecstatic sensation. If we read Dostoevsky's description of Prince Myshkin's epileptic attack – 'Then suddenly it opened wide before him like an abyss; an extraordinary interior light illuminated his soul. This feeling lasted maybe a split second . . .'[10] – we notice that it is a description of someone falling into a pool of gold. Suddenly. Abyss. Light. Illumination. A split second. We should pay particular attention to Dostoevsky's temporal calculation: a split second. This 'split second' has to imply, it seems to me, not only a psychic but a technical precision. That 'split second' is a measure of the velocity of the figures. No speech is possible in a 'split second'. At best, one is able to see something that words could only describe over many, many seconds. The 'split second' ensures an exclusively visual, thermal sensation, an auditory sensation even, if the principle is a musical one, which would be ideal. A word

---

9 For more on these ideas in Klein's work, see *Yves Klein, 1928–1962: A Retrospective*, Houston, Tex.: Institute for the Arts, Rice University.

10 See Fyodor Dostoevsky, *The Idiot*, trans. Alan Myers, Oxford: Oxford University Press, 1992, p. 246. The text above is translated into English from the Italian in Claudia Castellucci's essay.

What remains in the memory of a famous painting.

is an idea that has already been formulated; it is born in order to grasp that which escapes it; it is an instrument that is of no use at all when dealing with a split second's duration. We must abandon the idea of preserving and archiving. The rapidity of reception is the reason for the epilepsy that inhabits *Tragedia Endogonidia*, where activity and passivity have become synchronous. The rapidity is such as to make impossible any immediate restraining action on the part of the brain, those restraints that hold the personality together. Here is where we shall find the new man. And, in the new man, we shall find structures that don't even have a name yet. Because right now the time is too short.

MOULTING (REVERSIBILITY OF THE SKIN)

In *Tragedia Endogonidia*, there is always something that can be turned inside out, or turned into its own negative. Skins, hoods, sacks, sheaths, gloves, placentas and ski-masks extend the body into an ulterior dimension, through a change of form or sex, or through lines of flight that also function through disguises and masks and that slip through our attempts to intercept them, so that it is impossible to recognise the object anymore, due to this innervation of general communication.

There are two scenes in which the reversal of the skin is shown. In the first, a pair of childlike legs descends from above showing female genitalia. At a certain point, these legs are turned inside out like a glove, dispersing a great quantity of blood which pours down upon the stage. They are identical to how they first appeared, except with male genitalia instead of female. The second scene, which amplifies the first, is that of the Anonymous Mother: here the skin is entire and completely covers a young man with a female nudity, so that when he takes the skin off eventually, he reveals his own male nudity. This scene of the skin, put on like a glove and then sloughed off like a snake shedding its skin, is worthy of Merleau-Ponty's phrase 'the two leaves of the body', with the interior and the exterior sides of the skin articulated one upon the other. 'There is no need', he writes,

> of a spectator who would be *on each side*. It suffices that from one side I see the wrong side of the glove that is applied to the right side, that I touch the one *through* the other. The chiasm is that: the reversibility. It is through it alone that there is a passage from the 'For Itself' to the For the Other. In reality there is neither me nor the other as positive, positive subjectivities. There are two caverns, two opennesses, two stages where something will take place – and which both belong to the same world, to the stage of Being. There is not the For Itself and the For the Other. They are each the other side of the other. This is why they incorporate one another: projection-introjection. There is that line, that frontier surface at some distance before me, where occurs the veering I-Other Other-I. The axis alone given – the end of the finger of the glove is nothingness – but a nothingness one can turn over and where then one sees *things*.[11]

The exchange between I–other and other–I was already happening, thanks to the reflections of the body on the gold leaves of the walls, and now, in the reversibility of the skins, the Self becomes an object of contact, of the world and taken from the world.

---

11 Maurice Merleau-Ponty, *The Visible and the Invisible, followed by Working Notes*, Evanston, Ill.: Northwestern University Press, 1968, pp. 263–4.

It is because there are these 2 doublings-up that are possible: the insertion of the world between the two leaves of my body, the insertion of my body between the two leaves of each thing and of the world. This is not anthropologism: by studying the 2 leaves we ought to find the structure of being. Start from this: there is not identity, nor non-identity, or non-coincidence, there is inside and outside turning about one another. My 'central' nothingness is like the point of the stroboscopic spiral, which is *who knows where*, which is 'nobody'.[12]

SKI-MASK

The female figure, protagonist of the first episodes, has her face covered with a ski-mask. Her anonymity recalls 'no one', an indistinct member of the crowd who here has become the protagonist of the tragedy. This is not a hero: it is a whoever person. This state of asthenia, this weakness of being, however, also requires an ulterior weakness: she renounces her face. To cover your own face is to subtract yourself from the political experiment of the mass identikit. It is a form of inexistence, an iconological hole, a figural subtraction from the planetary encyclopaedia of faces. It is a resignation of character. And now everything begins from here: from anonymity. For Agamben 'removing the thin diaphragm that separates bad mediatised advertising from the perfect exteriority that communicates only itself – this is the political task of our generation'.[13] The mask, or *larva*, is something that has a certain similarity to the face and is often taken for one, but it is empty inside. The meaning of the word 'larva' is related to the face, originating in the insubstantial impression that is left behind by the dead. The pseudo-reality of masks appears also in the Kabbala, where they are called *Klippoth*, or shells. These shells without a nut inside connoted something impure or bad. But we see now with the commercialisation of the human figure that it is the face that is the mask: an empty shell capable of an obscure strength, impersonal, vampyric, but maintaining itself – as Florensky notes again when he describes the funerary masks on Egyptian sarcophagi – thanks to the reanimating forces of blood and face, to which the astral mask is able to attach itself, sucking up the face and presenting it as its own being.[14] It is the larval-face of glamour models pumped up with adulation. The negation of this larval-face, the subtraction of this cosmic and cosmetic catalogue, is, here, the covering of the face. But

---

12 Merleau-Ponty, *The Visible and the Invisible*, p. 264.
13 Agamben, *The Coming Community*, p. 65.
14 Florensky, *Iconostasis*.

the covered face is no longer a mask but rather the true face in a time when truth has need of strength. To cover the face is a new act of appearing, of making present. This, above all else, is the real scandal of the burka for the Western mentality, and hence the importance of covering the face when there is no obligation to, as with the Zapatistas. These days, theatre doesn't look towards the ancient masks, nor to the veristic faces of realism, but rather to the ski-mask.

MONEY AND ALPHABET

Money is the total *medium*, the system of communication that reduces interpretation – and, hence, the risk of disagreement – to a minimum. This is why there is a strong analogy between money and the alphabet: the impersonal character of mediation is present in both. They don't look anyone in the face, so to speak. They are amoral and apolitical. As casual as you like, they pass from one regime to another, without disintegrating or changing their function. For the rest, our having become accustomed to written words over such a long time is the condition that has made possible the Western use of money, which is linked to a specialist alphabetical technology that, according to McLuhan, raises to a new intensity the Gutenbergian form of mechanical reproduction. Money and alphabet set loose on the Earth the limitless power of the incommensurable.

The golden room, regarded as a treasure chest, becomes the treasure chest of time; that is to say, it contains the potential acts which money is capable of promising. Money is an appearance of the future, because it can postpone for 'later' that which it is already ready to realise. 'Realise' is, in addition, a technical term from economics, which refers to nothing that is actually real, but alludes to this actual, pre-futural power.

Also, through the projection of the final video, which shows a percussive sequence of letters of the alphabet, there is a demonstration of power, which is even more violent when the frequency of the switches between black letters and white background is increased. This sort of saturation of words which makes use also of the white space around them is a form of communication that aspires to the religious. Almost like the 'black fire on white fire' of the Holy Scriptures, which Moses Nahmanides wrote about, where the 'white fire' was the unwritten space which surrounded the characters of the text, where religious meanings could also be read, indeed all the more so because of the divine character of its silence.[15] The speed of this alternation of signs upon an empty surface overwhelms our 'capability', because everything becomes sign, even the white

---

15 Moses Nahmanides (1194–1270), Jewish thinker, leading Talmudist and founding figure of Jewish mystical tradition (Kabbala) in thirteenth-century Spain.

around the black letters, even the black Rorschach blots, which, in the end, alternate with the letters. Inside this furious demonstration of the mechanism, which is linked to the acoustic bombardment of an encyclopedic collection of human voices, there is the most beautiful poem, which, even so, must be locked in and never come to light. Because of the future that already is, and which is closed.

CC
January 2003

B.#03
Berlin, Hebbel Theater
January 2003

The stalls are filled with rows of rabbits. They are all the same, monstrous without exception. The public will have to be above in the gallery, far away. The curtain is closed.
The gaze of the rabbits is heavy, immobile and devoid of comment.
They know everything but say nothing.
For the audience placed up above the rabbits the desire to see is like an obsession.
The view is out of focus. Perhaps the theme of the episode is vision, its subject the physical gaze.
The effort is paradoxical: the figure becomes a shadow.
Its actions are performed in a grey space.
From inside an animalistic light fills the vacancies of the space.
The light is moved although not to illuminate a body but rather to hunt it down.
The light completes the action of the shadow, it prolongs it.
And then leaves it.
It grants a glimpse of an inside, but leaves the objects suspended in the void.
Such as the girl's body, such as the bed.

Music does not have the function it had in the preceding episodes.
It is not the language of the figures.
It does not open, but it also does not close.

RC

10 SEPTEMBER 2002

Dear Scott

The moment has come to talk about *B.#03*!!
    Thinking about Berlin and Germany, we'd like to work on the figure of Ulrike Meinhof, the revolutionary communist of the Red Army Faction, mysteriously 'suicided' in Stammheim prison camp during the 1970s. We'd like to work, not in a narrative or historical and political way but at the level of human strangeness. We've been asking a few friends in Berlin what this name stands for in Germany nowadays. We have a morbid fascination with this woman because of her dramatic biography, but we won't be narrating the events of her life, and there will be no commentary. We are very interested also in her being a mother (of two twins) who was separated from her children. We are also inspired by seeing Gerhard Richter's paintings dedicated to the last act of the Baader–Meinhof group. We are aware that the name of this woman is mythical in Germany, or an anti-myth, but we're worried also that this is an over-used figure, too much talked about, too much the revolutionary cliché. We know there are already some films and theatre pieces, and we know too, from the little we've heard, that they are mainly of a narrative and illustrative sort. What draws us to Ulrike Meinhof is her mute, tragic stature and, at the same time, her melancholia. We want to work on this figure in a way that her biography could be the biography of anyone. It needs to be about the things that Ulrike Meinhof did not do in her life and was never able or never knew how to do. This incapacity interests us and is what brings her close to us, what draws us to her. It is the void around her, and also inside her, which involves us.
    Every action of hers that was never written about must be brought to light. Because it's not about working on the character's mythic or heroic aspect, nor, least of all, her political thought, so much as those missing actions that were never written about because they never took place. It's about an excavation in pure abstraction, without commentary or judgement. It's a work about abandonment, about the

The Black Larva of the North.

Harangued by a demagogue.

vacuity of being. It is possible to imagine, in this respect, certain bitter-sweet and melancholy atmospheres.

The intention is to jam up the gears of tragic destiny that turn in anyone's life, opening out the emptiness and silence. The paradox is this: there needs to be an exemplary name (U.M.) in order to focus on the tragic structure of any of us.

It'd be good to work at the Hebbel Theater in a vertical way, using only the upper rows for the audience. We'd like to fill the main stalls with a crowd of black stuffed rabbits (a sort of simulacrum of the audience). The real audience will have to watch another audience watching a show. Ideally, the whole tragedy is performed for the rabbits. At the moment, we are checking the sight lines of the upper rows.

Dearest Scott, a long and, as usual, complex labour awaits us. The entire structure of the episode will have to be less fragmented and have fewer figures in it than *C.#01* and *A.#02*. All of the sound has to be like a monolith, giving weight to that other monolith that is the figure of Ulrike Meinhof.

Chiara and Romeo

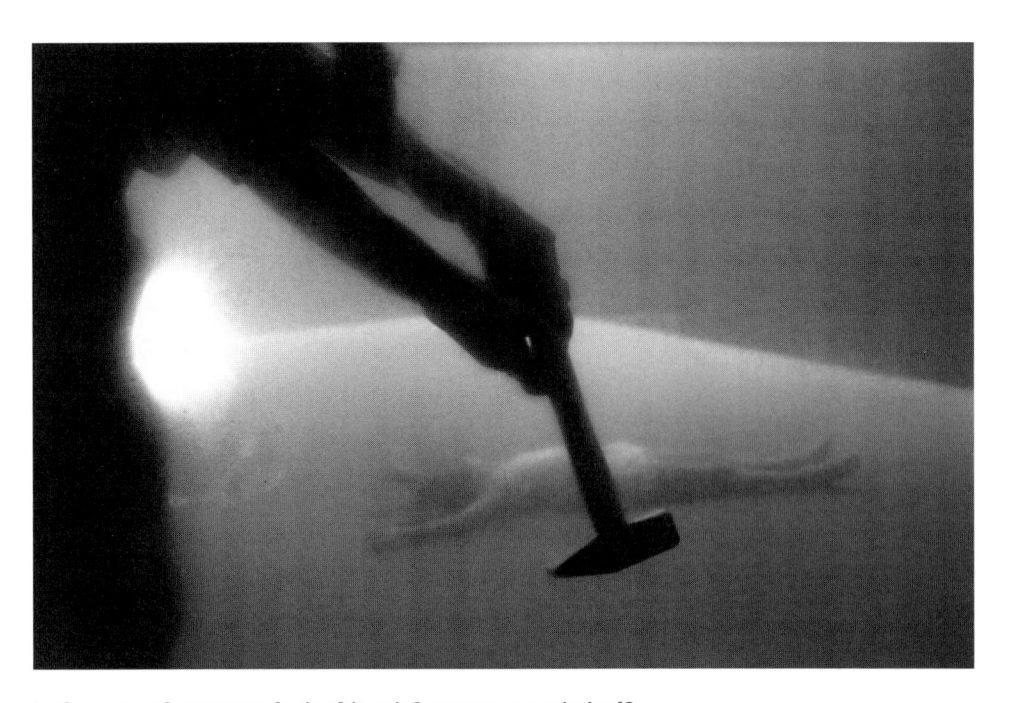

Is there no other way to be in this grief except as a criminal?

OCTOBER 2002

Dear Scott

We are now ready to leave for Melbourne and, in this overexcited period, between time zones and sleep, there's been a substantial change to the script of B.#03 regarding the figure of Ulrike Meinhof that we talked with you about. To understand better the effect this figure would have had in the context of a show made for Germany, we asked the advice of three German women, intellectuals who teach arts. Their letters have raised a very important alarm: in Germany right now it is difficult to approach this name without getting involved in a 'political' conversation. And such 'conversation' doesn't belong to *Tragedia Endogonidia*, which refuses any narrative or illustrative justification.

And so Ulrike Meinhof has now turned into a completely anonymous figure, without any historical reference. It's better to focus on the inability of this figure to complete any gesture or action, as if the action had got lost and become impossible to remember. Her brain sets an action going, but only to interrupt it immediately; the brain intuits a form but is unable to fully bring it into being.

This figure is tragic, melancholy and comical and sad at the same time. Sounds, noises and voices should accompany the woman's actions, synchronised with the actions like in certain action films.

Dear Scott, I await your reply, however brief, so as to know if we are thinking along the same lines.

Chiara

From the final script of B.#03

The beginning of the episode (Grey Room)

ENTRANCE OF THE AUDIENCE

The doors are opened.
The stalls are full of black rabbits; the Voyager image is projected upon the curtain.

GREY ROOM

Sound of silence: bass frequencies.
For a long time lights move behind the gauze and the PVC screen.
A double bed is lit in the centre of the stage.
There are two bodies in the bed. A girl's arm is visible.
The stage appears to be completely out of focus.
The light is flickering.
A woman appears. She gets up.
Silently, she collects her shoes and a dress from the floor and gets dressed, leaning on the bed. She stretches.
She kisses the girl and shakes her.
Moves the toy.
Picks up the plastic gloves and puts them on while still at the bed.
The woman drags the dead body of the girl down from the bed.
Gets on the bed and finds the hammer which she drags along the ground towards the PVC; then she stands it upright.
She carries the child offstage.
She re-enters, wiping the floor.
She returns to the bed, covers her face with the sheet.
She removes a shoe.
She grabs the toy again.
Masturbation.
She performs some other gestures sitting on the bed, then she weeps.
She gets up from the bed, comes towards the PVC screen and wipes her backside on it.
A rainbow descends.
Some further actions of the woman against the PVC and on the ground.
When the woman is on all fours on the ground, her legs apart, touching herself with her hand, the rainbow starts flickering.
The woman raises the PVC from the ground and speaks some indistinct words.
Darkness.

A play of grief

The Berlin episode of Romeo Castellucci's *Tragedia Endogonidia* is a play about grief. A mother awakes to lose her daughter and her grief erupts, in full view and straight on. It comes, though, with a glacial slowness and filtered through a haze of semi-transparent screens. It is sorrow played out like a history lesson we are unable or unwilling to comprehend, processed into a series of ritual actions: stepping out of bed, walking and rocking herself, before it all has to begin; putting on shoes and a dress; taking a child's toy (a wooden horse) from out of the tangle of sheets; attempting to wake the child; failing; putting on the rubber gloves; dragging the dead child from out of the bed and off the stage; showing us the hammer, balancing the hammer at the front of the stage (the weapon moves of its own accord); scrubbing the blood from the bed and floor; settling on the end of the bed to masturbate, or try to masturbate, first with fingers, then with the child's horse: an impossible attempt at self-abandon. As if history could be turned off at the tap and she could be in any other moment than this one, now. Already, this is a ceremony of grief, and she is locked into it, becoming a function of its repetition, the child having died before, countless times. But the ceremony is also hers and hers only to perform. It is a grief that looks and feels like guilt. Is there no other way to be in this grief except as a criminal?

Every time she awakes out of that terrible dream, she finds herself in this one, which seems to be the same dream, the dream within the dream where, out of the very nut of grief, forms appear to populate her despair. A formless form, a thing of electrified howls and liquid darkness, presses itself through the stage space, implacable and ungraspable. Already her grief has outgrown her, in league with a grievous remembering far beyond her individual scope. Three female figures appear from under the bed, clad in black with their black flags, their esoteric scripts, their cryptic gestures, shooting at blank grey targets: officiants at some sort of ritual of inauguration who draw their libations out of a deep well of historical amnesia. Or maybe not so deep: the scripts are Hebrew and German Gothic, printed on bedsheets, which the women lay back over the bed. Except we still may be unsure what these visitants intend, uncertain exactly of what these words remember or enact. Faced with acts of faith we are not sure we know how to 'do' and magic words set in scripts we do not know how to pronounce, it may after all be easier to be sad. The sort of sadness that recalls the forgotten things but holds them at the threshold of remembering, where the imagination conceives but cannot grasp its conceptions. In the wake of such sadness, the three female 'soldiers of the conception' throw a series of images that bob upon the surface of the scene like so much heart's garbage – a brief pornographic jig, the raising of the flag of German unification, the Mosaic tables of the law set down on the ground to look like a couple of gravestones. See what you will see. Use this as you will.

Meanwhile, the three women transform themselves into peculiar visitants: Barbarella girls and abominable snowmen, mythical denizens of the cold-and-distant, tour guides in grief's playland of guilt and recalcitrant hope. They will take her on a journey to the ends of the Earth, maybe even outer space, the stage floor shaking like the deck of a ship or a rocket, the 'weather' lowered from the flies like a three-sided box, the polar 'snow' rolled out as a rug. These guides will show her time passing in a pageant of the world's freezing over and a glimpse of history as an accretion of miniscule and major disasters that seem, from this distance, all of the same significance. Bread falls from a bird's beak. A black sun descends. And these things happen as if of their own accord. As if all of this, any of this, were not conceived in the space of our imaginings. As if our imaginings might not rebound upon us, exceeding the scope of our ordinary thought with all the enormity of a gift – born out of the disaster itself – we can barely acknowledge, let alone accept.

At the fable's end, the mother is reintroduced to her daughter in an outrageous anagnorisis involving a pair of red shoes and a child's dance on a coffin lid. The fable is propelled towards an unapologetic literalism that challenges us, as much as it challenges her, to give credence to what appears, now, 'alive', on the stage. The child is there after all. We can see her, dancing. Until, that is, she gets back in the box. Maybe, as at the denouement of another winter's tale of seeming magical redemption on the strength of the absurd, it just depends on how one approaches the site – or sight – of the offence. 'It is required you do awake your faith.'[1] Except here we know the child is gone. And, as the mother suffers the child's embrace, she is already barely even a spectator to the scene of their momentary reconciliation, turned towards the back of the stage, marooned, immobile. Her grief will not be scrubbed from the stage, no matter what fantastic transformations are affected. She does not need to look, she knows. Or so we persuade ourselves, as we conceive her grief for ourselves – which we cannot, and cannot help but do.

The theatre, though, is already ahead of us. In the Hebbel this evening, even our place as spectators is usurped. Every seat in the stalls is taken by a life-size (as in people-size: that is, spectator-size), stuffed blue rabbit. The rabbits loll and flop while the drama makes its play. It is like a game of seduction in which both parties have grown tired, lost the plot and no longer care too much where they left it. The rabbits are not exactly inert, there is a certain cynical animation to their postures. But, being stuffed rabbits, they exhibit no felt relation, nothing of critique or engagement or faith, towards the one relation (the stage–auditorium relation) that constitutes them 'as' spectators and thereby grants them whatever little animation they might have. They are, so to speak, here 'for' this performance, but they do not acknowledge the performance as 'theirs'. They are like the subjects of a corrupt and corrupting historicism, supine before the power of 'whatever happens', unwilling or incapable of conceiving it otherwise. When they are

---

1 William Shakespeare, *A Winter's Tale*, Act 5, Scene 3.

A brief pornographic jig.

harangued by a demagogue (later in the play the 'Black Larva' takes the forestage, barking some nonsense, dragging rabbits out of the front row, dispensing carrots and kicks in equal measure), it seems no less than fitting.

For the paying spectators overlooking the whole business from a few rows of the first gallery, whatever erupts down there on the stage in the way of guilt or atonement is short-circuited by those all-too 'material' sensibilities in the stalls. Later, after the show, we will prod at the lava at the far edge of the eruption: the cooling imprint of this or that image, the loosening links of a fable's 'cause and effect', the motile grain of a soundscape petrifying already into a friable, anecdotal crust. I remember the overpersuasive gesture of a young woman in a yeti costume rolling a stuffed snowball and the ungainly wobble of the Tables of the Law. With a little help from my notes, I can persuade myself I remember the passage of a whole scene: a black moon descends; there is the sound of night and insects; and a speech – the only speech in the play – accompanied by a

They are all the same, monstrous without exception.

tentative mime, a speech in German of gentle imploring and offering before the red shoes fall from the flies and the mother tries to put them on, a girl's shoes, too small for her, in which she attempts to stand upon the Tables of the Law like balancing on a sledge or a chariot that might carry her on, up and out of here. I am, though, already 'making it up'. My remembering does not grasp the thing that is to be grasped. Speculation too, even as it comprehends and articulates the dialectic, even as it grasps that dialectic precisely as a reflection upon its 'self', does not fail to miss something. It fails to grasp the exception. It fails to grasp what is not, and cannot, be given. It fails, in its intimations of the coming community, to grasp the specific reality of 'her', of 'that one' and her despair – and her inconceivable redemption.

Maybe something similar can be said of the theatre and its deployment of an offensive ostentation, blatant, brutal, and banal – a woman at the stage edge masturbating with a child's toy; a half-rainbow done in primary colours descending in front of the stage gauze like a parable for the stupid; the name of the Old Testament prophet stitched onto a bedsheet and laid out like an IOU upon the place of the loved one's disappearance. Belief, and maybe forgiveness too, or whatever means we might have to go beyond the hero's horizon of death towards a regenerative (though be it 'endogenous') conception, will have to go there by way of a negotiation with such offences. Put simply, speculation will have to face up to the facts. Meanwhile, grief – ordinary 'human' grief, the grief of the individual, each and any particular 'me' or 'her' or 'you' – has gone to the wall and is unable to turn back. And, at once, the facts are not so clear. Grief makes no ostentation at the end of the episode. Grief has gone to the back of the stage, to face up for herself (beyond the reach of sight or hearing) to the faintest breath of hope perhaps, or maybe just the blank of impossibility, the way one faces up to the surface of the theatrical scenery: its inertia, its indifference, its teasing impermeability.

JK

From the final script of *B.#03*

The speech of the Black Larva of the North (White Room)

The Black Larva of the North (completely covered in black fur) comes from the back and steps in front of the PVC.
    The sound of the earthquake stops and the sound of the white room continues.
    Then she turns towards the audience and is stunned by the rabbits in the stalls. She begins her text.
    Addressing the rabbits, she tells them a story in an unknown language. Every so often, she chucks bunches of carrots into the stalls. Sometimes, she grabs a rabbit, throwing it to the ground on stage, or goes down into the stalls to hit the rabbits with a stick, making them fall out of their seats.

Oh!!!
[*Then she begins to mutter*]
Rolloba mermina tappa?
Fol le alal alul
Yobbra folè font
Babra? Ah! Ah! Ma gnisdi Ki ezt o chisc Kooput?!?!
Moi meglatot hoghie mi fut
[*She stretches her back*]
[*Horse sounds*]

Officiants at some sort of ritual of inauguration.

Oh oh!!! Mierte la varra de la tirannu oh!!
Radulbi gnecche gnecche gnecche vienmi radulbi gnec
Senne?
BeKà eger variù hollo [*Sound of a girl's voice*]
[*Weeping*]
Vetrosso va là che si ma viende mi ralla na to bo là essemì tende
Senne??? Che ne te diende tabla porta a . . .
No siente!!!! . . . To to to to tò
Agliota! . . . Mi storca la spocca!!.
Mità [*Epileptic voice*] smeradaia muta trava, mità che su la gana travia la goria
Pope cura pope cura brrr
pope cura pope cura
[*Muttering again*] Brrr . . .
Gnecche: Lotzi te hollodè ier i dè
Ier o mondom ortoz corton u meghitten roz olemben
Mità: Rasciallà Resciai? resciai? resciai!!!!
Gnecche: Enne! Enne! Rabiu lo zatra viarsciu enne lo stiaco! Enne . . . Enne . . .
Mità: Rass..mo..tar..cas..taù!! Taù!! Taù!! Taù!!!
Enne!
Taù!
Enne, enne!!!
Taù! Taù, taù!!!!
[*Weeping, breathing*]
Vilvadle, snenne petè
Tl, tr, f, fafh, fif, pfi, ia, ala
[*Six kisses for the audience of rabbits, the last a blown kiss.*]

Note on the composition of the text

I link the phonemes together, forming a long uninterrupted chain.
I mark out the punctuation to individuate syntactic–semantic unities.
I design a pattern between the phonemes.
Every punctuation point breaks the chain, creating a gap where it is possible to take a breath.
A form emerges, which I emphasise with the line breaks.
I read some syllables then some meaningless words; a few I repeat; I emphasise exclamations with an 'h'.

The intonation is suggested to me by the phrases.

I separate bunches of words and it seems like a dialogue.

I then add some quotation marks and two characters emerge, one strong and the other weak.

The punctuation marks create a hierarchy between the two positions, and this syntactic function creates the dramatic node.

CG

On being there (in the beginning)

Each episode of *Tragedia Endogonidia* opens with a kind of breathing, as though there were a membrane between the stage and the auditorium through which, once we begin, breath may pass, that deep breath we take before we take the plunge. Scott Gibbons and Chiara Guidi process human breath into a sound that spreads through the space like a smoke, creeping into all the cavities and passageways of the stage and auditorium, opening them up to their own vibrations. Here, this time, in Berlin, it starts as a distant rumble, the long-since-accomplished aftershock of an exploding star reaching us through galactic time, perhaps, prefiguring the appearance of something that died long before human memory was born; or signalling, at least, that something of magnitude has occurred, something we were not there to see. What we hope to see and hear, here and now, is the transmission of some message about this event. And so we hold our breath, and we look.

Each episode also opens with an image. One might call it an emblem, appearing as it does not only as a projection on the stage at each venue but in the programme for each episode. A man, naked, stands next to a slightly smaller woman, also naked. The man's hand is raised, as in greeting. A set of lines converge on a central point, forming a sketchy star-explosion to their right, our left. Beneath them there is a series of circles and dots in a horizontal sequence. Like the emblem, with its motto and its explanation (sometimes in the form of dialogue), the action of the tragic stage often involves a doubling in which speech explains the action that is taking place, as it takes place, as though the one were always pointing at the other, saying 'Look there, look there.' Here, though, not only has the chorus been stripped out of this tragedy altogether (along with the messengers who bear witness to the deaths), but speech itself is almost always absent too. No explanation, no commentary, just the enigma of the action itself and of the image. In Cesena, a dubious messenger barked dubious Latin at an uncomprehending audience. In Avignon, the Ambassadresses of the Poet read in a language composed by a goat from its own

The yeti, then, is the thing that only ever appears when you are not looking.

arcane biological codes. Both episodes closed with a video projection in which visible letters, merging with Rorschach blots, sped past to percussive suckings, breathings, spittings and vocal clamourings, the amplified inside of the voice, as though what we were hearing was all the scraps and shards of breath discarded in the act of forming meaningful phonemes. A language in the negative, the sound of language in tatters and ruins, still desperately, urgently carrying something that must be communicated.

To return to the image, then, to start again at the beginning of the episode, we return to the image that appears without explanation. In place of the explanation, there is just this sidereal breath, the wreckage of language adrift in space. The projected image is of the visual message placed in the Voyager spacecraft and designed to communicate to an extraterrestrial intelligence what we consider to be the crucial information about us and our planet. A message of this kind poses a particular problem. The recipient has no means of understanding it. It must be self-explanatory because any supplement, in the form of a key or legend, would be equally mysterious and incomprehensible to the

From inside an animalistic light fills the vacancies of the space.

recipient. Its meaning cannot be produced by its relationship to a pre-existing and mutual system. It must produce its own meaning. That is to say that it must contain its own concept of itself. How else, after all, would it even be recognised as a message, let alone understood? Already this seems like a desperate throw, a tragic gesture commensurate with the silence of the hero on whose behalf we hope that somehow his absence of speech will speak to future generations, that there will be a time to come in which what he has to say in this silence or this enigma might make sense. And, fond hope, that there might be creatures still living at that time alike enough to make that sense, capable that is, of bearing witness. Someone, that is, will be there for us.

On not being there (Berlin)

It is incredible. I catch my breath. I cannot believe what I am being invited to witness, and I am breathless with the possibility. That after such pain, this. A group of abominable snowmen or yetis has come on stage. I am in Berlin, at least that is what it said on my plane ticket and on the sign at the airport departure gate. These messages I thought I had understood. But now I feel like I am somewhere else; that I must have misunderstood those messages and arrived somewhere I have never even heard of. I am witnessing the final act of a tragedy, an extended version of that moment, at the end of *Hamlet*, when the Norwegian Army appears on stage to clean up and make everything all right. We know they can do nothing of the sort – after all, they are the Norwegian Army, and no one expects the Norwegian Army. I certainly did not expect the abominable snowmen, and the point, perhaps, is precisely that. You don't expect to see them, and you don't really believe they even exist, despite all those television documentaries in which inexplicable giant footprints are found in Himalayan snow (the yeti as the result of reading the signs). The idea that we are destined never to see them is captured in a recent commercial on British television, in which a mountain exploration team, equipped with the latest in photographic technology, relax for a moment in their tent (to consume some of the product being advertised). While their backs are turned, a yeti appears and dances frantically for the camera, begging to be seen, but finally abandons the attempt to be recognised, leaving just its footprints for the luckless explorer. The yeti, then, is the thing that only ever appears when you are not looking.

Except here, for if seeing is believing – as perhaps, in the theatre, it might be – then here they are. It is incredible. I catch my breath. My eyes are wide open, and I am on the edge of my seat, feeling almost as though I might topple forward out of it, down over the edge of the circle and into the stalls. There is a state of wonder in which all you can do is slowly shake the head and mouth a long unbelieving 'no'. This is the no that dare not (quite) be yes, because what this wonderment actually expresses is that yes, I will go along with this, yes, I will say that I saw this, yes, I will bear witness to whatever miraculous event unfolds. I mouth 'no', but I will mean 'yes'. I want everything to be all right, but I know it will not. The gap between this wanting and this knowing, however, is tiny. The space of a breath. I almost know it will be all right. I almost want it not to be.

The little girl whose death (discovered, having taken place while we were not looking) begins the piece, will be brought back to life. In this mad hallucination, the threatening monsters of the mountains turn out, of course, to be tender and benevolent humanoids. They lollop amiably and make clumsily friendly gestures. They erect a low white fence across the stage, making a comfortable domestic space in the white wilderness. They raise the German flag. The girl dances in red shoes on the lid of her coffin. The voices of children sing a song about a cuckoo, and their song loops round and round. The flag is the most blatant sign that there is an allegory taking place, and allegory is both the most obvious and the most secret form of communication, its exegesis both the keying of a sacred meaning which is, of course, objective and universal but also a hermetic process which is entirely subjective. Walter Benjamin, whose work seems not only to animate this piece of writing but also the consciousness of the work I am writing around and about here, evokes another hallucination, that of St Theresa, who 'sees the Virgin strewing roses on her bed; she tells her confessor. "I see none", he replies. "Our Lady brought them to me", answers the Saint.'[2]

Perhaps if we keep looping the cuckoo song, spring and summer will always be coming and will never pass into autumn and winter. Amid the absolute whiteness of this winter scene, a parenthesis of sunshine will be forever erected, within which we shall live the eternity of the promise. In the deep freeze of the state of emergency, a new and benign rule will come. All that it requires is that we should have our eyes open when the yetis appear: it is that simple. This is not Marx's vision of history repeating itself as farce, but tragedy presenting history as comic alternative, for those who have eyes to see and ears to hear. Not, perhaps, these blind and big-eared spectators who occupy the stalls, however. Here, row upon row of stuffed rabbits have taken all the most expensive seats. They, it seems, have paid to have this promise acted out, but in their dumbly belligerent way of not being there, they make me all the more aware that I must, despite what I am feeling, be here after all. If they are not going to live up to their responsibilities to a tragedy that has moved the witnesses out of the dramatis personae and into the dark of the house, then I must. Must, not just logically, but ethically. I must be here because there is a message, a rose, here, for me and for me alone, and if I am not here to receive it, it will have been forever in vain. In his story 'Before the Law', Franz Kafka writes about a man who sits for years outside the door through which he hopes to gain admittance to the Law, but is always refused. Finally, as he dies, he asks why he has been the only person ever to seek to gain admittance here, and he is told, 'No one else could ever be admitted here, since this gate was made only for you. I am now going to shut it.'[3] This is the predicament that must be avoided at all costs. In B.#03 the door seems to be held tantalisingly ajar, daring an entry into the perhaps futile hope of this extended final act

---

2 Walter Benjamin, *The Origin of German Tragic Drama*, trans. John Osborne, London and New York: Verso, 1998, p. 234.
3 Franz Kafka, 'Before the Law', in *Wedding Preparations in the Country and Other Stories*, trans. E. Kaiser, E. Wilkins, W. Muir and E. Muir, Harmondsworth: Penguin Books, 1978, p. 129.

of redemption. The promise is that one day the time will no longer be out of joint. I, you, will be there, where it happens, as it happens, and we will understand it and be able to do something about it. There will be a *Jetztzeit*. A yeti-time.

NR

BR.#04
KunstenFESTIVALdesArts, Brussels
May 2003

The evening works like this:

- The baby and the mother must arrive 30–40 minutes before the start.
- When the show begins, the mother and the baby go into the wings of the stage.
- The show begins with the scene of the 'housekeeper' cleaning.
- After about ten minutes, the white curtain closes, and, very quickly, the mother (from a door on the right) takes the baby onto the stage, sits it down (or lies the baby down, as she prefers) and leaves immediately.

This is the operation. It is delicate because it must be done quickly, but the baby mustn't be made upset. For this reason, it is usually best done by the mother.

- The child must be clothed in white and may have some toys, or a blanket or some things that it likes.

The child, perhaps, awakes an impulse to possess, to claim, to rescue from the stage, to repatriate.

- There are no other actors in the scene, there is no music, the light is bright and diffused and there are no loud noises.

The only one on stage is Hans.

- After one to two minutes of NOTHING, Hans begins to speak syllables of the Alphabet (in Dutch), and usually this attracts the child who begins to look at him.
- If the baby is quiet, the scene can last up to ten minutes (maximum) during which the baby does whatever it pleases.

- If the baby is NOT quiet and cries, then Romeo orders the closing of the curtain, and the baby will at once be taken by the mother who is waiting in the wings . . .

FINISH

The reasons for Romeo putting a baby on stage are to do with the passing of time, and they are the same reasons why, in the same show, there is an eighty-five-year-old man: they are the same person, there is a passing of time, they are at different stages of life. It is the power of a mute presence, unselfconscious, white and microscopic, inside a white, macroscopic space.

SRS

25 MARCH 2003

Dear Scott

The Brussels work is totally different to the previous episodes. It takes place in a marble room (pretend marble . . .) varnished grey-green, with no openings.
 The figures come on one at a time, separated by long intervals of darkness. They are figures that 'stay' for a long time on the stage, alone, without provoking a theatrical dynamic, without creating expectations or developments.
 The sound mustn't be a commentary on the figures but an extension of the environment and the noises generated inside it. The figures perform some little gestures; they wear clothes that make noises and which, maybe, can be the basis of the sound. I've already talked to Marco about how to amplify these sounds, and he's bringing us some different microphones we can experiment with.
 Throughout April, slotted into the schedule in a strategy worthy of a Chinese mind, we are also rehearsing *BN.#05*. The episode takes place in the golden room which, in the first part, will be completely covered with a white PVC cloth. There will be letters and ciphers on the white walls. The environment should recall a laboratory. In the middle, there must be a live, flesh-and-blood goat. Is it possible, or interesting, do you think, to do it in a way that the goat itself determines its sounds (with its steps) in the same way it determined its language?
 The view of the white room at the beginning, and then later the gold room, is mediated by a series of cloths, which should offer a lot of possibilities for the play of

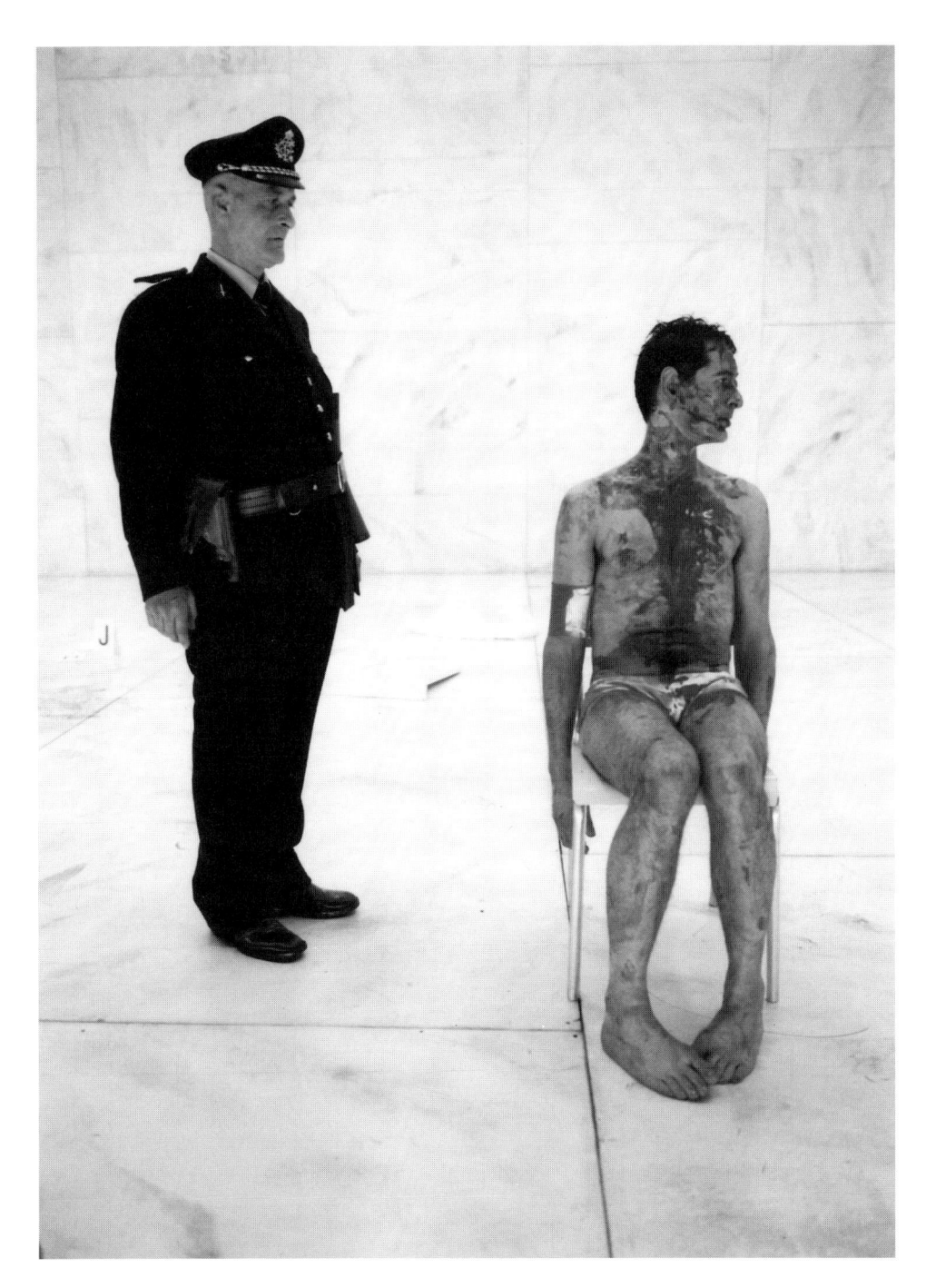

The beaten man is sat there and shown to us.

As though the act of our witnessing those actions, or these images of actions, were the point of the exercise.

light. As in Avignon, we're bringing back, with slight variations, the goat's text, the soldiers, the child and the skin woman in the golden room, and also the milk screen. Perhaps we'll add the figure of an old man, or an old woman. Many of the sounds we have already are perfect.

The goat text will need a lot of work, which is going to be recited again in unison by two women. This text needs to appear terrible and timorous at the same time, maybe through some effect of the two women's voices. Something Gothic, gloomy, even if the light effect is an incandescent white and there is too much light.

This is the summary structure for Bergen, with which you won't be directly involved. Anyway we will have to leave Marco with a precise and definite sound script. We'll need to work on this.

Chiara

Storytime

There is a large room built out of what appear to be grey marble slabs. The room is both imaginable and impossible. Three rows of fluorescent lights, familiar industrial issue, are suspended from the ceiling. However, there are no doors or windows, no way in or out except through the mouth of the stage where it gives on to the auditorium. From here, 'we' might attempt to project some sort of recognition upon the space, but these surfaces are too cold and resistant, too unparticular to accept our imagination. And so, already, any sense we might have of ourselves as a public, a collective, is fractured against this grandiloquent anonymity that might put us in mind of a mausoleum for an unknown dictator, or the redundantly ostentatious foyer of some unloved public building, or perhaps the grim exclusivity of an 'executive washroom' somewhere in some corporate headquarters. Places we don't get to go to, or don't care to remember. Places whose architecture is all rhetoric, all speech, all 'output', and in which, therefore, we cannot stay. These places belong to a nightmare of the city. In such places, you are on your own: you are in transit there, you are a worker only and not a dweller. You are not a citizen of this but a ghost.

Ghost

When the curtain opens on this marble room at the start of *BR.#04* there is revealed, in the centre of the space, the figure of such a ghost, a young woman, a contemporary labourer, dressed in a pinafore, with a mop and cleaner's trolley, cleaning the floor. That is the entire scene: she mops the floor, the mop is squeezed, and the trolley is trundled across the space. Perhaps, as she works, the light inside the room intensifies. Perhaps too, as the job comes to a close, she looks out towards the auditorium, as if something might be said, as if whatever she is wiping away were the traces of those very legends in which 'we' – those of us who feel ourselves addressed by her gaze – might constitute ourselves again, as citizens of whatever city we shall inhabit, in whatever real world we might feel ourselves responsible for. At the same time, that smear on the floor, for all its staginess, may be the trace of someone's suffering. Is that where our stories begin?

Infant

When the curtain opens for the second time, the stage is inhabited by an infant child, a mere baby, who sits there in her nappies, a small cup of toys beside her, surrounded by all that space. For this spectator, at least, the effect is startling. What strikes is the child's sheer unrelation to this place in which she finds herself, an unrelation that expresses itself just as effectively whether she plays out the scene like a 'good little actor', giving her attention in turn to the elements around her (including ourselves in the auditorium), or whether she howls impatiently as soon as the curtain opens. She does not appear born but put or left there, less an image of the hope of an historical awakening and more an historical deposit, some lump of actual humanity caught in the gob of the theatre's storytelling machinery. A piece of flesh in the throat, a gag of sorts, the gag of the little actor, around which the theatrical apparatus can only gesticulate like a rather ineffectual magistrate, assuming a sort of public responsibility perhaps, but essentially out of touch. And the baby is untouchable. She is as safe as the child Oedipus was, abandoned on the mountaintop with his feet bound together by frightened parents who had already heard the story of his maturity. Nothing will touch such children yet, the suffering consequent upon their actions has not caught up with them yet, and it is in this 'yet' that this particular child acts. She 'is' not, neither does she 'represent', strictly speaking, either the Oedipus child or the Christ child or the Moses child or the Freudian child of the *fort–da* scenario, or any other legendary infant we might think of whose suffering (and redemption) is already written, as it were, into the story of their infancy. That is because there on the stage she does not occupy her infancy as a story but as a slice of sheer enduring. From the point of view of an adult spectator, enduring is the infant's action, and it is by way of her action that she keeps time open for us. We are incapable of not watching.

The only other figure in the scene is a sort of abstract head and shoulders silhouette, cut out of sheet metal, at the back of the stage. At one point, this figure 'comes to life', three rectangular slots – eyes and a mouth presumably – opening and closing for the machine-like articulation of a series of phonemes, alphabetic scraps, the rudiments of a language, a rudimentary tutelage that only serves to emphasise again the child's unrelation to the play of patience and recall and anticipation, implicit in any language game. There on the stage, she is still an actor. Over here in spectatorland, however, where we manufacture legend and consume children's stories, the actor is history. In the end, the stage curtain cuts across the scene as sharp and as adamant as a blade, casting back at us a glare of white light and a blast of white noise, as if all our concern, our empathy, our interest were become a mess of gaze and interference, so much fractured and incoherent broadcast.

After this, to go back into the scene again is to rehearse something of the order of an Orphic transgression. It is to enter dreamtime. That is what appears to happen when a strange spectre of a woman, pale and balding, comes to stand in front of the curtain, as if awaiting entrance, before going onto the stage where the child is still to be found but accompanied now by a screen and a film projector. The folds of the woman's full-length

A series of arcane, baroque actions.

black dress are miked up to produce a sound as she walks, like the crackle of fire, or the crack of ice. She turns on the projector, and we see a looped flowing image: a stream or a flame attempting an ascent out of the top of the screen, or perhaps the ceaseless tumble through its depths of a woman's hair. She performs a dance, a simple choreography of stepping backwards and forwards between the screen and the projector. She gathers up, plays with and comforts the child. Here, among these Hadean rhetorics, caught in the beam from the projector, or brought to the very edge of the stage and introduced to the possibility of everything that exists beyond, the infant becomes the very embodiment of an historical awakening, a birth that is born, as Hannah Arendt wrote, not in order to die but in order to begin.[1] But, in the same gesture, she becomes definitively unreachable. Her experience, now, is dedicated to an education of the senses that no story – no mere biography – could ever encompass. It would take all of Hades, and more, to house it. And we will hear nothing of it. Like Orpheus, we have succumbed to the temptation to look back, and so we know no more of the child than we did at the start.

---

1 Hannah Arendt, *The Human Condition*, Chicago, Ill.: University of Chicago Press, 1998, p. 247.

Nor shall we know any more in the future than what we make up for our own songs' sake, laments, legends and children's tales, out of everything that has not happened yet.

Prophet

On the stage, memory is a garment. The actor puts on history just by turning up and appearing. As I have tried to suggest, though, the actor may also bring their silence with them. An old man who enters, dressed rather oddly in a floral bikini and sandals with pink roses on the toes. He is frail, a little slow and unsteady. He wanders the stage, going up against its surfaces as if testing the fact of those walls. He looks to his hands, as if testing too his own surfaces, their thickness, their permeability. We watch him, and he is whoever we want him to be. He dresses himself from garments on a chair at the side of the stage. At first, he puts on prophet's robes, bright white aprons and gowns and belts inscribed with Hebrew text, one piece of cloth wrapped over another, the words pressed upon the substance of his person. Secrets. Promises. Remembrances. Then, over the prophet's robes, he puts on a policeman's uniform, shirt, trousers, jacket, belt and holster. With the policeman's uniform comes the policeman's memory, whatever it is the policeman remembers. The actor has no need to remember anything, the clothes do it for him, as soon as he puts them on. In his police uniform, he steps forward to a pair of gymnast's rings that descend from the flies at the front of the stage and holds on with both hands. The posture is ridiculous, somewhere between a would-be hero testing his strength and an old fool hung up on a peg. He is – literally – suspended in his act, dressed up in the hopes and memories of the world and incapable of doing. There is a knock on the door. Another policeman enters the stage, carrying a small bottle of stage blood . . .

Police

I have suggested that the theatre, according to what appears there and also disappears in the actor's representation of his or her labour, may be a privileged site for the registering of a suffering that resides – as it were – in the image and that may force itself into the arena of our thought. This is even the case (in fact, it may be particularly the case) in relation to those occasions when violence is powerful enough to subdue its victims into speechlessness. At the same time, the theatre's intimacy with suffering may have something to do with its own 'primordial' relation to the means by which that suffering is inflicted. As the place in which 'it has not happened yet', however many times –

A rhinoceros appears?

countless times – it has happened before, the theatre is intimate with the police. That is its sadness. Its happiness resides in its power to pretend, to create itself out of its own creation, as an original, mimetic substance, whose blows don't hurt, whose actors are always 'making it up'. Its suffering, though, may be real enough, or real enough to be felt as it is acted out. Actions (such as silences) may be as loud as words.

Now, in Brussels, an actor in police uniform enters the marble room. He pours stage blood from a plastic bottle to make a pool. He lays out lettered cards around the pool, measuring the distances and angles with a tape measure, preparing the history in advance of the event. This is not a lying, it is not a cover-up. The event will follow faithfully upon its representation. It will be consumed in the memory of the police. Two younger policemen enter. One undresses and lies down over the blood. Over his body his colleagues take it in turns to mime a truncheon beating. The beating is interminable. The beaten man squirms under the blows, spreading 'his' blood about the floor. Each swing of the truncheon is accompanied by what sounds like an amplified thrash at a snare drum, accelerating into a nauseous crescendo mixed with interference, as if the white noise that accompanied the closing of the curtain between the earlier scenes was already anticipating this. The fluorescent lights in the ceiling flicker. If it was the traces of this occurrence which were being wiped away in the first scene, now the room is vomiting its memories at last. The younger uniform puts on gloves and unzips a covering from what look like conjoined gravestones. These are the tables of the law. They are blank. The victim's foot is wiped on one of the tablets. There is silence. A chair is brought over and the beaten man is sat there and shown to us. His face is swollen, his eye closed, his mouth bloated and broken. More blood is poured over his head. A black plastic disposal bag is brought on and laid out. The victim is sealed up in the bag so as to look like a black grub. A microphone is brought on and angled down to where his head should be. The other officers leave, and the man in the bag begins to speak.

And now we hear the voice of somebody who was injured and who suffered. Or rather, we hear something 'like' that. But how can we credit that? How can we credit a suffering that appears only in its repetition? We know already that the injury did not happen. Whatever we saw, and whatever we hear now, it did not take place. In the most obvious sense, the truncheons were plastic toys, the police were actors, the blows were not felt, the blood is a stage property, the wounds were applied in the make-up room, and the speech is an actor's task – written, rehearsed and performed on cue. Anyway, the injury and the speech, even if they did occur, could not have been witnessed unless by the participants themselves. After all, this is violence that takes place in a room without doors or windows. And all the traces have, already, as we saw in the first scene, been completely wiped away. This is mute violence indeed; and no less mute surely is a speech delivered through a broken mouth, from a disposal bag, in this same sealed room. In this bilingual city, language itself is, already, broken in two. So how is a true statement possible? Who will ever hear? Not only – as the police reports would be likely to declare – did this 'not happen', but it cannot be proved. All the same, according to the privilege of the theatre, these events have indeed been shown and, we should say, shown twice over. The police have seen to that. So, the evidence of the beating is set out before the act. So too, the broken-mouthed victim is given a microphone to amplify his testimony. However, as with those ghosts who shake off their legend like an unwanted aureole, or the speechless infant who cannot be caught alive within the limits of her life story, the actor whose appearance is a gift of the police wriggles upon the dish like something unwilling to be eaten.

The consequence of these events, rather than opening out into anything like a space of public action, collapses instead into a sort of hermetic allegory, the occult images of a nightmare. The strange balding woman from earlier appears again, accompanied by the actress of the first scene who is also now robed in a full, black dress. They are accompanied by a young boy in a strange garb that, when for a moment he is silhouetted against the back wall, seems to transform him into the outline of a certain old European folk bogeyman, another piece of the nightmare of history that has blood depending on it. These figures perform a series of arcane, baroque actions. A woman pulls a bloody tooth from her mouth into a little dish. A hunk of hair is combed from her head and is stuck onto a black, inverted parody of the tablets. An animal's heart is pulled from another black bag and dragged across the stage as if it were the heart of that young man himself, who wriggles and screams now in his own body bag as a siren starts up and a small paper house, like a lost child's drawing of home, afloat on the meniscus of the dream, crosses the front of the stage of its own accord. We observe this pageant. It passes before us. There is nothing to credit here other than what the stage declares, as literal, as self-referential, as histrionic as it likes.

Legend

At the last, an old man disappears into his bed. He has come into a space that is bare apart from a hospital cot and a simple wooden chair upon which his clothes are folded. A blaring siren has sounded over the previous scene, but that stops now, as if the important business, the emergency is elsewhere. Instead, we hear a sound like a rush of wind being sucked through a tunnel, as if some elaborate system, some construction of thought or concern or politics, were in hot pursuit of itself by way of its own intestines, disappearing into a world-swallowing emptiness of its own making. Meanwhile, the old man, frail as he appears, is calm. He sits on the edge of the bed, he looks at his hands,

Prophet.

he eats quietly from a piece of bread. And then he gets into the bed, covers his features with a ski-mask, pulls the covers over his head and allows the bed to absorb him. The disappearance is absolute. As the sound dies, there is not even the slightest impression of a human form to remember him by. The sheets are flat, the bed is empty.

The old man's time upon the stage is, already, legendary. Legend is a string of words and numbers, a weave of thought, which writes itself around the incapability of an image, specifically the image's incapability of living for itself. As a set of characters punched around the features of a sovereign on the edge of a coin, or in the form of the 'Life' of a saint or a hero, legend is – to appropriate a phrase from Alexander García Düttmann – a mode of 'over-naming', and so a form of that writing that 'deprives mimesis of all its power'.[2] For such figures, legend involves a suspension of their power: their inability to speak here, anymore, except in these borrowed terms, their inability to guarantee their own debts or to oblige the faithful, except by way of the legend. The subject of the legend – when and if the ghost comes – is, essentially, empty-handed. There is nothing we can take from him or her, except what we give back in advance, as credit, so to speak. And, indeed, that is the form, after the old man's disappearing act, in which his legend (his or another's) appears now on the stage, in the projection of what look like television or film credits, scrolling across a black gauze that falls at the line of the curtain while the empty bed is dimly illuminated behind. Meanwhile, beyond the gauze, a young boy in an old-fashioned black suit approaches the bed, the place where something is supposed to have happened but where nothing appears, nothing is said. The boy stays there a while. He sees what passes.

JK

Out in the open

/

Until we reached Brussels, everything had been mysterious. Messages had been enigmatic. Codes were in operation. Arcane languages had been resuscitated. Explanations were offered, but they explained nothing. 'There is no meaning here', read the message board in Avignon when, obviously, there was plenty, for those who could puzzle it out. Invitations to read were widely distributed. Interpretations were confounded by the

---

2 Alexander García Düttmann, *The Gift of Language,* London: Athlone Press, 2000, p. 60.

provision of supplements. The message board itself, for instance, in Cesena, in Avignon and, later, in Bergen seemed to offer a promise like that of the surtitles over a performance in a foreign language: the promise, that is, of translation into clarity. In Berlin, where the message board was not used, the entire episode seemed to operate as a single allegorical line, holding out its own promise of clarity: that enigmatic actions might, perhaps, be understood to be standing for other actions, available to us with the acquisition of the master code. The read-out thus produced would make sense, but, of course, when it came down to it, it did not; it did more, made less than sense or made too many senses of such sense. Until we reached Brussels, everything had been double, supplementary. All speech had appeared as writing, each episode inducing in the paranoid mind of the writer after the event the urge to explicate by further supplement, to build ever more elaborate fantasies, to allegorise ad infinitum.

Then, everything became very clear. The veils had been lifted, and we looked straight into the wide open space of a marble box in which every action seemed to have its own proper name and to need no explanation. In English, there is a phrase with which one can signal one's approval of this kind of straight-talking: calling a spade a spade. Suddenly, this theatre seemed to be presenting spades as spades. Each action of the episode took place, as it were, in broad daylight. With no gauze interposed between the gaze of the spectators and the action itself, everything that appeared, appeared to do so intensely as itself: lucid, in focus, most definitely here and now. In the marble box (on which more below) and often under the white light of overhead fluorescents, each action was announced and then concluded by the drawing of a white curtain, an intensification of light in the auditorium (lest we forget that we are here) and an austerely meaningless blaze of noise. Between these intermezzi, which seemed designed both to sear into the memory and to obliterate from immediate consciousness that which had passed before, acts whose meaning could hardly be clearer were performed.

Exemplary, for reasons that will become apparent, is the sequence in which a policeman is beaten. He stands with his back to the audience and strips to his underpants. First one and then two colleagues beat him with a truncheon. And then they continue. They beat him some more. Finally, they prop him on a chair before bagging him up. Then they leave him to us, with a microphone precisely placed so as to ensure that anything he might now have to say will be clearly understood. Nothing to be added here. No paranoid rage to write. If a spade is a spade then there is nothing to be written about spades. A simple scene of routine violence, of a kind that almost certainly occurs every day of the week in police stations around the world. Nothing strange about that, even though the theatrical effect of the action's duration (it felt like fifteen minutes) makes it unusually intense and difficult to endure. Indeed, the simplicity not just of this scene but also of others around it suggests that a certain experience of enduring is being engaged,

The outline of a certain old European folk bogeyman.

as though allotted hours are being passed on stage, the fact of their passage perhaps as important as the matter treated. As though the act of our witnessing these actions, or these images of actions, were the point of the exercise.

So the spade is a spade, but the spade is not the point. In concentrating in the description above on the matter of the scene, I have actually betrayed and misrepresented it. I have omitted the means of its production. For, although the Brussels episode appeared at first encounter to be direct, straightforward, literal, even brazen in its obviousness, in retrospect it turns out to be much more slippery than any of its predecessors, its literalness a kind of lure. Approaching the police station for a second time, then, as a memory image, let us meditate now upon how it was made to appear. First, a man dressed as a policeman enters the marble box carrying a plastic bottle containing a dark reddish-purple liquid, which he then pours into a pool on the floor. Then he places cards bearing capital letters at precise points on the floor around the pool of red liquid (which we may recognise now as stage blood), points whose relations he fixes with a tape measure. It is as though he is preparing for the arrival of a forensic team, marking the key spots so that they may be identified in subsequent photographs, so that what he is about to do can be properly and comprehensibly exhibited in a court of law. It is within this set-up that the beating takes place. Or rather, the imitation of a beating. The young man upon whom the truncheon blows are inflicted falls to the floor and as the 'beating' continues, his body is progressively covered in 'blood'. Each 'blow' of the 'truncheon' is accompanied by painfully loud bursts of sound. Sometimes, the timing is slightly off. The fact of duration ensures that the artifice makes itself visible and audible in such gaps between the visible and the audible. A shorter scene could, perhaps, have sustained its fabric of theatrical illusion intact. What we are witnessing is a kind of cinematic realism or naturalism but one which has already presented its materials as the materials of the stage rather than the materials of the world (although they are, of course, both, in both cinema and theatre, although the latter is less readily acknowledged). As Jean-Luc Godard once said, when it was suggested to him that his film *Pierrot le fou* contained a lot of blood: 'Not blood, red.'[3] Although the sustained shock of the simulated violence demands a particular intensity of attention for the action itself, the frame in which the simulation is conducted also compels a meditation on how scenes like this work. For it is not that the scene undermines itself. Although it demands that we pay attention to the fact of theatre, that is to say, to the fact that there is a system of representation at work that allows the matter of the scene to appear, and to matter, it does not do so in order to condemn us as gulls nor its perpetrators as mountebanks for participating in this travesty. It repeats Magritte's famous gesture: this is not a spade. It asks the rather difficult question: how do you call a spade a spade? Or, to put it more bluntly: how does theatre work? I reach for the spade I see. Is this a spade I see before me? It is but a reflection. My hand clasps water. All that is solid melts.

II

The curtain opens on a scene of contemporary slavery. A black woman stands with a mop and bucket in the huge empty space of a marble cube. The scale of the space suggests not only its own inhumanity but also the presence, beyond, of ever more imposing volumes. However vast it may seem, it is merely an antechamber, even though, so far as we can see, it leads nowhere. If not the lobby of a hotel, then that of a modern palace,

---

3 Jean-Luc Godard, 'Let's Talk about Pierrot', in *Godard on Godard*, trans. and ed. Tom Milne, New York: Da Capo, 1972.

an international bank, in whose depths we suppose power to be held, even if we momentarily, deliriously suspect that an endless sequence of antechambers may just be an elaborate ruse to mask some deeper invisibility.

One lunchtime in the financial district of Los Angeles, a hard sort of non-place, not unlike the marble room, a non-place in which only humans twelve feet tall could ever appear without discomfort, a group of service staff staged themselves. Protesting in advance in support of a pay demand, they appeared, in broad daylight, just as the financial workers – whose computers they spray and whose bins they empty in the dead of night – emerged in search of sandwiches. It was the simple fact of their appearing that mattered. They had nothing to say beyond the simple act of asserting their own visibility in a place where it was effectively if not formally prohibited. They appeared out of place to assert their place in this non-place. Is this opening scene, in which a woman cleans the stage, in fact, perhaps, the scene before the opening? Is she not supposed to be seen? Have we, perhaps, chanced upon her, intruded upon her labour, exposed her to our consuming spectatorship? Or has she exposed herself to us by staying late at work, beyond the opening of the house to the public that should compel her departure? Of

The child's sheer unrelation to this place.

course not, not really, but it starts to look that way, and since we are engaged by a mechanism that has its own particular way of calling a spade a spade, there is, of course, a sense in which it might just as well be so. In the face of an action that imitates an action, an appearing that mimes an appearing, there is always the possibility that we will, for our own satisfaction, take things at face value and stumble into some kind of vague recognition that in this doubling, someone really is somewhere they ought not to be. That is to say, that there is something wrong about being on stage, that to step onstage is somehow *unheimlich*, a step away from home into a kind of exile. Two of the next figures to appear intensify this suspicion that the stage is not the place to be.

The second of these to appear is an old white-bearded man, who will later transform himself via the costume of a Hebrew prophet into a Belgian policeman. But, first, he finds himself on stage wearing a pink and orange bikini and plastic sandals with flowers on. This is gender confusion as joke, of course, but also a practical theatrical action of exile. The old man appears to have fallen into one of those dreams in which you are precipitated naked into a high-pressure situation: performing *Hamlet* when you have never even looked at the text, for instance. All you desire is for the ground to open up and swallow you.

The first, however, to appear (after the cleaner, that is) is a very young child, revealed, sitting in the vast space of the marble box. Abandoned, perhaps, in the antechamber of the palace. Left on a giant doorstep by some desperate mother in an impossible predicament. To be discovered, perhaps, like that little boy with the pierced foot on the hillside, or that other little boy in the basket by the river, both of whom found themselves adopted by the rulers of their place of exile. Whoever she is (the strange thing is that I am sure that this is a girl not a little boy), infant avatar of the three great exile prophets whose lives are so tangled up in each other (and at least two of whom will appear later in their more familiar guise of white-bearded patriarch), her appearance here is something of an anomaly, or at least enough of one for some of the conventions of modern theatre-going to be suspended. How else are we to explain the fact that members of the audience in the front row in Brussels waved to the child as the curtains closed on its first appearance? Even if we believed actors are 'at home' on stage, which is far from being the case, this actor (for she is doing just what all the others are doing, no more and no less) seems to disrupt a sense of spatial propriety. It is not just that 'she shouldn't be here' (as the vocal protests of some spectators suggested another night when the child cried), but that, in being here, or rather there, on the stage, she seems not to wrap around herself the fact of not being here, in the same space as us, that other, older actors use as their most basic costume. Out of place, away from home, out of language: the child, perhaps, awakes an impulse to possess, to claim, to rescue from the stage, to repatriate. Exile seems to be where we are at, wherever we are at it. In the next action, this exile will

A woman pulls a bloody tooth from her mouth into a little dish.

learn, maybe, precisely what mother and father she now lives without, what land she will only ever look back upon, and we may get a glimpse of a clue as to why we are here, in Brussels, of all places.

First, the curtain closes. The white noise blazes. A balding woman in a black dress appears. She will take care of this child, for good or ill, and give her a place in history, even though she seems, herself, to come from some place quite ahistorical, the nightmare landscape of the child's sleep, the old tales of some dark mountainous Europe far from the sea where you are always lost, quite lost to recorded time. Her care for the child is a kind of education, and, like the scene of the beaten policeman which is still to come but which sets the scene for this attempt to understand, it is an education which may be about both matter and means. She shows the child a film. The image projected is a constant flicker like a column of smoke. Is the point of this demonstration to show representation at work, to induct the child in the secrets of Plato's cave, that she might aspire to philosophy and see clearly through the shadows of illusion? Or is this film, this already-antique apparatus of image-making and storytelling – emphasised here by the presence of the projector on stage – a way of reinforcing, restoring or developing a memory of something in the child's former life? I can't help but imagine the child being shown, in a mood of sorrow and lamentation, the images of the old country, pictures from home, and acquiring, thereby, some kind of home that would make sense of her exile. And so I am forced to think that the home that was lost was lost in an act of burning, to bring to mind the death camps, the atom bomb, the fires of the pogroms, Kristallnacht. At the end of the film and for just a few seconds, brief enough to miss if you blink, the image of a rhinoceros emerges from the smoke, perhaps walking towards the camera. Who could have shot this flickering black and white 'home' movie in which a rhinoceros appears? Is this perhaps the one cheeky, fleeting clue let slip for the paranoid writer to snap up and make much of? If so, then this is what he makes of it. Leopold, the Congo, Zaïre, Rwanda. A specific history of genocide, like the one fled by Freud, suddenly wraps its hot hands around the life of this infant. No matter that she is white-skinned: we have already seen her adult counterpart cleaning the floor. Oh. History happens now and we are in it here.

III

The child sets out for his new school. He is, perhaps, eleven years old, and this new school is a big school, full of noise and violence, new rules and inexplicable routines which everyone else seems to know. In place of the simulation of the home manufactured by his primary school, he finds himself in a place dedicated to the pacification, by coercion and, if necessary, physical violence, of the adolescent. He has entered, if you like, a regime of law. He has gone into exile for real this time, with no attempt being made any more to comfort him with homely furnishings. It is at about this age, too, that he could, if life took a disastrous course, be tried and convicted for murder. An arbitrary system engulfs him. It seems to have no foundation. He is treated as already in the wrong. He is an incipient criminal. Where is the statute that made this so, and what were his parents doing signing away their rights of care and submitting him to this violence? By what form of representation could he have given his own consent to such a horror? 'I don't like the way it is organised', he complains one evening at home, to the amusement of his family. In a chill moment, the logic of the law has entered even here.

This is the moment the sleeping child anticipates in images of bald women in black dresses. This is the fate he hopes to ward off in stories of child-catchers and bogeymen. These are the images that return the Brussels episode of *Tragedia Endogonidia* to the chill mists from which it emerged. Even the old man, who finally escapes from it all by vanishing into his bed, is haunted, it seems, by one of these apparitions. The childlike child-catcher in the black top hat, who had earlier joined two women in black dresses in some impenetrable rite involving the internal organs of some abductee, perhaps, even the beaten policeman, now stands over the bed, maybe regretting the fact that this one got away. Who can tell? This ghostly ending, in which, for the first time here in Brussels, our gaze is once again compromised by the mist of the gauze, feels at first as though it is not part of this episode, but something instead from the image world of the 'mysterious' episodes, far from the brutal, if slippery, clarity of the beaten policeman, the abandoned child and the Rwandan cleaner. But if, as Derrida suggests, today the 'police everywhere become, in society, the very element of haunting, the milieu of spectrality', if they are 'hallucinatory and spectral because they haunt everything; they are everywhere, even when they are not',[4] then maybe they were all spectres after all; however 'real' they looked, they too were revenants, coming back, again and again, doubling themselves over and over. The police are always and never at home, and we are all children when we dream of police.

NR

---

[4] Jacques Derrida, 'Force of Law: The "Mystical Foundation of Authority"', trans. Mary Quaintance, in Jacques Derrida, *Acts of Religion*, ed. with an introduction by Gil Andejar, New York and London: Routledge 2002, pp. 279–80.

BN.#05
Bergen International Festival
May 2003

Fluid earth

Ours is a fluid earth. Not just because, as we are constantly reminded, the waters cover two-thirds of the surface of the planet, nor even because we live in constant fear of inundation, seeking salvation on Ararat or in Kyoto. Ours is a fluid earth because of glaciers and lava flows and because we understand some intimate connection between the two. True like ice like fire. As a terrestrial, whose body, I am constantly reminded, is more than two-thirds water, I am probably not qualified to read the Voyager message that has accompanied *Tragedia Endogonidia* on its passage through Europe. All the same, I am struck, now I take the time to be thus struck, by a suspicion, no more, that the schematic communication of the nature of our world and our life here does not fully account for this state of fluidity. As the vessel floats off through our solar system, beyond the icy wastes where Pluto dwells, it seems to me increasingly unlikely that it would occur to any of its possible extraterrestrial recipients that the senders were the fluid inhabitants of a fluid world. But, struck now as I am by this apparent omission, I remember something about my own first encounter with the message system. I remember how hot it was in Cesena. Confronted by the glacial cool of *A.#02* and the literal snowscape of *B.#03*, I began to suspect that this very deliberate management of temperature was a kind of survival strategy for the work as a whole. Let us imagine that in Cesena we found ourselves just a little too close to the core. We felt on our skin the roar of the molten rock, got ourselves scalded enough to know for sure that an infernal liquid was driving the whole enterprise. In Avignon, in Berlin, in Brussels and now, of course, Bergen (where snow still sits on mountaintops visible from the city), we have come away from that 'burning burning' centre. But what we experienced in Cesena means we view the temperature differently. The chilly movements in these dramas may look like glaciers – indeed, they are glaciers – but they are also lava. They are the slow, cold movements of the surface, driven by the heat within. Ice like fire. In Avignon and Bergen, the golden room is there, or rather, here, but, for most of the time, it is clothed in white. In Berlin, where we are taken as far from the centre as it is possible to go while still keeping our feet on the ground – to the mountains of the Himalayas – there is no room at all. In Brussels, the viscosity of the golden room has increased to such an extent that it has become marble, set into that stone which, deathly cold as it is in the mausolea of the

Perhaps we'll add the figure of an old man, or an old woman.

I believe that it is movement that stirs up emotion.

There must be a live, flesh-and-blood goat.

empire, testifies in its swirls to some former hot fluidity, a molten state now arrested. Is this, perhaps, why it appears so frequently in the bathrooms of the modern world, or in those most fleetingly experienced of solid spaces, hotel lobbies? Might we then imagine the first appearance of this life form, *C.#01*, not simply as the molten core of a world but also as a kind of sun, around which the planets of the other episodes revolve, their temperature regulated by their distance from the beginning (or the end)? However we conceive or represent it to ourselves, we are clearly dealing with questions of time and weather, *crono e clima, de temps et temps*. The whole system is, of course, entropic. It cools. The older it is, the cooler it gets. The slow creep of the glacier will one day completely overwhelm the seething cascades of lava. The sun will burn out. All will be still on this once-fluid earth, and the Voyager message will no longer mislead.

NR

Stage blood from a plastic bottle.

A late-modern nightmare of some sort of *ancien régime* cabal.

P.#06 and *R.#07*
Festival d'Automne, Odéon:
Ateliers Berthier, Paris and
RomEuropa Festival, Teatro
Valle, Rome
October-November 2003

Here, in Cesena, after our return from Bergen, we are resting and trying, in spite of the exceptionally torrid heat, to prepare Paris and Rome and to do a little domestic work. We are very worried about the drought: it has been months since it last rained and the earth is arid, and everything is burned.

CG

Thrown down, his face obscured, beside him an overturned fire extinguisher.

It messes everything up.

Putting on the rubber gloves; dragging the dead child from out of the bed and off the stage.

Her grief will not be scrubbed from the stage.

'Not blood, red.'

Dramaturgy is really at work in the moments of crisis in the passage between figures.

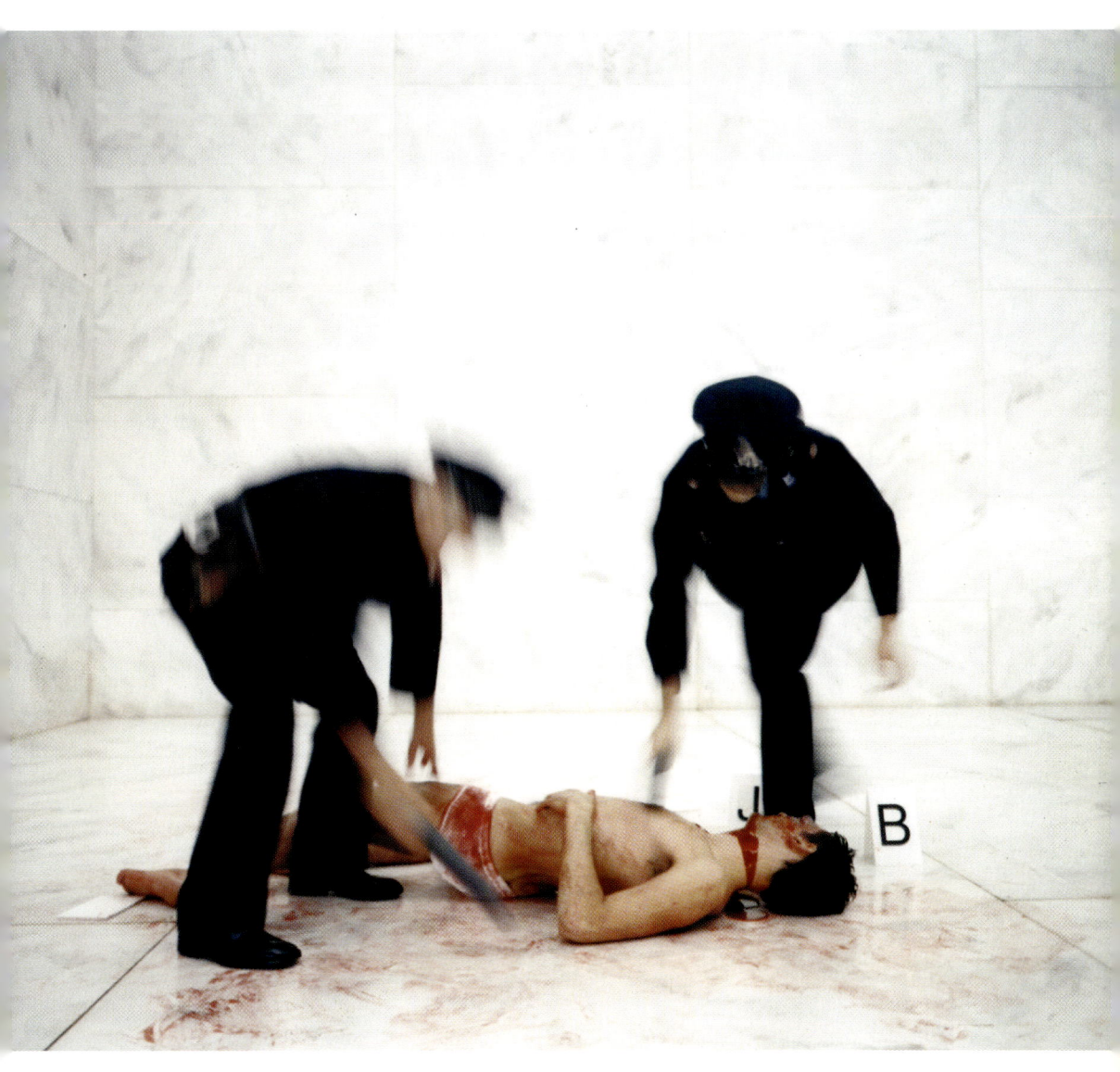

The beating is interminable.

Abraham raises the scissors and brings them down.

Mussolini, for example, will keep coming back; at least, this evening, he will.

He bites into the neck of Mussolini and spits a mouthful of blood upon the back surface of the glass screen.

No longer any revolution to fight for, no war to wage, no reason, no business being here.

She kneels down with her back to the audience, then lowers her head to the floor in front of her and weeps.

You know where you are from the wallpaper.

This distant voice which will get close, tear and harrow.

They were like the gangsters in films, with hats and long coats and hands in their pockets and heavy sharp-edged faces.

It seemed as if the man from the world had reached into the fairy story and pulled out a real boy.

24 JUNE 2003

Dear Scott,

We don't yet have a set dramaturgical structure for the two new episodes (P.#06; R.#07). As always, there are plenty of ideas (Romeo is a furnace!), but they will be organised on the basis of a central pivot, or rather on a basic idea, which can be arranged and developed.

The space in Paris is very wide and very deep. We thought of using its full size, including its walls. The auditorium seats 500 or 600. It's completely gigantic, open. It is the scene store of the Odéon Theatre, a great hangar of a building which doesn't provide the visual intimacy of Avignon and Bergen nor the theatricality of Berlin. The space pushes the figures away from the audience.

We would like to work on the figure of Jesus. This is an idea that vexes and bothers us because it creates so many doubts. We don't want to put the story of Jesus on stage. He should appear as a figure closer to the spectator than an actor. In fact, Jesus could enter from the back having paid for his ticket and go and sit out front in the audience accompanied by an employee of the theatre. J. could be an adolescent with long hair. Perhaps at the beginning Charles de Gaulle could pronounce in Aramaic those words of Jesus that contain within them the history of Judaism, the history of Christianity and of tragedy: 'Eloi, eloi, lema sabactani' (My God, My God, why have you forsaken me?) Jesus could encounter Oedipus's Sphinx and stand in silence before her.

There is a fifteen-piece orchestra between the audience and the stage but it doesn't make a sound. Like Jesus, it is a silent presence, dense, judging. Jesus and the orchestra communicate the sense of all those things that gather and settle, in their muteness and motionlessness, out of shifts in time and space.

As far as the sound is concerned, silence, even expressed by means of sound, is the true nature of the work.

In September, we will rehearse the Paris episode at the Comandini and the Rome episode at the Bonci.

Be well, Chiara

An act of purification.

1 SEPTEMBER 2003

Dear Marco[1]

In mid-September, we will go into rehearsal for the two new episodes of *Tragedia Endogonidia* (*P.#06*; *R.#07*), which will open in Paris in mid-October and in Rome in November. Just as for Brussels and Bergen, we will once again be working simultaneously on two productions.

Paris

The acoustic is very good. Romeo attended a performance there: natural voices came over well and amplified sounds – including those with bass frequencies – were strong and clean. In *P.#06*, the figures are volumes in the environment. There is not, then, a real scenography but objects, actors and animals who enter, take positions, act.

From the point of view of the sound, the show is in two parts. The first part doesn't have any music, or melody, but only noise produced by the objective presence of machines and objects. Silence is very important in order to expand the space and make it emptier. Few words are spoken and, if it's possible, it would be better if they were not amplified. In any case, if this is not possible, radio microphones will have to be attached to the costumes of a general and of a woman in a raincoat. The rhythm of the actions is slow, repetitive and interrupted here and there by the sudden and unexpected movements of objects falling onto the stage. Many sounds produced by the objects will need to be unamplified.

We will still need to test the sonic dynamics of each object to which we want to link a sound (in rehearsal and when Scott arrives around 22 September). For example, perhaps we will be putting two microphones in the wings (or one centre stage) to capture the signal from the poles of the flags which will be waving and banging against the wall. It may, however, be enough, as in the beating at Brussels, to follow the action with the sampler keyboard. We will know this in rehearsal once we have the objects. The movements of the flags will, however, be accompanied by sound.

Furthermore, on a long platform in mid-air we may want to have an object (a light?) run at high speed and crash against a wall. This action too is accompanied

---

1 Marco Olivieri, a sound engineer.

The story has gone horribly wrong, just as Kierkegaard imagined it might.

by a tone and an explosion, and it will, perhaps, be necessary to amplify the moment of breaking by adding in the smashing of a microphone.

These are all hypotheses, to which we will only find answers at the end of September. The second part, however, is supported by music which accompanies a complex choreography. We constructed the sound for this in Cesena in August when Scott was here.

Rome

The show is at the Teatro Valle, do you know it? It's an Italianate theatre, like the Bonci, but with a smaller stage. The scenography is a white box, like the marble box in Brussels, and the proscenium is completely filled with a glass wall (real glass). So the actors perform behind glass. On the acoustic level, the presence of the glass divides the idea of the sound into two parts. Because of the glass, the sound, the voices and the noises of objects placed on the stage are deadened, confused. At the Bonci, we will work out how to attach microphones to capture the voices of the

A new version of the goat-substitution offer.

actors and the noises of the objects so that the mixer can obtain the effect of being under glass. In August, we made some tests and some recordings.

When the glass is lifted, the sound obviously bursts forth and changes its nature. We will have to place a microphone close to a cafetière, which will be on an electric stove, in order to capture the sound of the coffee coming out. This is an important noise because it is the origin of a sound we have already made which will accompany the opening of the scene and scene changes.

R.#07 will be staged at the Bonci on 24 September, and only then will we know how to place the microphones and understand the sound parameters.

That's all for now, Chiara

Modern acting

P.#06 begins with the staging of an interruption. An orchestra is ranged across the front of the stage. Their music is prepared for them on their stands (the score of the work to be performed is displayed). They ready their instruments, and, just as I am beginning to contemplate a whole new dimension to the musical repertoire of the company's sound artist Scott Gibbons, they suspend their beginning, and some other piece of theatre begins in its stead. This suspension of one event in favour of a second performs an intensification of attention. Suspended, as it were, on the brink of something, I lean into the now-visible silence to witness what is coming. It is two men, on all fours, who enter diagonally onto the stage from upstage left. They wear identical black socks and underpants. As they draw nearer, it becomes clear that they also wear painted-on moustaches. But what compels the attention most strongly is the character of their movement. They appear to move as one, as though conjoined in flesh. They appear to imitate an animal – a horse, or perhaps two horses, similarly conjoined. Is this some strange take on the familiar entrance of the animals in the Ark, who came in 'two by two'? What they achieve is an uncanny reversal of the technique of dressage, in which immaculately groomed horses perform solo routines under the direction of their human trainer. Here, two humans imitate what the horse has learned from the human, and which, presumably, the human thought it knew. Yet, there is no such thing as human dressage. Well, yes, there is, in fact. One need move no further than adjacent venues at the Olympics to recognise dressage in events such as ice-skating, gymnastics, diving, synchronised swimming, in each of which techniques of human-body display are thinly disguised as sport. Examples proliferate, from sports arena to parade ground and through many locations in between. Let us not think too much about acting for the moment. So, the animal comes in, one by two, separating eventually to form two upright humans. One dons a black false beard to complement his equally stagey moustache. In the simple codes of stage facial hair, what we seem to have here is a father and a son.

In the sequence that ensues, the sacrifice of Isaac by Abraham is enacted. Two washing machines churn and mumble. The actions of the sacrifice are carried out with a precision that draws attention to itself in a strange way. Of course, the stagey facial hair has already made something of a mockery of the proceeding: we are already in the land of fabrication and repetition, even if the purpose of the act is unclear. But, in addition, every gesture through which the unfolding of the narrative is pointed out points also to itself: look not only at what I point to, look also at the pointing. Just watch me do some acting. See how I move, don't miss anything, judge me properly, award me good scores for technical achievement and artistic impression. Now, Isaac is bent over a washing machine, and Abraham raises the scissors and brings them down. Too late, a third man in black underpants has arrived upon the scene, applied black wings to his back to supply the necessary angel, and points, upstage, to where a small goat is revealed. But it is too late. Isaac is dead, and there can be no substitution here. The story has gone horribly wrong, just as Kierkegaard imagined it might. God called upon Abraham to give his only son, his one and only impossible gift of a son. And he's gone and done it. Once and for all. Oh dear. It seemed like a good idea at the time. Abraham and the angel raise their hands to their faces in a stereotypical expression of grief, and suddenly I realise what it is I have been watching. I have been watching mime, or rather, that particular modern form of acting in which the theatre and the cinema seem to coincide: the acting of the silent movie. In either case, an acting which is always pointing at things, shaping its gestures to draw attention to the way in which they are having to function as a kind of language. What the gestures point to, ultimately, is the unavailability of speech. At every moment where gesture would ordinarily develop into exclamation, and thus, as gesture, fall out of sight as the voice erupted into hearing, at every such moment the gesture must continue, extend its arc so as to encompass the fullness of the utterance. In standing in for speech in this way, the gestures of this kind of acting seem both original and derivative at one and the same time: original because they seem, at least, to arise from the body itself, as impulse itself, but derivative too, because however singular the gesture might be in its eruption through the body, it must also make of the body something that must be read – a hieroglyph or a quotation. The sequence in which Isaac is sacrificed is, therefore, both deeply sinister and hilarious at the same time, risking the utmost silliness in the fabric of its enactment, as, for instance, in the moment where silent-movie acting succeeds in alluding to its own inability to utter, in the joke 'utterance' – tsssssssccccchhh! – as a match is struck to light the sacrificial pyre. What on Earth is Abraham doing with a box of matches out here on the mountain, and by what magic may he imitate the sound of a match from within his world of silence? Only possible, of course, if this sequence is already understood as quotation, as a scene in which people are pretending to be Abraham and Isaac, rather than as a scene in which Abraham and Isaac do anything.

Now we realise that they are the police. They take their sodden uniforms from the washing machines and get dressed, and arrange themselves in a variety of obvious police formations. They hose themselves down. They burp. Black tablets of the law fly in, decorated with strands of black hair. The tablets are hosed down. A rifle is cleaned. Ceremonial candles are lit. Everything is being hosed down, and the whole business is being filmed/projected. This is a police operation. It is an act of purification that entangles itself with a sadistically comic second rendition, as hyper-parody, of the Isaac sacrifice. The trembling that began with the washing machines is spreading. A small black house shudders about the stage. The funnier it gets, this parody, the more fearful, concluding

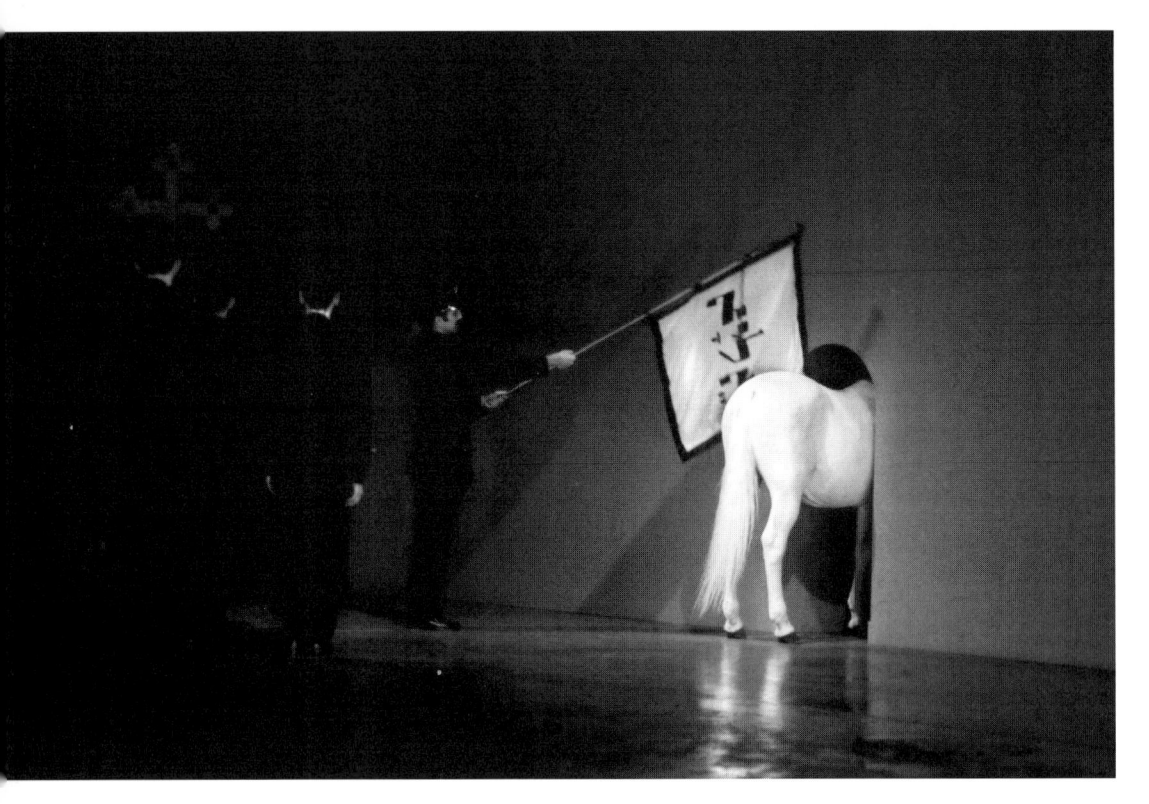

Across the stage, within a doorway, the hindquarters of a horse, an actual horse, between the on and the off.

with a new version of the goat-substitution offer, in which, in place of the goat (removed from the scene by the man in the red suit and top hat), a 'policeman' on all fours 'stands in' and bleats. The gesture of hands to faces is repeated, at the realisation that the angel has arrived again too late, and this time the hands cover faces that are only too keen to display a hideous kind of glee, as the 'policemen' laugh together with delight at their own performance. By now, though, some other force seems to be taking control of the house. The building is shaking under the pressure of a sound that seems to combine the magma rumble that we heard right back at the start of the sequence, in the foyer in Cesena, with the panic acceleration of exploding voices that accompanied (in Cesena and Avignon) the projection of the self-destroying alphabet. A fearsome trembling, then, an assault on the fabric of meaning-making, threatening to break open the theatre. And, with it, the demonic appearance of French tricolours, leaping and lurching in ghastly spasms from holes in the right- and left-stage walls. As though this parody of a parody of a ceremony, precisely because of its giggling distortions, had conjured forth some

Too late, a third man in black underpants has arrived upon the scene.

appalling spirit, as though in this police operation some absolute clarity of action had been achieved, apparently by dreadful accident, but more likely, by improvident and deadly design.

NR

Somebody, anybody

An actor stands at the front of the stage, silent, immobile, naked except for a white cloth wrapped around his loins, a twist of thorn twigs upon his brows. At one side of the stage, a woman, an anonymous mother, massages her breasts, her breathing forceful and rhythmic, as if lactation might be a mode of expression, *must* be expression sooner or later. Across the stage, within a doorway, the hindquarters of a horse, an actual horse,

Ecce homo, he says.

We don't want to put the story of Jesus on stage.

between the on and the off. And, over all, a deadening, ungenerative grey light, more like a gloom than an illumination, spacing out the pieces of the tableau, soaking the interminable moment into which . . . a car falls, out of the roof of the theatre, onto the stage. Smash. The figures in the tableau are unmoved, but we gasp, we utter noises: brief ejaculations, trickles of laughter, a short buzz of chat. And here's another one. While we attempt to assimilate, another car crashes onto the stage behind the first one. And then immediately another one, beside this one. Smash. Smash. These cars fall in a way we might suppose meaning, or understanding, to fall. With the weight of an event, set into motion and apprehended. And it happens now, not later. There is a phrase in English 'the penny drops', referring, I've always supposed, to a mechanical entertainment – an automaton – that might be set in motion by inserting a coin in a slot. Idiomatically, the phrase implies the rending of a veil, as in: Ah, now I comprehend. The penny drops, and then . . . we see, and hear. And these are such heavy pennies, loose change out of the pockets of the gods maybe, but heavy enough to have gouged a dent in the stage over the first few days of the show's run. Maybe – at the level of metaphor – these are the machines of the gods, crashing out of the heavens. So there will be no *deus ex machina*, no last minute (and forever after) resolution, no resurrection, for instance, no rescue, no reprieve, and we must resign ourselves to that. And how can we not resign ourselves to the fact of the event? Look at these things, so familiar, so ordinary: everyday traffic, mere vehicles, mere commodities. Surely, as the coin falls, along with the crash (once, and then at least once again) of the mechanism itself, we 'get it'. Nothing is suspended anymore. *We* are not suspended anymore. There is nothing left, now, to decide about. We are switched on. (Ah, I comprehend . . . 'thinks' the automaton.) But switched on to what? What do I 'get'? The figures in the tableau, him, her, and the animal, I notice, are still immobile, and mute. Still sad, I suppose. They are still giving nothing away, as if there might still be something to give – in this moment – if only 'we' had an adequate language to give in return, in which the gift, the true gift, might be exchanged, and heard. As if, let's say, the exceptional thing wasn't there, where we thought we saw and heard it, flashing and banging in *our* sky, not even in the marvellous *coup de théâtre* after all, but somewhere else, for example, in the sort of place where language cracks up a little bit, away from the stage at the very least, as this or that spectator, registering a gasp of surprise, registers at the same time the closeness of their neighbour. Or – to project another sort of example upon a theatre that precisely does not *speak* its uncertainties – a place on the stage, a particular spot, where an actor might be less willing to stand (knowing, as he does, that a car is suspended above that spot): *un*exceptional instances like that, ordinary upsets, things that you don't look forward to.

 The unexceptional, anyway, haunts this exceptional-looking and exceptional-sounding theatre. The Christ actor is given an armband with the figure '5' on it. Christ number 5?

Things went very well in Paris.

That many already? I remember how he came here, breaking open a window at the back of the stage, using a crowbar to do it, climbing into the theatre from the street outside, like a burglar, Christ the criminal, letting in all of that ordinary, marvellous, everyday daylight. As if unexceptional light might touch us more closely than anything. A moulded Sphinx appears downstage. He stands before it, a long time, in silence. He presents the Sphinx with a human skull, Oedipus' answer to the Sphinx's riddle (who is it walks on four legs in the morning, on two legs at midday, and three legs in the evening and speaks with the one voice?). *Ecce homo*, he says of himself with this gesture, mankind, me. Any of us, that is. Me, especially, although I am anyone else. And, perhaps, one who is yet to arrive. The same answer Oedipus has arrived at before, and will arrive at again, later, in his own tragedy, in answer to another question, in another theatre than this one, in another fiction; where on that occasion it will be his own skull, masked in red, offered up to the monster that demands such spectacles. But is it Oedipus who brings such knowledge? Is it really him? Is he really himself, as he is named? And, anyway, doesn't that naming, that unmasking, reveal him, *not* as a stranger, an alien amongst us, but as one of us after all, 'a native Theban', as unexceptional as ourselves? The police come onto the stage, to conduct a forensic test. One operates a mock-up movie camera, out of which is extracted a cylinder of light, 'sent' across the stage, as if the image – *his* suffering – were *their* composition and theirs to play with. As if the fiction were their only concern. His piss is collected in the same cylinder. An insane, literalising, paranoid alchemy: mixing the appearance with its juice, as if that were a way to capture the substance of the image and save it for later, to store up affect like some sort of bio-psychic fuel or weapon of mass destruction. Essence of myth. Concentrate of power. And then, the police abandon him, and he stands at the front and stares and says nothing. A man of sorrows indeed. Abandoned to his pose, and sustaining his abandon as a 'true' pose, the last pose left. Christ the actor. Later, after all that ordnance has fallen from the heavens, he will go and take up the pose of the crucifixion, on the roof of the central car, in imitation of all the countless, familiar representations of that scene, including every subsequent, 'post-Christian' travesty. The latest travesty, anyway, occurs right here. The car on which he is crucified parks itself at the back of the stage, the machine's last reflex, making space for whatever spectacle is to follow. Later still, he will be picked up in someone's arms, in the arms of a man dressed in red, and carried and put in the front seat of one of the other cars: a crash victim, one of so many (has anyone counted?), remaining there in a dark corner of the stage for the rest of the show, almost out of sight, almost out of mind, as unexceptional as you like. Somebody something happened to, nobody you know.

JK

27 OCTOBER 2003

Ciao Scott

How are you? Things went very well in Paris, and people really liked the show, not just the audience (always busy) but also the European co-producers and the scholars who saw it. The cars fell straight every time, but the middle one made a dent in the floor several centimetres deep.

We've looked at Rome again, and next week we will start rehearsals again. I'm sending you the text of the commands. They need to be angry, malicious, violent, choral and must have a completely unexpected effect in relation to the climate of the stage. The actress has to receive each one like a kick.

Text:
Come here.
Drink my water.
Metal.
Ash.
Listen to my line of fire.
Make yourself seen.
Jump.
Don't look.
Don't look.
You must not look.

Rome will be a concert of sounds which will carry the emotions and give blood and life to the images. I hope the rehearsals will be less chaotic and confusing than those for Paris. However, we will be living in the same house, which is close to the theatre, so it will be possible to develop a good part of the work there.

Ciao Scott, Chiara

From the final script of *R.#07*

Bell

When the white drapes have all been removed, the priests gather up the carpet, and Mario and Salvo bring the bell on stage.

'You thought the monkey was real?'

The bell is raised up.
All the priests gather on stage and dance slowly in a circle.
Luciano approaches the bell and strikes it.
Then he rejoins the others in the dance.
Once Luciano has made one circuit, Ofelia throws basketballs from offstage, and the priests start playing with them again.
Salvo throws a ball once against the PVC.
After a minute of playing, Luciano approaches the PVC and looks at the audience.
Then the sound of the bell.
Luciano pauses.
All the priests let the balls fall to the ground and roll downstage so that they are held onstage by the PVC.
Luciano stops the bell from ringing and raises the PVC.
The balls fall into the auditorium.
Once the balls have gone, Luciano sees to it that the bell is raised.
Once the bell has been raised, Fabio enters and puts a microphone in place on stage.
He touches it to make sure it is working and the amplified blow of his hand on the microphone is heard.
He exits.

Stage break

The stage rips open.
Sounds of breaking.
A gun emerges through the floor of the stage.
Harlequin emerges walking backwards, grabs the weapon and carries it forward to the proscenium, undresses, puts the gun back over his shoulder, looks at the ceiling of the theatre.
A Harlequin painted on the ceiling of the theatre is lit up.
The commands are issued again:
'Don't look.'
'You must not look.'
The curtain closes.

Flash

Photographic flashes go off against the white curtain at the same time as the text of the commands.
The sound of the flash is amplified.
When the flashes finish a bass frequency remains until the house lights come up.

Monkey business

Theatre has this way of tricking you into making a fool of yourself, tripping you up on the most straightforward questions, generating confusion where everything is plain to see. How else, then, could I be so uncertain, here in the Teatro Valle in Rome? Why don't I believe my own eyes? After all, there doesn't seem to be any attempt to hide anything. There is a white curtain, for sure – one that we have seen before in various presentations – which opens in the usual way to reveal what I am supposed to be seeing. The curtain parts, and behind it there is a window, or rather, an array of windows, stitched together in identical glass rectangles to form one single window with many panes. In this typically Italian theatre, this means that there are already at least three frames in play: the frame of the proscenium, the frame of the parting curtains, and this additional frame, or set of frames, provided by the window or windows. Everything that is placed between me and what is to appear is designed, or so it appears, to facilitate my seeing of what is to appear. And that which does appear appears unambiguous, in an even white light that seems to insist that there is nothing to hide and no place to hide it: in a white box, there is an ape or monkey. A chimpanzee, I think. But from the very first moment of its appearance, I am questioning it, doubting the evidence of my own eyes and feeling myself a fool. If I fail to make up my mind about this monkey, this monkey will have made a monkey of me. I absolutely have to be sure this is the monkey I think it is because I cannot run the risk of being deceived: 'You thought the monkey was real?' I imagine someone laughing at me afterwards, exposing me as the dupe that I am, to fall for such self-evident trickery. I pay very careful attention as the chimpanzee goes about its business, doing those monkey things that monkeys do, and doing them so convincingly that I still can't help feeling this is a perfectly staged deception. After all, a real chimpanzee wouldn't need to toy with a banana or make chimpanzee noises in order to convince me that it was a bona-fide chimpanzee, would it? Surely a real chimpanzee would do real chimpanzee things instead of conforming so readily and so exactly to my expectations? The chimpanzee doth protest too much, I think, as my hermeneutics of suspicion give themselves full rein. And where are those chimpanzee noises coming from, amplified, so that they can be heard through (or is it, rather, around) the glass wall? The chimpanzee comes downstage and looks out through the glass. It looks pretty convincing, I tell myself, beginning to feel more confident in my judgement. Someone behind me (in one of the boxes?) is shouting something I don't understand, and there is laughter and some remonstration from people closer to the back than I. Is this some kind of protest at the presence of a live animal on stage, or is it, instead, a protest at the blatant act of deception being perpetrated here? For a moment, I even wonder if this disruption itself is some kind of simulation, but only for a moment, really, after which my sense of what is real and what is not begins to consolidate. Now my foolishness starts to operate in reverse. Instead of worrying that I might have fallen for a deception, been taken in by a human in an ape suit, I start to think what an idiot I must have been ever to think that a representation so exact and complete could ever have been accomplished. Of course, this is a real ape. How could I ever have been in any doubt? I am just coming to terms with this revelation when the curtain closes.

During a game played by novice priests.

A familiar message board descends into a position within the frame of the proscenium, so that its text will sit above the scene that has just taken place. It begins to transmit a message. It starts something like 'O . . . OH OH . . .' This is somewhere between a literal rendition of a human cry (of delight, of despair, of astonishment or recognition) and the literal (again) transcription by which we might conventionally expect an ape's 'speech' to be transmitted. 'SONO FELICE' ('I AM HAPPY'). Happy that 'everything is going well', that 'the last scene was perfect. Perfect.' Who might be speaking here? It is the machine of the theatre, of course, but the logic of the situation also makes it the chimpanzee. In an earlier episode (*BN.#05* in Bergen) the message board, appearing at a similar moment in the dramaturgy, after the departure of a goat from the stage, had claimed, 'It is I – the goat – speaking.' Earlier, in Avignon, the idea that the goat, a poet, might be able to speak to us via the medium of theatre was worked through by means of the translation of the goat's own passage across a floor marked with the codes of its amino acids into a series of syllables sung from a glass tablet. The chimpanzee's message seems to have been easier to transmit, but what has the ape to be so pleased about? What was 'perfect' about the scene in which it made its appearance? What, really, has been happening here?

That the ape and the machine of the theatre should be taking joint credit, as it were, for whatever has happened, seems just. For it is their collaboration that has been so felicitous. The ape has aped itself. It has passed itself off successfully as an ape, it has appeared on stage and convinced. It is not the fact that we – or I at least – remain convinced that this was, indeed, the ape we took it for, that impresses, but rather the way in which the ape's presence within the rhetorical machine composed of the theatrical frames (the windows, the curtains, the arch) has permitted it to perform the act of aping. In that aping, the ape has not just been an ape, it has done an ape. One might even go so far as to suggest that this ape has actually made an ape, that this animal has performed a mimesis in excess of the simple mimesis (of copying) for which, as an ape, it is famed. The ape has not copied, so much as made a copy. In aping nature, thus, the ape might be said to have reproduced itself, endogonidically. Perfect. Immaculate, even.

NR

From a conversation about dramaturgy (24 July 2004)

Chiara: If I have to talk about dramaturgy, I think of a symphony . . . When we listen to a symphony we feel the fullnesses and the emptinesses you were also speaking about before, the changes of rhythm, the slowings down and speedings up . . . The fall of the cars in Paris could very well have been placed at the start of the show, but

A ridiculous miracle.

what a difference in weight and significance that would have been from the point at which it was actually placed! It would still have been a very strong image: get the audience seated, wait, then – boom! – a car falls to the floor, immediately. However, placed as it was, after the entrance of Jesus, who had come from outside, breaking through the window, so that you could hear the sound of passing cars, where the figure of Jesus, in this way, I don't know if this is right, is not rhetorical, carries in itself no rhetoric.

Romeo: Jesus is always rhetorical.

Chiara: No, because like this you avoid the problem of the name, which was the problem with Mussolini in Rome, you avoid the problem of narrative . . . and this fall of the cars is as if it made for us a kind of mode of knowing not only the technique of the theatre but also the technique of the audience's perception. The second phase of the dramaturgy doesn't just settle accounts with reality, I take the idea and transfer it here, but you must also reckon with the perceptive capacity of the audience, with the human brain, with our brains because the figures, above all, must be able to surprise us.

Joe: When I saw the cars fall, after that moment, it was as though someone else and not me had seen it. The emotion is something which is there.

Chiara: Exactly. That's why I said before that emotion has something profoundly tautological about it, it is not sentimental, because you see it from somewhere, because you are looking too . . . it's an emotion that you experience, but that you also see.

The Italian comedy

Getting at what happens, after it has happened, involves an attempt to stay faithful to the event, although that is a fidelity that can only express itself perhaps by way of a betrayal. I cannot, in truth, say what I saw. It may be, though, that the *staged* event – as it imitates suffering, as it composes the elements of false appearance – anticipates that betrayal with betrayals of its own. It has to do with torn fabrics, broken promises and memory that overwhelms itself, like a landscape that can't help but mean more than it says. Writing at home in London, some three months after the Rome performance, I remember the structure of the episode in the following way: it is as if a geometrical abstract painting – a minimal patterning of black lines and masses, horizontals and verticals mainly, against a white surface (recalling, therefore, as well as a modernist painterly tradition, a landscape of print, of messaging, but blown up large, too large to 'receive') – were morphed, through a certain sort of pressure being applied, a force of attention or need or, indeed, magnification, so that black forms and white planes appear, over the course of the evening, to secrete what is immanent to them but otherwise concealed: movement, and sound and colour.

In a theoretical essay of 1920, the painter Piet Mondrian – a champion of just the sort of work I think I am finding an allusion to here – characterised the historical task of the 'new art' as a struggle with the 'tragic'. The tragic, for Mondrian, was a condition of 'disequilibrium' in which the 'individual', the 'corporeal', the 'natural concrete' had been dominant to the detriment of the 'purity' of art, a condition in which the 'expression of form' had tended to be 'veiled . . . by the descriptive', and from which the 'new spirit' must seek to 'free itself entirely' by way of a plastic art dedicated – as he puts it in an earlier text written during the Great War – to the 'expression of immutable relationships'; or, as the 1920 essay has it, a mode of composition 'in constant and neutralizing opposition'.[2]

---

2 Piet Mondrian, 'Dialogue on the New Plastic' (1919), trans. Harry Holzman and Martin S. James; and *Neo-Plasticism: The General Principle of Plastic Equivalence* (1921), trans. H. Holzman and M. S. James, selections in Charles Harrison and Paul Wood (eds), *Art in Theory 1900–1990*, Oxford: Blackwell, 1996, pp. 282–7, 287–90.

The early twenty-first-century theatre we are concerned with here shares, we might say, Mondrian's intuition of a modernist 'tragic', but remembers something too of what was perverted, of the terror that was turned loose and turned to the advantage of power, in the world (and not just the art world) and with 'corporeal' results, in the very sublation of the tragic that Mondrian imagines and, indeed, by means of the institution of certain formal and supposedly 'immutable relationships'. Specifically, in this episode, the focus is upon a 'tragedy' of modern Italian history, imaged, as we shall see, in terms of the 1929 Concordat between the Catholic church and the Italian fascist leader Benito Mussolini, an alliance that established the Vatican as a sovereign state and legitimated an ordering power (the bad dream of Fascism) that still haunts contemporary Italian public life.[3]

Whatever its allegiances, however, and precisely on the principle that a space cannot have two different contents, or at least not at the same time, the theatre is always going to have a problem with the expression of immutable relationships and the composition of constant and neutralising opposition. In the last account, the theatre doesn't work like a painting, if only because it has to unfold its matter over time, piece by piece, minute after minute and can only 'abstract', can only unpack the tragic (along with its need, like Mondrian's need, like Italy's need perhaps, to be born *out* of the tragedy, to be free of its domain) after the fashion of a sort of paranoid farce. Things keep coming back and have to be worked over. Mussolini, for example, will keep coming back; at least, this evening he will. Although, so too will figures of vulnerability and uncertainty, as well as belligerent refusal. An example of the latter is a young woman, hobbled by stereotypes – naked as an allegorical nude in a neo-classical painting, pushing a shopping trolley, with one trendy high-heeled shoe and a black scarf wrapped around her head in the old style, as tradition demands – who faces up, bewildered, to a series of impossible commands barked out in the dictator's disembodied voice: Look at me! Don't look at me! Listen! Sit! Don't listen!

Things keep coming back, but there is no way of answering adequately to the demands they make. Which is why, in the theatre, the picture is anything but immutable and why, perhaps, its 'relationships' can never be fully accounted for in any sort of 'plastic' expression. If watching the performance is like looking at a picture, it is like staring at a picture for such a long period of time – it may be a picture that you love although you don't know that yet – that you notice things that aren't actually given there (hence, the paranoia): shimmerings, polyps of delinquent thought, leakages of the spectrum right against the edge of a line. Meanwhile, you hear something in the picture of the murmur

---

3 See Italian Premier Silvio Berlusconi's interview with *The Spectator*, 13 September 2003.

Chocolate.

of the world or believe that you can hear it, like a sobbing somewhere, like a plucking of tones, like animal chatter: like 'the distant rumble of the world and its demons in the midst of the ideal city of human communication'.[4] It's like a worldliness returning – as a gift, an interruption, an embarrassment – right where we separate ourselves from the world, right there where abstraction makes its most rational calculations. The difference being that in the theatre this worldliness is given, deliberately, explicitly (and hence the farce) according to a dramaturgical calculation that has to pace itself alongside the progress of *our* thought, leading us on a little, shadowing our steps, as we get lost, fall over each other or seek to arrive too soon. In the theatre, 'we' never see the same picture, if only because when we look at the picture there is always someone else over our shoulder.

Things begin, when the curtains open, with an asymmetrical grid of dark lines upon a white field – a partitioned glass right across the front of a white box stage – and an adult chimpanzee: a living mass of slowness and darkness and relative unpredictability, who inhabits the box and moves around there, checking it out, eating stuff. The

---

4 Alphonso Lingis, *The Community of Those who Have Nothing in Common*, Bloomington, Ind.: Indiana University Press, 1994, p. 105.

chimpanzee is an invader of sorts, a 'separate' and 'particular'[5] corruption of the abstract environment but an invader who appears to belong there all the same; as if the aesthetic construct cannot sustain its immunity to the fantasies – as brutal or productive as those fantasies might be – that at some level or other have fed its production. Already, it's like watching history leaking out of the picture, as if 'history' were some sort of actual substance, something oozing and collectable, that emerges haphazardly enough in the motley of a range of imaginary figures and forms: a Darwinian ancestor (the chimpanzee), and then later in the evening a school of priests, the dictator Mussolini, that composite 'woman of Italy' (the only woman in this particular episode), as well as a chameleon Harlequin from the Italian popular theatre of the *commedia dell'arte*. However imaginary though, these are forms that, once released, won't quite disappear back into the pattern – although the pattern, as we shall see, will adapt to try and accommodate that end. They are figures that can't be brought completely into line – although there will be lines, specifically, stripes of colour, a colour for every figure in the play, that will be organised later around the stage precisely so as to order and assimilate these relapses into the historical mess.

These figures are shapes that emerge from the picture as agents (Mussolini included) of a potentiality of thought, a militant thought even, that can't altogether be killed off but that, just as that thought begins to realise itself, realises in the same moment something of its extreme vulnerability to whatever resists it, to the thought, we might say, that resists its own thinking. Mussolini, for instance, appears for the first time adjacent to a ridiculous miracle, when a basketball gets stuck above the hoop during a game played by novice priests, multiple figures in black who will succeed the single figure of the chimpanzee. Mussolini comes forward from the back of stage, literally 'emerging' from invisibility, robed in white like a prize-fighter, white against white, wrapped up like a larva, newly hatched, wingless, but ready for change. Or even (more pertinently perhaps) like one of the ancient Roman *larvae* or *lemures*, malevolent, unexorcised spirits, that returned to the places left behind by the dead, and with the faces of the dead, but which could be placated – for a while anyway – by throwing beans in their way at the nighttime festival of Lemuria. In other words, persistent ghosts, perpetually fading, perpetually coming back again to bite. If we want to suggest, after the contemporary Italian philosopher of potentiality Giorgio Agamben, that the potentiality of such figures to appear, to be, to do, goes hand in hand in hand with a potential 'not to be', we might have to say that in the theatre these figures bring their impotentiality with them, even as they appear before us, caught upon a threshold, there at the skin of the image. Or – to borrow a

---

5 The terms are Mondrian's.

thought from Aristotle cited by Agamben – shall we say they bring a potential 'to suffer', to suffer 'destruction' of a sort even in the process of being given to creation? But also, in creation – in that moment, at least, of coming on to the stage, that moment of birth which is nothing like a birth, where one is always born full-grown and, therefore, loaded up with memory and forgetting – to suffer the 'salvation' there of all of the cruel possibilities, of everything that remains in potentiality, that remains unborn but finds itself reflected nevertheless in 'what is similar to it', out here in the world, in our places and times?[6]

We should, anyway, beware of imitations. From the first moments, the stark patterning of black and white is already corrupted by the motility of a fleshy, earth-coloured element that wanders around behind the rationalised sectioning of the picture, like a loose atom at first, but then settles, fixes into the narrative, as this element of pigment is translated through a succession of similarly coloured objects that displace each other in turn and coagulate upon the scene: a chimpanzee's backside, a basketball, a man's hairless face and head (Mussolini's when he takes off his hood) and a jug of drinking chocolate. Throughout this process, there is an emergence of sound, sounds of life it sounds like – the ape's voice and movement miked up from behind the glass screen, the thump thump of a basketball game, the mutter of debate – although these sounds are not given us to hear for ourselves, to read and recognise, but are muffled behind the sealed-in stage, like rumours of the world, like reserved business at a meeting that we are not party to. There is one exception. At a particular moment, a priest removes a small disk from the glass and whispers to us through this hole, sharing a confidence or two, before pouring a cup of chocolate through the gap so it smears down the front of the picture, between us and the scene, a dirty protest, a libation, a desecration, a sweet and shitty stain upon the whole affair.

Even as the signs of life are spattered about the stage, however, those signs continue to be organised into a pattern, a pattern that perpetually erupts and recuperates, as if life could not be grasped – can only be grasped – in the machinery of representation, which keeps attempting to get at the root of things, only to break what it recovers, before turning everything back into the soil. And so, for a moment, as the element that references our clay becomes encrusted upon the surface of the spectacle, we are given a cut of a deeper colour altogether, a shock of primary red, as if the theatre itself had opened an artery. A black-clad figure uncloaks an all-over scarlet costume, topcoat and top hat, a figure we recognise – those of us who have been following the sequence – as

---

6 Aristotle, *De Anima* 417b, cited in Giorgio Agamben, *Homo Sacer: Sovereign Power and Bare Life*, trans. Daniel Heller-Roazen, Stanford, Calif.: Stanford University Press, 1998, p. 46.

Make yourself seen.

a regular denizen of *Tragedia Endogonidia*. This is the red pastor who, since the fifth episode in Bergen, has been responsible for taking care of the abandoned life: the suffering child, the 'symbolic' animal, the life that remains, that survives its signifying function. In Paris, it was he who carried the crucified Christ away from the place of martyrdom and into the shadows at the back of the stage. Now, as if in reparation for all the abandoned life, he bites into the neck of Mussolini and spits a mouthful of blood upon the back surface of the glass screen: a red stain beside the brown, a stain which, as soon as it appears and sticks, abstracts the 'life' that is represented there, renders that life as the mark, the gesture, the scream, which, even as it enacts remembering, forgets *what* it remembers, casts that into the dark. So, already, the mark is not blood: it is red, paint, image merely. The scream, when it comes, and a silent scream at that – as this same figure puts on an ape-mask taken from the dictator and then doubles up, contorted into a simian posture – is a borrowed scream, someone else's, a figure of pain transferred as if from one sufferer to another, suffered on trust, acted out. As for the gesture, as this same figure in this same moment passes Mussolini a bone, from hand to hand, in an action reminiscent of the famous 'cut' in Kubrick's *2001* (it looks like a leg bone: an ape bone? a human bone? an actual 'missing link'?), this gesture pre-empts the dispersal of the figure who makes it, into the *mise en scène* itself: a sovereign dispersal, we would have to say, the projection of a domain, but a projection that squeezes the actor, the sovereign subject, literally out of the picture.

Again, this is worked out through a dramaturgy of colour. To explain: the figure in red, after spitting out the blood of the tyrant and leaving his mark, had uncloaked again, another layer, to expose a diamond-patterned multi-coloured harlequin costume, as much colour – it may be – about one body as we have seen in any episode of the *Tragedia* to date. And, in that costume, this figure takes charge, becomes the dominant character upon the scene. By this point, we have had our lesson in modern Italian history, we have seen the contract between the Fascists and the church sealed in *cioccolato*, and it is perhaps appropriate that it is the enigmatic Harlequin, an archetypal *theatrical* principle, 'first poet of acrobats and unseemly noises',[7] a peculiar figure of disingenuous subtlety, who arrives to assume command of this unholy alliance. What follows now, though, in the moment of collapse into another and – as it happens – earlier 'life', is an explosion of the theatre and an establishment of the spectrum, according to the livery of this regent Harlequin. In effect, there is a taking apart of the stage's white environment, an army of priests dismantling walls and ceiling and floor, to expose a cathedral of colour – super-precise vertical stripes of yellow, pink, green, red, brown, white, blue, orange . . . around the entirety of the stage – acknowledged with the chiming, onstage, of an enormous bell and attended by the busy movement of scurrying figures in black. As if life – and world – were a catastrophe that had to be 'redeemed' by abstraction, absorbed again and again into a pattern of system and command. As if the rainbow, for instance, were not a promise of life and world, an accident of appearance, a miracle of encounter, but the imposition of law, of ocularity and order. As if, in the theatre, there were, indeed, some sort of sovereign principle at work, that feeds off the forms of life it gives birth to, even as it depends upon these forms – figures, dreams, memories, acts – to redeem it from itself, to actualise its potentiality (or at least to prosecute its interests), in the world, after all these moving pictures are put away.

So, at the conclusion of the spectacle, the stage is shown to harbour still a sort of outlaw life – specifically, an Harlequin, the same actor but 'another' Harlequin, a bandit

---

7 Pierre Louis Duchartre, *The Italian Comedy: The Improvisation Scenarios Lives Attributes Portraits and Masks of the Illustrious Characters of the Commedia dell'Arte*, trans. Randolph T. Weaver, New York: Dover, 1966, p. 134.

We should, anyway, beware of imitations.

Harlequin, costumed, after all that, in black and white again, but now with a rifle, and an attitude, and a silence. Agamben has written of the bandit, not set outside the law but abandoned by the law (and so abandoned to its full severity), as a figure that ambivalently links sovereign power to 'sacred life'. That latter is nothing other than the 'bare life' that constitutes sovereign power while being designated so to speak as beyond the pale, and therefore exposed to harm, as much harm indeed as there is to inflict. Agamben goes further in linking the bare life of the bandit to the Hobbesian concept of 'the state of nature' and its relation to the foundation of the modern city, a relation which Agamben insists is nothing like that between a prior and a subsequent stage of development but rather a 'non-relation' that is never settled, never finally resolved, by which the state of nature 'dwells within' the city as an 'always operative presupposition'; 'in truth, a state of exception, in which the city appears for an instant . . . *tanquam dissoluta*'.[8]

---

8 Agamben, *Homo Sacer*, pp. 106, 109. See also pp. 28f, 58–60.

The bandit Harlequin appears to be of this provenance. He breaks into the theatre by smashing a hole up through the floor of the stage, in the exact place where a microphone has been placed, for the orator, for his demagogue predecessor presumably, his previous self. He climbs out of the hole, dusts himself off, and then he shows us – where a spotlight picks out the image, up there on the ceiling (our ceiling, over the auditorium) – himself as he appears now, and mounted on a cloud, a black-and-white Harlequin, one figure amongst many in an altogether more old-fashioned genre of painting than the one we have been considering here, an eighteenth-century decorative allegory: a representation that his life – let loose here, set at large in the theatre's maw – pays ambivalent tribute to by standing and breathing and making ready to depart. Harlequin tips his hat to the image, shoulders his rifle and prepares to move: towards the back of the stage for starters, wherever that leads. From out of that darkness comes again a series of barked commands, in Mussolini's tones: 'Guadarmi!' 'Non guadarmi!' Look at me. Don't look at me. Harlequin stops in his tracks. It is as if an intelligence – a brutality – of the theatre itself speaks here, and it *knows*. It knows that it cannot put a limit on what it shows, cannot calculate that limit, and knows that the external world, the city, for instance, from which we thought we were sealed in here, and *its* bad dreams, along with whatever else rustles and twitches out there, has already squeezed in to this place – however thick the walls, however torn we are from what we were (however broken the connections between us) – and attached itself to the picture: the rumble of the world amongst us and touching us, almost touching us; an infection of sound like a bacterial growth in the ear; a human stain on the surface of the eye; life let loose, unconscionable, unstoppable. And starting over again.

JK

S.#08
Le Maillon Théâtre
(Le Wacken), Strasbourg
February 2004

In *Tragedia Endogonidia*, each show inaugurates a language of its own. Each episode has its own narration, or reinvention of a narration. I can recount what I have seen on stage. This becomes a dramaturgical fact. The act of telling. I can write down what I saw. That is an act of dramaturgy. I can write a theatrical text after, or according to what I saw. This I count as a pure dramaturgical act, arising from the elimination of the chorus: work on the episode alone, work on the action. Here I can always write and tell what I saw, thus inaugurating a new dramaturgical language. Every show has its own dramaturgical language. I believe that the rhythm may be, in *Tragedia Endogonidia*, the dramaturgical language of each episode. Each episode has its rhythm. Each episode is recognisable by means of its rhythm.

CG

4 JANUARY 2004

Dear Scott,

Here are the first ideas and suggestions for you for the Strasbourg episode.

The theatrical space we will be using is an immense hangar which we want to use without a set and without a stage. The space is equipped with an aerial grid of metal poles and tubes supported by broad columns. The floor is cement, and we will be covering it with a lot of earth, particularly in the central area. The roof is sheet-metal, and when it rains the sound disrupts the silence (we know this very well because we've played most of our repertoire in this space). The walls are perfectly white with various doors in the side walls. At the end, there's a big glass wall (like the one we used in Rome), which gives on to an exterior courtyard. The whole audience can easily see the courtyard, and on the left-hand side, a busy road. The courtyard is enclosed at the far end by white buildings with doors and windows, one of which is an ice-skating rink. The light outside is the orange of street lights.

We want to stage a double show: one outside and the other inside.

Chiara

26 JANUARY 2004

Dear Scott,

We have listened to the MP3s that you sent. It is a good start for this episode which we will only be able to be sure of in Strasbourg. The rehearsals in Cesena are partial because there's no earth, there's no external space with forty extras, and, of course, there's no tank. The four black women we've started working with in this period have an ideal stage presence, precisely because they are not actresses. Their voices are extraordinary: fragile voices but full of pathos. In the show, they will sing and speak in their own languages. They have sincere tones which are fascinating and surprising. I am thinking of recording their voices with the DAT so that at Strasbourg you can have them available straightaway to insert eventually between the radio interference and the rhythms. They are voices that will enrich our library. In the show, we will use them without amplification, but I fear that the poor acoustics in

Strasbourg and the delicate and gentle voices of the actresses may yet present us with unwelcome surprises.

Regarding the last e-mail you sent us, there's nothing new in the structure of the show, although rehearsals have given rise to some doubts about the sound. What's worrying us is the use of African rhythms, because this sound completes, in descriptive mode, what is already happening on stage and doesn't complicate it. Perhaps some interference and your tracks of stone sounds can come from the radio. It seems that what is happening is a putting-into-relation of the sound of the show and the earth that covers the space. It's good to see the earth by means of the sound, and right now the stone sounds seem perfect. The heartbeat of the stones that you created could be used as the heart of the earth. Concentrating the sound on Africa and on the black women seems to me too simple. The African rhythms could break out while the tank leaves, at the end of the show, when the black women are no longer on stage.

Another doubt which has arisen during rehearsals is the use of *Psycho*. We believe that a long passage of the show needs to be dedicated to showing the film. The sound should be distantly attached, recognisable but perhaps without selecting the most obvious moments of the soundtrack. Then the film will have to be transformed into a fire, and the sound will have to change too. We don't yet know whether we will use the ink-blot video from Bergen as an image of fire or some actual fire.

Chiara

Earth and glass

The episode begins in darkness. We take our seats in a large shallow-raked auditorium that faces down to an unilluminated stage area. This is a deep space, but apart from the fact of its depth, it is hard to see what the space contains. I can make out some broad and very basic forms, some sort of mounds. The stage seems to be contoured, like a landscape. Towards the front, there is a spillage of soil, ordinary grey-brown dirt and stones, as if the earth itself will have something to say for itself this evening. But that is all that is visible for the moment. Meanwhile, my gaze is drawn beyond the area of the stage. The back wall of this playing space is glass, right the way across, exposing a parking lot behind the exhibition complex, and beyond that various unspectacular institutional buildings. These, in turn, give on to the city itself: a motorway cutting into the view way over to the left, car headlights punctuating the perspective as they come towards us and pass by, the rumble of traffic doing what it does at such a distance, dissolving specificities in an indeterminate aural fill.

A man walks across outside, from right to left, smoking a cigarette. Has it begun? Of course it has, and possibly ages ago. Because look, there are already sightseers. A coach, a tourist bus, pulls in from the left and stops just beyond the glass. All of the people on board – there must be thirty, forty of them – pile over to the near side to peer through the bus windows towards where we are, inside the theatre, staring back at them. They seem livelier, more engaged than us. They seem, in a way that we do not, to know what they are doing there. If tourists, they behave as if in the first flush of tourism, still able to absorb, not bored yet by marvels. When they get out of the bus and the bus pulls away, there is much laughter and chatter, indistinct, but audible, even over the vehicle's engine.

It is hard to make these people out, they are largely silhouettes, but I can see there are children, women, men. They are all in dark coats, scarves, hats. It is cold out there; we know it because we've been there ourselves, and I can see their breath condensing even now. Signs of life, then. Although there is also something ghostly about those figures. They move further away, into the parking lot, and arrange themselves into a sort of formation, two groups, divided in lines. At one point, a little girl appears, isolated at the centre of the arrangement, noticeable, something to remark upon, but the moment passes as groups form and reform according to an improvised game, a game of stepping and measuring and counting, which – am I imagining this? – seems less like something playful and more like an ordering, a fixing and determining of movement and the meaning of this movement, moment by moment. A complex body of disparate figures is organising itself out there, as if subject to some sort of commanding force which they conjure from amongst themselves. And which cuts me out.

We see chairs being taken out and set in rows facing away from us, and then the entire group of citizen-visitors sit themselves down out there and watch Hitchcock's film – projected onto the back of a building a further fifty yards or so away. We watch with them, right from the opening credits – there is nothing else to do, as the projection cuts a monochrome corridor into the night, a zone of manifest immateriality within which our attention swims – hearing what we cannot help but hear of the dialogue and the soundtrack and Bernard Herrmann's score as these leak in to the theatre space where we remain sitting, trying – for what seemed a good fifteen or twenty minutes as the projection continues without interruption – to take it all in.

There is a sequence, before she ever arrives at the Bates Motel, where Marion sleeps in her car beside a desert road and awakes to see a traffic cop, peak-capped and sun-glassed, whose face fills her car window and also fills the frame of the film. At that moment, the screen outside the theatre in Strasbourg goes white (and remains illuminated the rest of the evening), as if the film were torn; or as if the rest of the movie,

I encountered that form again.

the familiar part, can afford to go by unshown. What happens then, although it had started to happen already and will continue throughout the evening, is that the group of people watching outside drift away from the site of the spectacle in ones and twos, wandering off somewhere to the side or far away across the parking lot, dissolving between the distant buildings.

Each spectator leaves at his or her chosen moment, and takes their reasons with them. We must do our best with what is left, unable to say for sure – unable to confirm here in writing – what it is these departures mean. Whether, for instance, those people outside depart in indifference, their rage and pity and amazement and grievance all used up (like tourists indeed who have just seen that there is nothing new to see). Or whether their movement is a way of keeping faith with the world by refusing to produce the image that is demanded of it. Whether, that is, we can imagine each of these spectators choosing to walk away from the film at a moment before the tragedy has to be accepted on its own terms, a moment when – for her, or for him (the exact moment would be peculiar to each) – it might still have been possible to conceive that this woman was not yet destined: as victim, as scapegoat, as murder statistic. As missing person.

JK

Just at the point in Hitchcock's movie where the McGuffin falls away, like the final section of rocket booster propelling an Apollo mission towards the moon, to set me on course for the thrilling trajectory through the space of pure action, I find myself dumped back into the theatre where there is nothing taking place. Or rather, where whatever does take place, even if it be some kind of nothing, must take the place of action.

As if to start to deliver on this promise, some light comes up, for the first time, on the space that ought to be the stage. The mound or earthwork dimly discerned before, and across which I have been watching 'the other event' of spectatorship, turns out to be just about what it seemed: a pile of rubble, not quite earth, but some rough agglomeration of soil and what could perhaps be the blasted remains of some human construction, as though the concrete of a long forgotten city had mixed itself in with the earth on which it once stood. To the rear and the right of this heap of world there is a small group of tents, a minimal camp from which, little by little, five or six figures eventually emerge. All women, I think, all African, and all dressed in military camouflage. They emerge onto the heap of world with a movement beyond weariness and busy themselves with various activities – preparing food, burying sanitary towels in the ground, establishing radio contact (with a distant command centre?) – all accomplished with the economy of routine but no urgency. They appear as the remnant of a rebel army, out in the wilderness of a country that perhaps no longer exists, still going through the motions of maintaining an operation even though there is no longer any revolution to fight for, no war to wage, no reason, no business being here.

If this is the 'action' I have been waiting for, preparing for, it is an evacuated action, without meaning or purpose, struggling (but there is not enough effort for struggle) to rise to the occasion demanded of it by its place in the dramaturgy and the demands of the spectators. Any movement towards narrative development runs into a dead end: the radio contact produces no new orders, provokes no change in the state of the camp; guns are cleaned, but their preparation leads to no intention to use them; when one woman digs in the earth, all that she finds is a spade. Perhaps not so much a cul-de-sac as a circularity. They can do just enough to maintain themselves here on the stage, but no more. The spade will allow more spades to be found. Throughout this activity, there is a persistent sound of nature – birdsong or insects – but it is somehow unusually evident that this 'soundtrack' is a simulation, that these signs of life are simply proofs of a total morbidity.

Out there now, in the night, there's a rumble of an engine and the flash of a new light. Towards the theatre, heading directly for the glass wall, comes a tank, latest in a line of 'chariots': from the baby buggy of *C.#01* and *A.#02*, the cars of *P.#06*, the shopping trolley of *R.#07* and the coach of earlier in this very episode. As this latest char approaches the glass, a panel lifts to allow it to enter the stage and mount the rubble. You want 'action', 'spectacle'? There. Now, how do you like it? It's both imposing, alarming and intrusive and also slightly stupid, clumsy, flimsy. It's the real thing, all right, but it's somehow just a little less convincing than it ought to be, almost as though the image of a tank were more powerful than the thing itself.

This tank is neutralised, perhaps, by having become a theatre tank, a fake tank, even, constructed out of armoured metal and wheels and tracks and whatever it is that real tanks are made of, but nonetheless not quite adding up to a real tank. But it does just what a real tank does. It rolls up the top of the mound and points its gun into the auditorium; it manoeuvres around and swivels its gun turret so that it can see out of the back of its head. In a costly and entirely grotesque parody of cinema's equation of the camera and the gun, this fake–real tank starts to look like some misshapen apparatus with one very long cylindrical eye, misconceived, misconstructed, maladapted. And then it leaves.

NR

After the tank has gone from the building, the theatre lights come down, all apart from a spot that lingers and then fades slowly on a large polyhedron, like a white concrete-and-plaster diamond transposed onto a human scale, or an irregular carved stone block – a piece for a peculiar corner of a larger structure, perhaps, or else a chipped and twisted platform, devoid of the statue that would have adorned it and tipped over on the earth towards the back of the theatre on this side of the glass screen. Whatever this object 'is', or represents (basically I presume a prism that mediates the passage of light between one world and another, or else, indeed, an opaque mass that interposes itself between the 'here' and the horizon, a block on all appearances), it is given upon the stage in the form of something inaccessible, an enigma, a hieroglyph. It invites our attention but says nothing of itself. It bears no inscription on its surfaces, it does not crack open to expose an inside. As such – and this is *whether* we imagine the translucence of a prism *or* we imagine an opaque block – the polyhedron functions as a peculiar sort of diversion of the work of 'making appear', even as it is itself so exposed, so 'given', so available. That is to say again, *it was there*, I could not help but see it, it was even pointed out to me by the spot of light at the very end, i.e., it was performing its full share of the mimetic labour, but somehow, at the same time, it remained outside of my attention.

Just enough to maintain themselves here on the stage.

I encountered that form again, the day after the performance, reproduced in an art gallery near Strasbourg. German artist Albrecht Dürer's early sixteenth-century engraving *Melencolia I* shows a young woman with wings on her back – an angel therefore – sitting in apparent dejection, her head on her fist, her elbow upon her knee, surrounded by a disorder of tools and instruments, along with evidences of the most advanced scientific and technological endeavours of her day, a day which represents a certain emergence of the 'modern' as such. Here are the representational means, the devices of measuring, counting, shaping, making, all of them scattered round and about her: the timer, the scales, the plane; the globe-describing compasses held loosely in the free hand of the melancholy angel herself. And here, too, are the proofs, the applications, the capabilities. Here is the ladder against the side of an architectural construction that towers out of the image. Here on the wall is the magic square that incorporates the date of the engraving (1514, which was the year also of the death of Dürer's mother) into the inevitability of its numerical pattern, as if grief and history might be bound together as necessity, in a mode of mathematical destining. Here is the perfect sphere in the foreground, beneath the nose of a sleeping domestic animal. Over there, on the horizon, a marine landscape glowers under a star that seems to gather the world's dark towards it and then spear that back as spikes of negative illumination, not unlike the baleful projection upon the Strasbourg sky that has been suspended over every element of the spectacle this evening.

JK

A conversation about dramaturgy, contd.

Chiara: And this is the initial inspiration . . . this was clear from the start, that there would have to be a diptych separated into two distinct realities and that there would need to be a great deal of earth and that a tank would have to enter the theatre. In a certain sense to unite the outside and the inside, but in a very elementary manner. And Strasbourg is the simplest example of the show because the initial inspirations stayed just as they were, they didn't change at all. The fundamental structure was always this: Hitchcock film, black earth and tank. There were the three elements, put together properly. Then there was the dramaturgical quality of the thought in the interior of each action, according to which the tank had to enter in a particular way and turn in a particular manner and disappear in a hurry. The fact of the presence on stage of the tank is a question of dramaturgy, too. Whether or not you had the black girls sing. We tried having them singing on stage from the very beginning. Then, however, at Strasbourg, it was very clear that they absolutely should not sing . . . but these were questions internal to the individual blocs.

Romeo: Then the stone of melancholy came from outside, and then the relationship with the earth. First, there were the traces of feet furrowing the earth, then the tents, the encampment, then the provisional attachment to the earth, and then the tank arrived, which had been conceived as possessing the earth, assaulting the earth. And also the sounds were amplified, were theatrical. There was a microphone right inside the tank, so that when it came in, it was its own sphere of darkness, and then from the noise of the tank we arrived at the silence of the girls. In this sense, the tank was considered even in the most subtle, little aspects of dramaturgy.

Chiara: So, to turn also to the examples of a concrete dramaturgy . . . For example, we had numerous discussions over whether or not to have tents on the earth, whether the camp should be an instantly recognisable location, with its tents, or whether instead it should be recognisable gradually as a result of what the women were doing. We thought about this at great length, because the more the dramaturgy wrapped itself around the conceptions and became almost dramatic in certain moments, everything untangled because external elements arrived.

Joe: At Strasbourg, there is some kind of dramaturgical narrative, the Hitchcock film is narrative, and in Strasbourg the film stops just at the point at which the narrative begins. The camp too. Perhaps something will arrive, perhaps the revolution . . . There is the possibility that the catastrophe might arrive, we know that it is not the possibility, but we know that the story is arriving, because the narrative will come.

Romeo: Will come. Will come – exactly. It's true that in the film *Psycho* there is a double narration, because there is the first story of the woman who steals money from her employer and the second story which . . . the story that must arrive.

Nick: Chiara spoke about the rhythm with which the women walked. It seems to me that their rhythm is absolutely particular; it is not a rhythm of bored women, nor is it a rhythm of tired women, but of the beyond tired, the beyond boring. What interests me about this rhythm is how this rhythm arrived at the start of rehearsals and was not something that was developed or that you imposed. That's true isn't it?

Chiara: It's true that they moved freely, yes. With the black women, we followed a working method a little different to that we used with the other actors. We already knew that they had to walk in a physical place which would be earth and that on this earth there would be the sleeping zone, the cooking zone, that there would be geographical points and points of reference, and so, with them, we talked about these points of reference, coming out of the tents and going to the kitchen. We gave them these errands, we taught them four different errands because there were four of them and we set them working . . . Immediately, the rhythm of the show became apparent, because they had this slowness.

Romeo: The slowness of this super-tiredness had in itself an element of waiting that one might say is typical, an African waiting, the waiting of a land that awaits.

Chiara: However, to return to the previous concept of the pregnant figure, it was a surprise to see this slowness because already the figure in itself, even if it was not logically envisaged in advance – the walking of the black women on the earth, containing this thing, was so pregnant that it surprised us – was already dense because at the level of intuition it was perfect. We were also surprised by the expressions of calm on their faces, because the rhythm is not expressed solely through action but also by means of other elements of the theatre.

Nick: What is extraordinary for me is that in this rhythm the physical sensation of melancholy is discovered.

Chiara: It is what I said before. The figure comes to be played on the stage, and like a musical instrument, the figure, in this sense, it is played thinkingly like an instrument.

Romeo: You are contradicting yourself, because before you said that we discovered it. I know we accepted whatever rhythm was already there. We saw it, we didn't create it.

Chiara: Yes, because once you see it, you say, good, that is the departure point, that is my instrument, now it is my instrument, and I move to slow it down, create little accelerations, I become conscious of my instrument, I know it.

Romeo: Yes, but the idea of rhythm was already contained, if you like, in the choice of working with the African women.

Chiara: Yes, because I knew in the moment I put them on the stage, and in that moment, I knew I had to bring together what I played and what I knew.

Claudia: Yes, Chiara is right in a sense that practically nails down the initial distinction that was made about a dramaturgy divided in two, the first totally free, the second constrained. So it could be said that the synthesis of what Chiara says is that the rhythm is conceived like poetry, the rhythm of the theatre is like a canticle.

L.#09
LIFT (London International
Festival of Theatre), Laban,
London
May 2004

A conversation about dramaturgy, contd.

Chiara: London has two blocs with atmospheres that are not very different from one another. What is it that determines the splicing of these two worlds? It is the objective presence of the team of cleaners who the moment there is a mention of blood in the theatre appear at once to clean this blood, which is colour, which I have poured on the ground. This is an objective break, but then the performance plunges back into an identical atmosphere. When the curtain opens on Francesca[1] or on the atmosphere

---
1 The actor Francesca Proia.

of Saint Paul, we have two figures, and so two rhythms, which in a certain sense are equivalent to one another. What is it that breaks the rhythm of London?

Romeo: Perhaps we need to reach an understanding on this question. What is rhythm? I think rhythm is the contraction of a body, how many beats there are in a movement, essentially.

Chiara: Sure, or at a more distant level, rhythm is the numerical coherence of the figure with its ambiance, its location . . . there must be a very strong relationship between the atmosphere you want to create and the presence of this figure.

Romeo: Then it is this: rhythm is the phases of movement of a being who can be actor-human or actor-machine. Because these same phases can appear different, modified at a second level by colour, by light, by sound. Because very often the sounds Scott makes are deployed as counterphases. If there's a rapid movement here, Scott's sound can be in counterphase, and it can be slow, or vice versa. Or it can go in phase, and there you get maximum amplification.

Chiara: Because in London, they were in phase with the woman and amplified the woman because the dramaturgical work on sound was carried out to the millimetre, particularly in London, it was worked out to the millimetre . . . We spent a whole Sunday in the theatre with the sound, working on three tiny details which were the key to Francesca's action. And, perhaps, another thing: the rhythm of the show has a very strong relationship with the blood of the audience, the vascular, cardiac rhythm of the audience.

Romeo: Like at a disco: boom boom.

Chiara: But not at such a simple level. In London, I think, there is a laceration of the air that can't be seen. There and then, the audience doesn't get this idea, doesn't read it in these terms, but experiences above all a pouring forth of tones, the discharge of a kilowattage into its body. Above all, it's a matter of the impression, printed on the self.

Nick: In this example, it seems to me that it is possible for me as a spectator to sense with my own body the force of Francesca through the air. Feel in the body the precise force, something similar to what Chiara has spoken about as regards the particular rhythm of each episode. Perhaps it is as if each episode had a pulse, not a regular pulse, but a pulse that changes and that it is possible to sense.

From the final script of *L.#09*

Woman flower wall

The curtain opens. (Salvo.)
A gauze fills the proscenium.
A woman wearing a white dress in nineteenth-century style is on her knees in front of a wall covered with floral wallpaper.
Her wrists are tied together with a silk cord, with a pair of elegant tassels the same colour as the wallpaper.
Her head is lowered.
She raises her head and looks up.
The cord is pulled upwards. (Marco, on Chiara's signal.)
The woman makes numbers with her hands.
She turns her head backwards and signals no.
The cord is pulled up once again.
The cord pulls until the woman gets to her feet.
She turns around on the spot keeping her arms raised.
She returns to a position with her back to the audience.
The cord is pulled so that she can free her hands.
She frees one arm and then the other.
She massages her wrists, and with her right hand touches the ends of her hair down her back, while with the other she touches the top of her head.
She straightens her hair with her fingertips.
The tassles are pulled upwards until they vanish. (Marco.)
The woman brings her hands down to her sides and pulls hard with her fists.
She turns her head in three snaps towards the audience (she has a black face), then touches the flower wallpaper with her finger.
Thump.
Very loud thumping noise.
She scratches a nail against the wall and raises her right arm.
The wall is flown out. (Salvo, Luciano, Fabio.)

On the idea of *crescita*

. . . from something or of something.
   Growth is the fourth way that we know of putting a form together:

sculpture: by way of removing;
plastic arts: by way of adding;
fusion: by way of percolation;
and growth (*crescita*): by way of endocrinal accretion.

In this case, it has to do with something that grows *from* a body and develops on its own, although remaining linked to that body. *Crescita* is a theatrical action that endows the entire arc of *Tragedia Endogonidia*, on which it depends, with its particular way of bringing things into focus.

Crescita, therefore, is not an autonomous action: it derives from the episode to which it refers (in the initial of the title) and develops one aspect of it, one object.

The idea behind *Tragedia Endogonidia* is, in effect, that of a thought which moves around and multiplies; it is moved from city to city and multiplies from spectator to spectator. Its movement is that of ramification, like the delta of a river. Its tendency is to conquer the land around. It is, like every organism, ideally without end.

Crescita is a circular dramatic action, a rotating push that produces concentric ripples. It is like the engraved cylinders of the Sumerians which, when rolled over a tablet of clay, tell a hero's tale that has neither beginning nor end, that has no need for beginning or end. The fundamental trait of the *crescita* is the transversal structure of an action that can surprise with its intensity and brilliance. The spectator is inserted into the action at a tangent, and what she sees is the fact of being before an action in this precise and synchronic length of time. This is what gives back the idea of being surprised, of surprising oneself in the act of seeing. To be there by mistake. Hence, the choice of an action that can be repeated in a circular fashion 'without end'; and, hence, also, the choice of an audience on foot, which represents this same idea of walking and passing without pause, without reflection, 'through' the image. The experience of the audience is, thus, closer to that of a sudden dive, immediate and unprepared, into another dimension, into an atmosphere with a different density, an unfamiliar gravity.

Having abolished the Chorus, whose classical function was to explain the events that were taking place, it now comes down to the spectator to explain, to 'unfold' in the true sense of the word, to put her own hand into the theatre's most hidden parts. But, today, the dramaturgical problem resides in the folds, not in the unfolding of explanations. The eyes see well enough what is happening on stage. The lack of words, however, seems to muddy up this clear vision. In fact, vision remains clear enough, and the incomprehension simply betrays a habit of granting only to spoken language the key that can unlock the story. What is needed is a suspension, not an a priori abolition, of words. It is simply a silence, that isn't so much a not-speaking as a speaking without words. The fact is that the word, at the moment, is an instrument soaked in a form of analogy that

She immerses herself in the black liquid which the sarcophagus contains.

kneads it into the banal violence of power. It would be wrong to trust in it and confide in its presumption of an exclusive communicative capability. Today, communication is a tragedy that comes disguised as a comedy. And theatre, which is the cradle of tragic and comedic representations, cannot ignore this reality and must put right this deadly confusion which leads equally to belief and indifference. If the theatre today has a function, it is to get right to the bottom of its own specificity, which is not communication and analogy, but revelation and interruption. Personal revolution and personal interruption, of course, which may be participatory or shared, but which derive from a personal relation with the stage, not preprepared or orientated by an external mediator.

And so it is that what at first sight seems arbitrary and absurd can, little by little, *speak*, can open perspectives of thought and revelatory interpretations of what is happening on stage and catch the spectators unawares, like autonomous *artists* of thought.

RC

Francesca and the machines

On Crescita XIV Prato[2]

The start of the Prato *crescita* (which develops material from the London episode) has the performer Francesca Proia playing out a movement sequence that involves her after a short while stepping out of her clothes and dancing – mainly with slow and deliberate turnings and 'facings' of her shoulders, her back and her sides, along with a few minimal, indicative arm gestures – dancing what seems now, at this distance, to have been a sort of dance of defacement. I say 'sort of'; I might also say literally. Proia has her back turned towards us for maybe the entire sequence. We only see her face briefly when, for a moment, she turns her head over her shoulder as if to challenge the gaze of the spectators with her own gaze. What we see too, though, in this moment is that the face of this white woman has been blacked out. Indeed, throughout the sequence, it is not the performer's actual face that does the work of facing, but rather her backside, especially when at one point she kneels and presents her bum to the light, her hands reaching

---

[2] The *crescite* are short performances developing specific images from the major sequence, each devised for a particular location (in this instance, a bare and rather sterile white-walled room in a newly built modern art gallery devoid of actual works of modern art) and performed in a loop for small audiences who are brought in and out of the event with little of the rigmarole or comforts of the formal theatrical occasion.

behind herself over her buttocks as if in imitation of Man Ray's photograph *La Prière*. Like Man Ray's still image, the movement sequence is unsettling, not least because even as it appears to expose an explicit nakedness, to perform its being-there as it were shamelessly, at the same time, there is a sense – a feeling, a sensation – that what the gesture 'says' is that nobody out there knows how to look at this. I am disregarded. And so, I turn my face, and I make a face of my flesh, for all of you, as if to say, the shame is yours – if shame there be – back on you.

Proia performs at the far end, as I've said, of a long white-walled gallery. The rest of the space in the gallery is taken up by a phalanx of gymnasium machines, all matt black and chrome, heavy and articulated, lined up against the gallery wall that stretches down towards the spectators. When Proia has finished her dance, the machines go into action. Powered by compressed air, with much hissing and clanking and whirring, they appear to 'comment' upon the action like a mechanical chorus in some sort of weird constructivist ballet. Like a chorus of critics, perhaps. Except, they don't *comment*, because there is nothing to say. There is nothing that is not already exposed in the enigmatic fact of the performance that has been given. And so, instead of commenting, they display. They display their capacity to move in the way that they can, and do. This movement is funny – to me – but also dimly terrifying. These are machines that a person – a dancer, for instance – might use to help her train and shape her body. But whatever a person's ends or motives for that training, the machines should have no part of it. They are machines. They don't have ends or motives or intentions. Here, though, as they move – as it were – by themselves, it seems as if they may well have an incentive to move, to act, after all. The machines would appear to be needy or greedy for something, in need of a function – greedy for the still body of the dancer a few feet away that might fulfil that function. They appear capable of making a grab – perhaps the 'gesture-like grab for reality' of art, to borrow Adorno's resonant phrase, that 'draw[s] back violently as it touches that reality'[3] – anyway, the hyper-articulated gesture of a mechanism that is all limb, itself fleshless and faceless (and shameless) but ready to serve as a harrow *for* the flesh, ready to put a face on us, if we ever care to strap ourselves in.

JK

---

3 Theodor W. Adorno, *Aesthetic Theory*, trans. C. Lenhardt, London and New York: Routledge, 1984, p. 399.

From the final script of L.#09

Woman white room

The environment is now all black, and on a white square column hangs the mask of comedy, and attached to it a black ribbon.
Upstage and to the right, there is another much larger white cuboid, reminiscent of a sarcophagus.
The woman lifts her dress and shows her bottom to the mask.
She undresses. Her body is incredibly white.
She leaves her dress on the ground.
With one foot she pushes the dress away, and it is then pulled offstage with a cord.
She shows her bottom to the mask and strokes the column with her foot.
She kneels down with her back to the audience, then lowers her head to the floor in front of her and weeps.
She raises her torso.
Elbows back and hands at her sides, she then lifts her bottom.
She approaches the mask with her bottom and rubs one of its eyes.
She lies down with her back to the audience.
She beats twice on the ground, calling 'Who is it?' and replying 'It's me!'.
She creeps on all fours, showing her bottom to the mask and then reaches out a hand towards it.
She keeps her back to the audience.
She takes hold of the black ribbon she has taken from the mask and places it between her legs and moves it backwards and forwards.
Then she springs into life and removes the mask from the column.
She looks at the mask and passes it between her legs to put it on her back.
She sticks the mask behind the black ribbon and walks on all fours.
She brings her legs together and then stretches them apart, then gets up on both legs.
She walks towards the back of the space with one hand held out in front of her.
She fixes the mask to the back wall and then walks on her knees along the wall until she is behind the sarcophagus.
Here she puts on the ski-mask after getting rid of the wig.
Minimal flickers of light.
The PVC comes down behind the gauze in the proscenium.

Sarcophagus

The woman approaches the sarcophagus.
She climbs onto it.
On her feet, she slides the black ribbon she has between her legs and puts it on the sarcophagus, taking up the position of the Kuros with the right foot forward, on the ribbon.
Then she kneels in a sphinx position.
She executes rapid and symmetrical movements.

Press

Another cuboid comes down as though to crush the woman. (Marco on Chiara's signal.)
The cuboid glows.
Just as it is about to crush her, she gets down slowly behind the sarcophagus.
The press comes right down for a few seconds and then lifts away.

Sarcophagus opening

The woman reappears behind the sarcophagus, opens the cover and climbs up to get into it.
She immerses herself in the black liquid which the sarcophagus contains, by turning around in it.
She gets out of the sarcophagus.
She comes towards the PVC.
The press is hauled up and out. (Marco on a signal from Chiara.)
She presses her bottom against the PVC and then exits.

Cleaning team

A man dressed all in white with a logo on his back from the cleaning team Raffaello Sanzio Cleaning Corporation comes on stage and with a cleaning spray, cleans the PVC the moment the woman stains it black.
The PVC is flown out. (Salvo and help.)

Other people dressed in white enter. (Three extras and Salvo.) One has a cleaning trolley and everything needed for removing dirt.
They clean the floor and then cordon off the sarcophagus and the column with yellow and black tape.
The sarcophagus and the column are carried off stage right and left respectively.
After having taken the sarcophagus off stage, Salvo returns in order to exit immediately on the other side of the stage.
This is the signal for the entrance of the little girl.
The three other members of the cleaning team turn to stone on the spot.

Little girl

A little girl in a long white dress enters.
She lies down on the floor.
After a while, a stain of blood starts to spread on the floor around her head.
Then the girl gets up and looks in front of her.
She is bloody-faced.
She counts to five and exits.
The cleaning team starts to move again.
They stand in a circle around the blood and make one rotation.
Each person puts their arm over the shoulder of the person next to them and hums.
The blood is cleaned away.
They all exit, apart from one of them who puts a sign where the bloodstain was, a yellow sign warning of a dangerous slippery floor.
Then he exits too.
The trolley remains on stage; it is illuminated, and gradually a sound builds up reaching its apex when the curtain closes.

Curtain closes

An incandescent light comes up on the white curtain.
Then, all at once, the sound is interrupted by loud blows and photographic flashes illuminate the curtain, accompanied by the voice of the girl who says 'Don't look'.

A theatre dream

You see, through a gauze screen that puts everything into a haze, yourself in fancy dress, a straight white wig and a white full-length gown that billows out from the waist, kneeling down with your wrists tied together, in an eighteenth- or nineteenth-century English drawing room. You know where you are from the wallpaper, which is inches from your face, a creamy flock pattern that extends as high and as far as you can imagine, like the wall of a prison or hospital compound. It is hard, though, to say whether this is indoors or outdoors. Everything 'speaks' of a domestic interior, but there is already weather at work there, something like an old English fog from the age of manufacturing or a mist in from the sea, and when you knock against the wall soon with your fist, you will be answered by thunder. For now, though, your wrists are bound together by a bell-rope that hangs down from the darkness overhead, the sort that might be used to alert the servants. You are chained to this dream of servitude, like those paintings of the Ethiopian princess Andromeda chained to a rock in the sea, waiting for the rescuer hero Perseus, the Gorgon-killer, an image that will be repeated for century upon century. Call the time of this image the time of empire, a 'period' of history that seems, like the flock wallpaper, to spread, if you are living it, indefinitely, deep into the borders of the dream. Except that dream is not your dream. And the knot around your wrists is just a loose loop. You could let go at any moment, although you allow a tug upon the rope to pull you to your feet before you do so. You bend, and extend yourself slowly, getting your breath back, and then turn suddenly. You see your – her – face, over there on the stage, facing you for the first time. The face is painted black, which Andromeda's never was. It is a face that hides a face, your face, her face among others, even as it exposes a face for the first time tonight. It is an actor's face. For the record, her name is Francesca Proia. There is, though, no way of knowing that face – or claiming its gaze or its expression as an image of one's own – without making divisions, black/white, mine/yours, here/there, on/off, etc., like in one of those dreams that come between sleep and awaking where nothing can be approached except by dividing it into its parts and those parts into further parts interminably, an impossible series of calculations, until the only solution is to remove yourself – to remove yourself from repetition – by throwing yourself in, as yourself, pressing your own parts – hands, face, tongue, skin – against the surfaces of sleep's exhibition.

The scene shifts, deepens. You are in a milk-white room, simplified almost to abstraction, except for two forms, which have just enough about them of reference, world-historical stuff, to keep you hooked. The one is a pillar on which hang a ribbon and an open-mouthed classical mask. Watch yourself, naked now, as you press yourself – it has to be your back, your bum, your shoulders, whatever part of yourself *you* can't see when it's 'just' you – against the floor, against the side of that pillar. Or turn your back in this direction, towards the spectators beyond the gauze, feel these eyes upon you. Try to tie yourself together with the ribbon. You can't. You don't *go* together. Watch yourself as you reach sideways for the mask, the way one would reach out blind for the Gorgon's head for fear of being turned to stone, and take it into your hands. Its groan cracks through the theatre like something being torn from itself. You press it behind you, over your backside, and crawl like that as if to escape a beam of light that follows you anyway, your own silence divided by the wordless articulation that howls around it.

The atmosphere thickens; the air itself is like milk now (a second gauze descends) as you – is it still you? – approach the second form, a rectangular stone block, a sarcophagus it may be, upon which you lie, weaving your limbs slowly like a ghost swimming back to the beginning, as you imagine another block descending upon this first one like a press, like a purification machine, to render you formless, to force from you a concentration of bright white light. Except already you are there again, standing, dividing the dream again, heaving the lid off the sarcophagus, dipping yourself into its hidden substance, pulling yourself out again, dripping with the stuff, as light and noise – the sound mixed now with traces of melody and percussion, even some fragments of song – splash onto the stage in irregular interruptions, overspill from the dream's reservoir.

You approach the screen at the front of the stage, leaving marks where *she* treads, an indistinct human form, dark from the waist down, pale above, who rubs her backside against the gauze and leaves a small stain before departing. A smudge of actuality to put between us, between the ones who watch and imagine and interpret and 'make it up' in that way, and the ones on the other side who make it up in the way an actor 'puts it together', performing a sequence of tasks, doing this and then doing that with whatever care and deliberation, as the theatre grabs the lot of us and makes us up too, introducing us even as it divides us from each other. Although it also suffers that mark to appear, a smear of real pretending. Something somebody did. Something that doesn't pretend to be anything *but* theatre. The suspended lure, doing nothing itself, which you might or might not fall for.

JK

M.#10
Théâtre du Gymnase and
Théâtre des Bernardines,
Marseille
September 2004

From Marseille sketch

Bernardines

Black table, black figures: enigma.
Twelve people at table.
Dialogue.
Black horse slowly washed with milk.
Masks of light.
Black drapes that fall to the ground.
Glass panels that explode.
Lights from above, reflected.

Gymnase

Screens of coloured light.
Lights from Berlin.
Vision: classical song which comes out of the audience.
After the song, as the scene fades away, black shapes, silhouettes, complete a strange gesture.

Sound:
Trembling
Rippling
Pulsing
Crescendo and Diminuendo.

18 AUGUST 2004

Dear Lavinia,[1]

On the eve of your departure for Paris, I thought it would be good to quickly recap what we have been talking about over the past few days. The time for preparing the show really is very short, and we will only see you again at Marseille, which is why while going over again the structure of the work, I will also try as best I can to anticipate any questions to which we might quickly be able to respond.

As we've said already, when the audience comes in, you will already be in your seat in the stalls. Your presence is anonymous, and no one should notice you. The dress you will be wearing will have to be dark too, easily camouflaging you among the audience. You spoke to me on the phone and said that the woollen suit you already have is straight-cut. This could work well. However, when you are on foot with your back to the audience, you will have a black veil on your head like in those Boecklin pictures.

We will know in Marseille when exactly you should step out in front of the audience, but I suspect that the colour of the stage images will either be the dark

---

1 The singer Lavinia Bertotti, who plays 'The Voice' in the Théâtre du Gymnase part of the Marseille diptych.

green or the afternoon purple. If we decide that the song is to be drawn from the repertoire of Hildegard, the timing of the images will have to be made to fit with the chosen song. If the words are too readily understood, we will have to modify or deform them so as not to attract the audience's attention to the symbolic significance of the words. Don't you think so?

It would be good to send Scott the Hildegard track you've chosen as soon as possible so he can create the foundation for your song. On the telephone, you told me you were thinking of recording it yourself: I think this is an excellent idea because that way Scott can work on the basis of your interpretation.

After your song, while you are still standing like those people who stand and gaze in the Friedrich paintings, the voice of the entity will surge forth from the sound that has been accompanying you. This distant voice which will get close, tear and harrow, is born from the tone of the song which has just finished. If it is the Hildegard song, then after the initial attack, it maintains a single breath which holds the soul in suspension, while the voice of the entity, by contrast, makes the emotion more human. The voice of the entity will last perhaps two or three minutes. Your voice will continue to echo this voice and will approach, wordlessly, so as to gather in the last breath of the giant luminous being which, in the course of this evening, comes to know the waning of its own life.

Your voice could be tinged with compassion and follow the slow rhythm of an agony. The harmony should lead to the lamentations of classical song. If, at first, your voice will have increased the vision of the light, now, after the entity's response, this same voice becomes the only human possibility of touching this self-consuming glare.

Chiara

Asking for it

Two large dark rectangular objects slide into view: one rising from the floor, the other descending from the ceiling. Their movement suggests weight: they appear three-dimensional. As they approach one another, they recall an image from the preceding episode (*L.#09*), in which a woman climbs onto a white sarcophagus or tank and a second massy block descends towards it, to press her, enclose her, bury or drown her. A glow of white light fizzes between the two blocks as they near contact: some kind of charge of energy, perhaps, like the explosion of a flash gun or an X-Ray machine. The woman seems to vanish in this electrical coming together, reappearing, once the second block has departed, to steep herself in the black ink of the first sarcophagus/tank, coating the lower half of her naked white body in a dark liquid with which she makes her mark (the mark of her buttocks) on the transparent screen that hangs between stage and auditorium. Photography: writing with light. Ventriloquism: speaking from down below. Here, in Marseille, it is impossible to tell whether the two dark blocks are two- or three-dimensional. Perhaps it is only the memory of the London sarcophagus/tank that lends substance to these shadows. Perhaps they *are* only shadows passing across the surfaces of the scene, and the whole sequence is an elaborate play with 'smoke and mirrors'.

While they – the rectangular blocks – seem to promise the coming of substance to a stage which, until this moment, has seemed all light and surface, this promise is only barely redeemed. No one will (dare) step into this stage and the only thing of any substance – the only thing to which I can confidently ascribe matter – to appear here will be a glass tank filled with transparent liquid. The liquid, apparently under the influence of an electrical current, synchronised with the intensification of fierce light and nerve-shaking noise, bubbles and toils as though about to trigger in itself some chemical reaction, produce from the folds of its seething liquid some form, some matter, some life, even. This tank hangs in the frame of the screen as a mockingly solid clue as to the nature of the space into or at which I am compelled to stare. The stage itself is a kind of tank, a huge developing machine. The black rectangular shapes are being dipped, it seems, into the hot chemical seething of the developing machine, as though some deranged photographer were trying to manufacture some new life form, develop something from this light, something, anything that might inhabit this world, as though the palpable alchemy of the photographic dark room might indeed be a place of conception rather than replication, as though this light-writing process might not merely capture what the naked eye cannot make out (the great perceptual promise of photography) but actually bring new life into being.

Or reanimate the ghosts of those who were once here. For this space – the latest in the sequence of chambers (the golden room, the marble hall, the white box) – is void of life, suggesting either some moment before the first one-cell organisms were bubbled into life or some post-human space of catastrophe. The place of this episode in the affectual arc of the *Tragedia* sequence overwhelms me with the sense that it is the latter, the aftermath of catastrophe, that is at stake here, with the painful twist that the manner of imagining our own human erasure so vividly calls to mind visions of a planet on which no life has ever taken hold. Our little life is rounded with . . . what? With the eternally impersonal vibrations of the universe. This hot yellow light, these flickerings of electrical discharge, these rumblings and stutters and sparks of signals that are only noise, forever noise, with no one left who might receive a signal (through the flames). The promise with which the whole sequence began, back in Cesena in December 2002 (*C.#01*), was

174

But we had to look.

that we might signal beyond the grave, beyond our comprehension of the universe: that in the carefully composed diagrams and calculations propelled aboard Voyager out of our solar system, there might be an intelligible message by which our life here might be registered by an alien intelligence. The desolation with which I witness this inhuman spectacle tells me what, in truth, I knew all along, that the promise was only ever a fantastical lie. We have been utterly forgotten: we were never here.

By the end of this panel of the Marseille diptych, I will be longing for just a tiny sign of human presence. Please let me see the human beings, please let me see them, just one more time. The theatre seems to be caught up in my desperation. Even leaving aside the idea that the theatre might be a machine for the production of just that – human presence – this theatre seems to be insisting upon its inability to summon up and into our presence even a remnant of the human.

Eventually, my desperation – perhaps it has calmed now to a resigned longing, an hour or so into the performance – produces something new. Not a response, as such, but rather a precipitation of my feeling into a theatrical figure. Out of the audience and onto the forestage steps a woman. She looks into the space of the stage, into the developing machine, the spirit tank, the chamber of catastrophe, as though she too were longing for someone to appear there. As she sings, she raises her hand – in the hope, perhaps, that there might be a greeting to be made and exchanged – and although no miraculous child steps forth from the flames, something stirs within the cauldron. Her song and her gesture form an evocation of sorts. They come from an already existing repertoire of organised sound and movement, presented again here in the hope perhaps that this organisation might draw from the relentlessly a-signifying sound and light machine some body-with-organs she might call her own, or at least recognise as a being of her own species, if such a thing were conceivable.

The response that comes brings nothing in the way of solace, however, as if we ever expected, really, that it might. The response, it seems, in the end, after various promising shifts in climate and the emergence of new configurations of light and sound that seem to portend revelation, is simply to mock our desperation with the old Rorschach routine, with yet another trick done with smoke and mirrors. We have, of course, been here before. In Bergen (*BN.#05*), this was the film that the girl was shown, and we looked, as it were, over her shoulder as she watched it: a cascade of transformations, doubled either side of the centre line, an onrush of always-symmetrical shapings, misshapings, flows and blobs and seepages, of liquids in liquids, twisting themselves about, curling momentarily into mockeries of faciality: for a moment, a mountain scene becomes Donald Duck, leering out at us with filthy intentions. And always, always, our perception working away, constructing these fleeting figures of the ghastly, preying on our appreciation of the symmetrical and our desire for the face-to-face by serving up for our fantastical construction whatever moments of recognition we convince ourselves we might desire. This film sequence, which in Bergen seemed to form part of a pedagogical programme designed to acclimatise the infant to the otherness of the world, now comes across as a malicious taunt addressed to my own anthropomorphic desire, to the selfishness of my spectatorship: Show me, show me, show me me! I want to see myself up there.

NR

From the final script of *M.#10*

Bernardines

HORSE

While the curtain is closed, the horse is brought on stage, and the five men in front of the curtain stand up and chat among themselves.
Guillaume opens the curtain.
A large black horse appears.
After a few seconds, Sergio enters: he wears a black smock, black gloves and a gas mask and carries three petrol cans and a white plastic bucket full of milk.
He starts to wash the horse.
The milk that spills on the floor forms a perfect circle.
Sergio exits. The horse remains on stage for a few seconds and then the curtain closes.

LADDER

With the curtain closed, the horse is taken off stage, and a white ladder is leaned up against the back wall with its base on the ground at the edge of the circle of milk.
While the curtain is closed, the nineteenth-century spectators chat and stretch their legs.
The curtain reopens for a few seconds on the image of the ladder.

PLASTIC RUBBING

The curtain closes.
The ladder is taken off, and a length of white elastic is stretched between the top of the right wall by the proscenium and the left edge of the circle of milk.
The length of elastic forms a triangle with the line of the floor.
Francesca places herself in front of the elastic, dressed in a white nineteenth-century dress and a long blonde wig.
She turns her back on the audience and breathes heavily.
While the curtain is closed, the nineteenth-century audience whispers, and then, suddenly, Charli climbs on stage in front of the curtain, picks up a little plastic bag of rubbish, indicates the number one with his finger and rubs the bag against his head, near his ear, then indicates number two with his finger and rubs it for a second time.

FRANCESCA

The curtain opens, and Guillaume ties it to one side and resumes his place among the nineteenth-century audience.

Francesca, with her back to the audience, touches her hair with her hand, makes three movements with her head towards the public and shows her black face.

She shows her bottom to the audience and covers her face with her hand.

She carries out movements, cries and breaths continually, covers her face, takes off a shoe and touches the elastic with her foot.

She lies on the ground.

When she takes off her dress, Sergio comes down from the stage towards the nineteenth-century audience with a tray of glasses and a bottle of liquor.

He shares this out among the nineteenth-century audience.

Francesca approaches the circular pool and drinks, then lies prone of the floor, covering her face with her own dress. She says 'Please, Please'.

She gets to her knees and says it again.

STRAPS

The nineteenth-century women enter quickly.

They whisper and laugh.

They have straps of leather in their hands, with little bells attached.

Julie puts a leather collar on Francesca, while Fanny, after having taken off Francesca's second shoe puts an armband with the number 5 on her right arm.

They put a black blindfold on her.

The women strap Francesca tightly with buckles. The strength of the women is palpable.

When they have run out of their straps, they leave.

Elise puts the two shoes together close to the circle of milk.

They put Francesca on her back completely trussed up.

When they have all left, Francesca moves a little, producing the sound of bells.

Beware what you wish for

In the second part of the Marseille diptych, it is as though someone were responding directly to my earlier desperation: 'You want to see humans, you say? Well, we'll show you what seeing humans is all about, and then we'll see how you like it.' This is part, perhaps, of the effect of the doubles who soon appear: equal numbers of men and women, identically dressed in their sexualised costumes, proliferating like viruses around the dining table, functioning as both many (individuals?) and one (swarm?). 'This is what you wanted, isn't it?' And then come elaborate choreographies of group portraits (riddled, it seems, with some underlying pain or trauma) and a dinner of animated choric discussion, in which I think I detect a reprise of the almost unintelligible conversation between the original couple. This conversation, like the tableaux that teetered on the brink of expressionist desperation, carries with it some freight of profound anxiety: speculation about something that might or might not happen, someone who might or might not arrive, representative of all the anxieties of time and place and coming and going that drive dramas such as Ibsen's *A Doll's House*, to cite just the most obvious example. Just as this is all getting a bit too much, a little too suggestive of a form of torture by dramatic convention, the gang of doubles vacate the stage, to be heard (if it is them) in animated offstage cocktail-party chatter while the stage from which they had derived their life, or rather, their life-likeness, sits waiting, full of its own emptiness. They were already dead, of course. Just like all the people I couldn't see back there at the Gymnase. This theatre, too, is a developing machine, a tank for the production of ghosts. It's just that, for a while, I didn't see it that way, failed to attend to the power of my own desire to have something different here, and to the way in which this theatre too had been set up to give me just what I wanted, precisely the way I would never have wanted it. And it gets worse.

A black curtain has been erected at the front of the stage. On my side of this curtain sit five or six of the male doubles, smoking cigars and drinking, as though attending some *cabaret-danse* event of the kind we imagine impressionist painters to have frequented every evening. Various images have already been presented by the withdrawal of this curtain. This time, the curtain is drawn back to reveal a familiar figure: Francesca Proia, reprising for you her role as 'Yourself' from the preceding London episode. Wearing a long stiff white dress, hips and bottom accentuated and a blonde wig, she is holding onto a cord (not the same bell-pull cord as she had clung to in London), but occupying the same place in a repeated choreography of gestures and glances, one of which reveals her black-painted face, others which expose the whiteness of her buttocks. As in London, she appears here in what looks like willing subjugation to an invisible social system, one which here, for this audience, doubled by the smokers in the front row, also involves the enactment and display of this submission. The composition of this woman as image is already painfully evident in the transposition of the London material (performed just for our eyes) to this new specular economy (in which we are made to see the terms of our seeing in perhaps the most bluntly objectifying way imaginable). You see 'Yourself' exposing 'Yourself' to your own devouring eyes, in a closed circuit of pornographic pleasure. The closed circuit of this composition will play itself out differently for each spectator: for every 'Yourself' that comes here bears with them the histories of their own

The milk that spills on the floor forms a perfect circle.

gender and sexuality. It is, ultimately, the mechanism by which this sacrificial apparatus is set in motion, rather than the individual disturbances it might provoke, that makes itself available to critical discourse, but this should not occlude the real personal difficulty the predicaments evoke. The final phase in the composition of the image involves the return of three of the double-women (perhaps these are the same women who appeared in Berlin to perform a ceremony combining girl-on-girl action pornography and militia funeral) who this time bind 'Yourself' into a position of extreme restraint, leaving her as an almost completely disarticulated non-human body with whom, in turn, double-men pose for souvenir photographs. That the target of this illusionist *mise en scène* should have been this deranged reduction has a certain inevitability: we have seen it coming; we had it coming to us; this is what, apparently, we desired for ourselves. If only we had listened when we were told not to look. But we had to look.

NR

The picture, the place, the drama, us

When a figure manages to reach a spectator with precision, it gives to the latter the sensation of being an object. Subject and object fuse but without confusion. Activity and passivity become one and the same. The figure is planted in the spectator, giving the latter the sensation of being taken on before she can take it all in. But before all this, a field is needed. The place which 'holds' paintings or sculptures has always involved a problem of the coessential, although it is only since Modernism, or more exactly since the Parisian salons of the Impressionists, that painting and sculpture have drifted in such a way as to generally lose sight of this essential religion of the elements, to the point where they often don't know where they are. They haven't been able to *shape* a place for themselves, which is to say a general human framework, a system into which these same means might enter and re-enter along with the spectators. It is the works that have the power to recreate a place, to give it a meaning and orientation. If a picture does not have the capacity to recreate or, better still, to emanate the laws of a place, it will remain nailed to the everyday jurisdiction of the fashions and costumes of the century. The greatest artists have always held up not so much the internal relation between the various elements of vision, but rather the estuary of gazes that emanate in and from a picture as in the optical and psychic density of gazes in Velasquez's *Las Meninas*. The great painters and the great sculptors have always considered the *theatre* of their works; they have always thought about the dramaturgy.

To think of drama when making art doesn't, however, mean thinking about the spectators and imagining them prey to an effect which is sought in them. The spectators are a destiny, not a horizon. To imagine a spectator would be like having before you that which you miss in yourself; it would be an equivocal exchange, because to create in this way means to fill in what isn't there. But creation is not the result of an operation. There is no operation; there is no knowing what is missing nor what it is that one wants. There is no education. It's about conceiving an embrace, not a reflex – and certainly not a reflection. And this embrace pushes together alienation and intimacy. It brings together in me that which is intimate (that which I have understood since I was born) and that which is at a stellar distance, but which, nevertheless, draws me like something equally intimate (because I have understood it since before I was born? – to be precise, because I have always felt myself to be 'held' by a world that has only just expelled my body into the immense sleeping universe, because I myself can think of me and think of it).

CC

To live episodically[2]

Towards the State, towards the Law, we live, *theatrically speaking*, in a condition of conscious apathy. We have no wish to get into dialectic either with a law or a tradition: not even the most just of laws, not even a tradition inaugurated by ourselves. Socially and politically, things change a great deal when regimes change, on which basis one lives better or worse in this world, but *theatrically speaking*, one must be perfectly indifferent, whatever the regime. A theatre that is possible or even conceivable *thanks* to a regime or *thanks* to a law would automatically be a state theatre. Any industrial action by the 'entertainment sector' is, in this sense, equivocal. The theatre, too, lives better or worse according to the government of the day, but this must remain, *theatrically speaking*, a simple and stubborn background, to be resisted and broken through, always and no matter how, but not a goal to be hoped for. The origin of hope is fear, and fear is ill adapted to the danger towards which, in every epoch, the arts are called so that they might forge another world. Always and no matter how: another world.

If we ask for state funding, it is because, *politically speaking*, we are obliged to do so. The republican state is obliged to concern itself with aleatory things, that is to say, things that are not linked to a product. Into this group fall scientific research, public instruction and the theatre: all of them activities that advance solely through aleatory encounters. The finances of painters, writers and pharmacists are excluded because all of these people produce tangible and lasting objects. Once this principle is recognised, it necessarily becomes a secondary, although deadly, matter who governs. This means that we are, and wish to maintain ourselves, solely as passive spectators of how the law treats the theatre. It is not at a theatrical level that one struggles for justice. The theatrical struggle is played out only at the level of language.

Patience and impatience of immediate politics

Political parlance should make itself cognisant of a profound and capillary activity going on these days, but not immediately apparent at the state level; patient and impatient at the same time: patient with respect to the hidden and direct (and, therefore, concentrated) work that needs to be done, impatient as regards the life to be created and lived immediately, a life freed from the perpetual comparison with models; with a memory

---

2 Written for the programme of the Santarcangelo Theatre Festival, July 2004.

empty at last of the names that weigh on the brain; with a will no longer prey to the crushing events of history that pulverise any attempt at change and any perspective on the future; and free at last of the neo-religious wave which technologies, as impossible these days to understand as they are to take hold of communally, arouse with their miraculous products. The progress of the microchip towards a state of insubstantiality shadows the bewitching power of the spiritual, something which commands without even being there.

A new political topology must seek to strengthen *places* as opposed to unconfined space, which has no part among small social realities. Small in terms of dimension not intention, which put together can be effective and immediately incisive. Not sects, self-enclosed in their own worlds; not micro-syndicates, dedicated to defending their own workplaces by excluding the weak; but places where it is possible to express one's own idea and choose how to live – exercises of liberation from the sort of work that is fatal to real waiting, which is the proper way of relating to the world. This, *politically speaking*, is what we have to do, without concern for any popularism or spectacle that is not part of the political activity itself. The only political spectacles that make sense are mass demonstrations. Then, and only then, in a double activity that combines the small and the big, the smallness of an effective grouping and the bigness of a visible grouping, will there be a rethinking of republican theatrical politics. Politics, meanwhile, *theatrically speaking*, means getting right to the bottom of the specificity of the language. As we see, for example, in the pictures of Gustave Courbet, activist in the first rank of the Paris Commune.

Anarchy of the episode

In a July 2003 minute of the Theatre Commission, the reduction of the state contribution to Socìetas Raffaello Sanzio is justified by the fact that *Tragedia Endogonidia* (the company's three-year cycle subdivided into eleven episodes) is more 'ideological' than theatrical. A morally neutral adjective is used: 'ideological', so as to suppress the principle of all human creation, which is based on the sensate linking of ideas. The motive behind this measure is political, since it affirms that the theatre's relation to the world cannot be ideo-logical, but only ana-logical. And since the general system of current Italian politics is monarchical, the job of the analogy is to sanction this system. Hence, the attempt to root out the *episode*, the *episodic* concept, altogether, because to live episodically means living without reference to any monarchical principle whatsoever, like Speussipus who refuted the necessity of a supreme and unique principle of things and who, for this reason, was reproved along with his companions by Aristotle, who said of them, 'they reduce the substance of the universe to a series of episodes'.[3] These days, it is no longer a question of aesthetic evaluation or administrative and bureaucratic evaluation, let alone the evaluation of 'contents'. Rather, this is where the ideological procedure strikes directly, furnishing the equation – deduced from all this – of either a lobotomised art as far as the production of ideas is concerned, or, vice versa, a dangerous art, to the extent that it is ideo-logical. Repression had already got to work on satire, whose improper exorbitance, whose improper absence from the ranks, was deemed unacceptable. Now, at last, tragedy was also going to be taught a lesson, protected until this point by its austere and noble language. A tragedy, based on episodes and orphaned of the Chorus that might have explained what it was about, is an art that goes everywhere at once multiplying its theses. A tragedy in which the episode is in force is a tragedy without principles (and also without princes).

Once more, and once more again, let us take care: let us not be intimidated by money nor by those who – without the strength to use it – hold the power. We must, indeed we must, expose this repressive intention towards ideas, but at the same time – and without any dumbfounded consternation – we need to carry on as if these blows couldn't hurt a fly.

The bureaucracy of the avant-garde

The theatrical model which the Ministry holds dear is that of a facile – but not innocuous – 'socialoid' drama. A lawnmower of socialoid culture. The media monarchy experiment makes a neo-fascism appear plausible, an intravenous and sentimental fascism that aims at a complete similarity of its subjects. The condition of the *complete spectator* is the political project of the new 'citizen', with a temporal dimension that is stuck to a centripetal present.

The other political tendency of the Italian state is that of an anti-traditional bureaucratic avant-gardism which tends to turn everything into merchandise, even aleatory activity, and which is the reason why soon even the theatre, public instruction and scientific research will no longer be financed by the republic but will become just like products: so much artificially aged novelty. To desire the new is 'to think', not to replace. Everything will be sold, on the American model, except with a massive dose of incapability, laxity and slovenliness which Americans don't have. The theatre will be paid for

---

3 *Metaphysics*, Book XII, 1076a.

from the military budget, or, if the republican concept still holds up, by the regions and cities. It will be the return of the city-state.

Significant parts of the state patrimony, the witnesses of our history, will be sold off, including the documents of the state archive, without the least scruple towards tradition. Artists – natural enemies of tradition – will then be the ones struggling to defend it, trying to tear it from the claws of those who seek to reduce it to a *tabula rasa*. How strange it will be to see the historical artist struggle against the avant-garde bureaucrat! And to see the roles of tradition and revolution reversed! The artist needs tradition in order to go against it. The State doesn't need tradition in order to be capable of answering only to itself. The ministerial programme is neo-futurist but without being able to count on artists of that calibre, because, in reality, there is no movement towards the future, merely the centripetal pull of a chocolate sweet.

Towards a poor theatre of the world

Facing these likelihoods, companies must, as they sense the problem, begin to make politics in every way, or in any way that best suits them. There's no point in hanging back in little self-made assemblies of solidarity, within one's own little world, as if the best thing for it were to form some sort of quasi-union. They must prepare themselves for a new catacombal period, living towards a poor-poor theatre, attempting the utopia of a liberated labour and living a neo-communist economy. Young performance-arts graduates in the democratic cities will have to churn out project after project; they will have to go out and discover places; they will have to put on festivals, microscopic at first, but then bigger and bigger; with continual work mounting up on the sides, they will have to force the administrators to finance ideas which, in the meantime, will root themselves in the earth. The deeper its actual culture, the more resistant a reality can prove. Whoever is without culture gets swept away by a breath. That is why it is not Lombardy or Veneto but Lucania that has recently demonstrated some political capability. Areas and societies considered insignificant, like Scanzano and Melfi, have experimented with cultural autonomy in the face of large-scale political and economic interests that have had to stand back incredulous. Rooted culture is still stronger than the trade-union tradition. Lombardy and Veneto, in spite of the League, which tends anyway to express an unconscious despair towards its own land, have sold their way of life to the strongest tendencies of a fashionable whim. These regions don't have what it takes to resist; they were overwhelmed, and now they have to content themselves with putting up street signs in dialect. All they have in their hands now are some local festivals and the sense of a social body curdling with the most banal hatred towards the outside world – that is, when it isn't turning on itself by way of familiar, countryside crimes. In the north, the Val d'Aosta, Liguria, Trentino and Friuli have not been reduced in this way: they still live expressively in an expressive land. The tragic dilemma bifurcating ahead involves, on the one side, a 'folk' consecrated to tourism and, on the other, cultural dispersion, incapable of inhabiting a land founded upon a way of living, of speaking, of eating. The political project of the Italian Ministry of Culture is, at the moment, one of eradication, notwithstanding the patched-up rhetoric of national identity and Christian roots, which are the other face of the tricolour flag.

CC

C.#11
Teatro Comandini, Cesena
December 2004

It's a tale about childhood and native land. A tale about a family and a little boy, to whom one comes to say goodnight and who is dreaming about an aeroplane. And every night, as soon as he goes to sleep, the dream becomes reality. It's the tale of a bedroom, as intimate as any bedroom, but which we have to leave behind, where the familial drama is knotted, where the adults make up a story about the things they don't know how to say, about the true and the false, about the world, about being in the world, about nature and about the animality of humankind. It's the tale of the permanent duality of imagination and reality, their reciprocal influence which leads, at times, to genuine confusion. It's the tale of a crime, of the murder of the child lost in the forest, the original tale of the paternal crime, a detour along a path that a child takes without having been asked to. Because this is how, in the end, love and law manage to perpetuate the generations, as the hope of escape, whether through the ritual crime or through the chance event of being born.

SRS (programme note)

From the technical script for C.#11

PART A

The curtain opens (Salvo).

DOMESTIC SCENE A ginger cat is visible on the bed.
   Cosma enters, picks up the cat and takes it out the door (someone will have to put it in the basket).
   The mother enters.
DARKNESS Cosma exits and takes the cat basket to the kitchen where he will get changed and then go to get ready in the woods.
   In the darkness Sergio moves the plastic panel.
WIND Luciano is at the wind machine on the right, Salvo at the one on the left, Fabio brings the central one in through the door.
   After the wind, Fabio exits, where he can lay the carpet on the outside landing and then go to the horse-handler to tell him to get ready. Finally, Fabio goes into the garden. After the wind, Salvo can put on the oilskin poncho and pick up the little paper bag with the cat's head inside.
CLEANING WOMAN cleans the floor of the boy's bedroom with a vacuum cleaner.
DARKNESS
BUTTERFLY A butterfly moves in the lampshade (Luciano).
OLD MEN All the men enter except Claudio, who enters a moment later. A short while after Claudio enters, he will give Salvo the signal to enter. Salvo must have the paper bag and cat's head and must be wearing the poncho.
HORSE After all the men have gone out, Romeo brings the horse on.
CURTAIN Salvo closes the curtain when he sees Claudio come back on to look at the horse.
SCREEN Salvo brings the screen down.

On make-believe

A perfect traditional naturalistic box set. Carpet, ceiling, ceiling light, table lamp, bed, telephone, door with a frosted-glass panel. Everything you might want for a good game of naturalist make-believe. On the bed, there's a cat. Yes, it's real. A small boy enters. He puts out the cat and settles into bed, reading from a picture book that looks like it's one of those graphic novels, still very popular in Italy, which we might think of as little

A tale about a family and a little boy

handheld domestic cinemas. His mother (we suppose that's who she is) enters, prises the book away from him, replacing it with a teddy bear and encouraging him to lie down to sleep. As the lights go down on this scene, a white curtain is pulled across the front of the stage, and the mother backs away from the bed towards centrestage. It is completely dark. Here in the Teatro Comandini, Raffaello Sanzio can play it their own way with no need to obey health-and-safety regulations. There are no exit lights. I can't see anything. I can't even tell whether my eyes are open or not. A sound starts to rise. It sounds at first like a little motor, rather tinny, regular, mechanical. Soon it increases in both volume and depth. Its sonority thickens into a vast motor roar. The air is moving in the auditorium, blowing a breeze across my face. This is both terrifying and exhilarating. I remember a terrifying dream from my childhood in 1970s America, a dream in which I was hiding with my brother and sister and mother and father underneath the kitchen table as a sinister aeroplane came high overhead, clearly about to release its atomic bomb. This time it is a thrill, a ride, as though I were suddenly in the plane myself, full of power, hurtling above the world on an unimaginably vast and thrilling journey. As the theatre vibrates around me, I feel that I have never flown so far or so fast. Gradually, the sound starts to subside, returning towards its initial tinny grating. Surely this sound must have some utilitarian function: covering up an elaborate and noisy scene change, of course. As the lights come up, the white curtain is drawn to reveal the amazing new location to which the theatrical machine has transported me. The same room. Exactly the same. Except that the boy is gone from the bed, and a woman is now hoovering the carpet. In the intensity of the restored experience I have been deceived into believing that I must be somewhere else.

Such deceit can be deadly, as the little boy (whoever he is, but with whom I find I have identified myself) will soon find out. It is not me, but the boy, my double, who has been transported. Seduced, it seems, by the mimetic lure of the graphic novel he has been drawn, it seems, by fairy magic into a place that really is (and yet is not) somewhere else. For in the second half of the episode, the audience is conducted from one theatre space to another. In the second space, there is eventually revealed a dark and sinister forest, with rain dripping through bare branches, car headlights on a nearby highway flashing through the gloom and, finally, the probing torch beams of the men who are hunting the boy down. Caught in the forest of his imagination, the boy meets his death at the hands of a merciless child-killer, make-believe victim of a make-believe murderer to whom he was led by his own belief in make-believe.

NR

From the final script of C.#11

Transfer of the audience

Sergio says: 'I've something to show you. Follow me, please'. He invites the audience to follow him. The audience is led into the other room.
The Arvo Pärt music continues, still at the same volume.

PART B

Spermatozoa

The man who led the audience into the other room puts the reel in the projector and shows the film.

Film of spermatozoa (interrupted very quietly by the Arvo Pärt track in the other room).
The film ends.
Darkness.
The screen is raised.
The scenic space is surrounded by a large black frame.

Night garden

A flash (car headlights) lights up the stage. (Fabio.)
The noise of tyres on wet asphalt.
In the mist a night garden appears; during a flash the outline of a fawn appears.
Noises of distant dogs.
Drops fall, it is barely raining.

Search

Four people covered in ponchos enter with torches in their hands. They are searching for someone. They have a dog.
They pause for a long time. They scatter. They don't find who they are looking for, so they go.

Crying child

Through the branches, we can catch a glimpse of the outline of a child.
He is hidden, doesn't want to come out.
He is crying.
'I can't go back . . .'
The boy stands up and sees there is no way out of the woods, raises a hand, puts his hand over his heart and goes back to hide because cars are stopping near the garden (red headlights).
Crying stops when it begins to rain.

Assassin

In the background, a hooded man returns.
He approaches the boy.
It begins to rain.
He comforts him, kneels beside him quietly.
Gives him a slap in the face.
Britten Track 9 begins.
The boy is on the ground, and the man gets a knife from his pocket.
Other hooded figures come in.
Confused scene with commotion.
It is the death of the boy.
The hooded man gets up from the ground where the boy's body is lying.
He has a cat's head in his hand; in the other hand, a dagger. The cat's head is put in a sack.
The body is summarily buried with a few kicks of earth.
As the men go away, one of them finds the boy's teddy bear.
He turns in his tracks and throws it on the boy's dead body.

The Britten song ends with just the boy's body on the ground in the garden under the rain.
When the song ends, the lights in the garden go off.
The rain stops.
Darkness.
The back-projection screen is raised.
House lights.

The enchantment

A fantasia on Romeo Castellucci's C.#11

The boy settled down in the bed, his teddy bear beside him on the pillow, and opened the picture book. It was made of thin grey paper, and the pictures were printed throughout in the same cheap ink. The ink was so uneven you could hardly call that black a colour. All of the books were like that. There was even less colour in these small volumes he kept in a cabinet beside the bed than there was in the world, and there was little enough in the world. Most of what there was – in the bit of the world with which he was familiar – seemed to be concentrated in the body of the cat (he called her Cat) and even she was not much more than a sort of dingy brownish orange smudge of a thing. He had found her, as he always did, lying on the bed when he came back into the room this evening, and, as he always did, he had picked her up and carried her outside before coming back in to say his prayers. He shouldn't say in the body. On the body. Her fur. Who knew anything about in the body? Of course he knew about insides and things and that there were colours there too, reds and blues and purples, with bits of white fat like spit or drips from a candle. But it was hard to believe it when you had your own skin on and you were walking around and breathing. He imagined that the cat's insides and his own were pretty much the same, hidden but alive like when the lights were turned off in the room. Right now the light was on, a white globe in the centre of the ceiling like a full moon, but even so he switched on the light beside him as well – a smaller but otherwise identical globe that stood on the cabinet – so that he could read the pictures in comfort, propped up on the pillows, his legs tucked under the sheets and blankets. The book was about gangsters. They were like the gangsters in films, with hats and long coats and hands in their pockets and heavy, sharp-edged faces. They showed their teeth when they talked, but not their eyes. In the story, they were looking for something or someone, in a wood at night. There was a full moon in the story too, although you couldn't say it 'shone'. It sort of gaped in several of the frames like a hole scissored out of the picture, curved around with black. It was the same with the gangsters' teeth and the beams of car headlights when they cut between the trunks of the trees. Anything that was supposed to stand out was bare paper. Everything else that wasn't was black. It meant, though, that anything was possible. He could feel his eyelids slipping. Already he was having to stare hard at the pictures to stay awake. You could make up a world just with black and white, just by putting something together with its opposite. Together and separate. Like shining a light in darkness. Or the other way round, painting darkness onto light. He couldn't hold onto the thought or where the thought was going. His head felt like a weight, like a ball of stone, ready to topple. And it was only in the possible worlds that real things really shined. Moons. Headlights. Teeth. A cat's eyes. Except you wouldn't be able to be sure, would you? Could you tell which of the things that seemed real really were? Even when you were there, here and there at the same time, you couldn't be sure. His mother came in to kiss him goodnight. She, too, in her maroon dress and thick stockings looked sometimes like a character out of a film, as did he, the little boy in the white nightshirt, falling asleep by the globelight over there in the corner of the room. That thought, though, no longer belonged to the mind that had conjured it. The boy was asleep. His mother took the book and switched off the light. She watched him lying there, in the dim light. She took a step back from the bed, and then another step and another, her hands rising to her mouth, slowly, like someone about to be sick

Maybe it was only a bit of woodland along the side of a road.

or someone incapable of screaming. She continued to back off as if there were something emanating from the child's body, a negative glow or a sort of leaking, seeping darkness. In this moment, as the woman was seized by her terror (or was it instead a sort of astonishment?), the darkness crept up and devoured her and her son also. Into the pitch black a chill wind blew, as if the outside had found a way in; and a din arose, unorganised as yet, building towards a screaming intensity as it sought out its proper form.

The same room. A young black woman with a vacuum. She looks like a cleaner, dressed as she is in that grey smock dress, that apron, those gloves. (Was she wearing gloves? She should have been, white cotton gloves perhaps, or plastic protectors. And was that what the noise was, the motor of the vacuum machine amplified?) Everything in the room is as it was, before anything happened, as if nothing had happened. The same wood panelling halfway up the walls, the same armchair, the same door with its single pane of glass, the antique telephone on the quaint three-legged stand, the bed over there in the corner freshly made, the cabinet beside it with its white globe lantern.

If anybody was ever here, you would have to say now they were gone. Even if they'd left their ghosts behind, you would say, at this juncture, that the ghosts had long since slipped out of the window. If, that is, there was a window – which there wasn't. Isn't. Maybe, though, no one has ever lived or died here. It is clear that the woman with the vacuum does not live here. At least, this is only one of the many places she belongs to, although 'belong' is the wrong word. The room, its ghosts, if there are any, are incapable of including her in their dreaming, which is what enables her to work at the surface of things, dealing with stains and traces, tears, whispers, minor invasions, eruptions on the skin – anything that might signify for somebody who comes looking or germinate in an untouched corner. A sign, a seed. She turns off the machine and relaxes in the armchair, taking advantage of the fact that she is the only one here, as good as unimagined, as good as invisible. She kicks off her shoes. If only it were that simple. She knows that there must be eyes upon her; she can feel them. She grins, making her face into a rictus mask, turning up the whites of her own eyes, challenging the pictures behind her eyes to put on their stupid flesh and present themselves, here, one more time, in all their pitiful actuality. She dares them to do that.

The man looked up at the globe on the ceiling. It did look like a moon. A bit. He still had his hat on, maybe that's what made him think of it. People assumed you didn't have to be too clever to do this job, but he wasn't an idiot either. And it was obvious there wasn't anybody here, nor had there been for some time. You could feel it. Of course, he'd search the room anyway; it wasn't like it would take long, he could do it pretty much standing where he was just by turning around and looking. Even so, he checked every corner up close. He even went over to the wall behind the bed, just to make sure, and had to draw back smartish. There was something rotting – or growing – down there. Some sort of stuff. He had to cover his mouth and nose with a handkerchief. It could be a dead animal. He didn't want to know. He picked up the telephone receiver and dialled the number. When the voice came on, he told them. There's no one here. If they were here, they're gone, gone for good. The voice in the receiver talked for a while, issuing instructions. Basically, it meant he had to wait. He didn't have to wait long. The others, four of them, when they came in, were also dressed in the same kind of double-breasted suits, heavy coats, felt hats with the brims turned down. They were older men mostly. Old hands, you would say. They knew each other; they belonged to the same life. It was a life that went back centuries. None of them could see an end to it. They exchanged a few words and walked around the small room, taking the measure of the strange space, each of them getting a feel again for the familiar steps, the gestures, the poses. These were the simple easy deliberate movements (not so easy to carry off, of course, it took a fair amount of skill and precision) that would bring one of them face to face with another for a moment, or turned away just so, so that the arrangements – as they appeared

– seemed to form of their own accord, out of the range of possibilities given by the situation. The discussion. The contemplation. The recognition. The pity. Whatever was called for. It wasn't, though, so much a matter of meanings as of catching the reflections of things, picking up the ripples that spread out from events, decisions. Even if those events and decisions were deeply obscured – long gone – by the time they touched you. It wasn't an idiot's job at all. While they were waiting, two of the men prepared the room, which in this case simply involved unfolding the red sheet and covering the bed. And then another opened the door for the boss, who came in slowly. He was an older man, although not the oldest amongst them. He took his hat off, the only one to bear his head; already – as the others could not – taking his place in the room as if he knew how to be there, the same easy way he took on the authority that they conjured for him simply by standing back a step and granting him their full attention. The boss filled them in on how it was, how things were, or as much as he thought they needed to know. They had the mother. She wasn't saying anything, but presumably she could be persuaded. There were other interests involved, higher powers you might say. Think of them as the fairies. Think of this as a fairy tale. He might have smiled when he said this, but he did not laugh. Neither did anyone else. Ourselves, we can only do whatever is in our power to do. With faith, though, he added, or so they imagined him to imply, our power is not nothing. He motioned to the door, which was immediately opened, and a figure came in, covered head to toe in an oilskin cape and dripping with rain, his face obscured by a hood. Maybe it was the weather he brought into the room with him, or the black plastic bag that hung from his left hand, but this new arrival – in spite of his obscurity, his obvious insignificance – seemed to be more sharply of the world, more a thing of the present moment than any of the rest of them. Maybe the game was nearly up. Maybe, after all, this time they were starting to fade, just a little. The bag was handed over, and the stranger left. The object was unwrapped and put on the three-legged stand in place of the telephone. It was a severed cat's head, a pathetic little trophy. There was nothing left to think about any of this, there was only the procedure now to be followed through. Maybe, indeed, they were fading, their sorts of pictures and their ways of conjuring a world. It felt like everything that meant something, the arrangements, the moves, the deals, was seizing up, turning into so much statuary. This is a world of men, they used to say. Or, if they didn't say it, they believed it. But maybe it never was, not really. And maybe they didn't believe it either. The boss had been stripping and was now naked. He knelt down in the centre of the room, facing the bed, turning around to grin (the old goat), his hands together in prayer, like the patron in an old painting. A supplicant abasing himself before 'higher powers'. It seemed too for a moment that the room got brighter, as if the substance and feel of things were reduced briefly to the appearance of something spiritual, something asserting itself, as it were, from outside, against the grain of whatever was happening, inserting itself into the scene the way a meaning might be inserted into an allegory. But, just as quickly, the moment passed. One of the men scattered dust over the boss's back and shoulders. A supply of straw was laid over the red bedcover, and the horse was brought in from outside and tethered to the bedstead. A gorgeous white beast. It was impossible to imagine a more beautiful animal. The thought of that beauty could make you feel vaguely nauseous. But the image was complete. You could bring the curtain down now. It didn't matter, though. None of them would be able to save himself. Their power was nothing really. Behind the pictures, their world was nothing more than what rings out from a bullet striking a stone in a forest. A brief puncture in the universe that heals as soon as it appears. A fast receding, high-pitched tone. It was like being suspended in a vertigo of doubt.

Meanwhile, in the real world, arms got twisted, heads got kicked in. In other words, there were interrogations. Of course, an interrogation could not happen in full view. If you ever caught a glimpse, it might be of shadows struggling behind a curtain in a lit window, nothing where you could be really sure what it was that was going on. Or else it might be something that took place on an upstairs landing, so all you could see from downstairs were the feet, like a truncated puppet show. That's how it was on this particular evening. The men – I'd say there were two of them at least – were holding the mother between them. That's how it looked. They might even have dragged her there, holding her up to keep her from falling, but I can't be certain. The other woman, the one on the right (my left, their right) who was asking the questions, I think she was in charge, of all of them. Like I said, though, I couldn't see their faces, so I can't identify anyone. But I do remember some details. The woman on the right changed her shoes. During the argument. Or maybe it was before. She had on these pumps, like a cleaner would wear, and then she stepped into a pair of elegant court shoes. And that's what made me notice too the hem of her skirt. I couldn't see clearly, but it looked like a sort of grey tweed. Expensive cloth. I don't know if any of this is significant. Something else also. At the end, there was a trickle of blood down the leg of the other woman, the mother. Why do I say the mother? Because they were asking about the boy, her son. I can't remember now if they said boy or son. I'm just assuming. Is it important? I'm sorry. They wanted to know where he was, how they could find him. That was the gist of it, I'm sure, but I can't remember the exact words. Also – this is going to sound odd – it didn't sound like it was their own voices speaking. Maybe this won't make any sense, but the argument, the voices, sounded like a recording or a radio broadcast or something like that. Almost as if what was happening wasn't really happening but was being played out or played back or however you say it. Like an image of itself. Like actors in a theatre, except without an audience there. Which is why, I think, I didn't do anything, didn't intervene. Except – and this is strange too – that's what made it seem more actual. It's like they were

I can't go back.

making a film, or copying a film, and that's what I try to do, run the whole thing through in my head like an old film, a gangster film maybe. But after the studio credits and the fanfare, all I can see is . . . it looks like spermatozoa blown up under a microscope. They're sliding, like something being washed across a window, all of them kicking their tails, wriggling for all they're worth. And then they stop moving. They are alive for just a minute, and then they get washed off. Dead stuff, just like that. Has anybody found the boy?

    Maybe it was only a bit of woodland along the side of a road, but it might as well have been a forest. You couldn't tell what was near and what was far away. The darkness and the din of rain, which was never going to stop, made it seem as if all the world must be like this right now, and not just this enchanted corner. He didn't know what time it was. The only way you could tell how slowly or quickly things were happening was from the sound of traffic back on the road. It was separate from the sound of the rain, and it wasn't all the same noise, you could still imagine individual cars, and sometimes the beams from the headlights came through, passing over the ground for a moment like eyes that weren't really looking, but lighting up the trees and the darkness, like a photograph of invisible things. Animals, even. Invisible, but there. Like he was. He could feel himself there. He could feel the cold up close, it must be what was making him shake, and although with the branches tangled densely above him he wasn't soaked through yet, he could smell the wetness of everything, and he could also hear it. The world was even more astonishing than he'd imagined it would be. The water was dripping all around, close up like the cold, in thick drops as if the trees were leaking. He didn't know what to do, whether to move or to stay here. What did boys do in the stories? Maybe it was best to stay invisible. The first time the men came, they didn't see him. They had flashlights. The light from their torches arrived ahead of them. When the men arrived, there were three of them, in long oilskin capes and hoods. One of them had a dog on a chain. Even with the dog, though, they wouldn't find him. It was so wet, so dark, the woods went on for ever, and he was small. Not invisible, but small was almost as good. He started crying. It happened just like that, without him meaning to do it, without even trying. Against the rain, which was everywhere, and the distant drone of the traffic on the road, his sobs were the only sound in all that vastness that belonged to a particular place. A flashlight flickered through the trees again, and one of the figures, one of the men, came back. The man stopped about a metre away and directed the light down into the roots where it was just possible to make out what looked like a little boy hiding. The man didn't have a face, but he reached out a human hand from under his cape towards the small shivering figure in knickerbockers and braces, who came out timidly, his face as white as a moon, clutching a teddy bear, into a brief clearing between the trees. It seemed as if the man from the world had reached into the fairy story and pulled out a real boy. The man put his arm about the child and drew him towards him while, with his other hand, the hand holding the knife, he stabbed the boy in the chest. He was sawing at the neck when the other two came back. The man held up the object to the scrutiny of the flashlights. The head seemed so tiny now, like the head of an animal, an ordinary domestic cat, which, as far as they were concerned – as the man dropped it into the black plastic bag held out by one of the others – is what it was. Anyway, the job was done. They kicked some twigs and soil and wet leaves over what was left of the corpse. The man picked up the teddy bear and, after a thought, threw that down on top of the little mound. They moved off into the woods. The darkness gathered around again, thick as ink, interrupted only by whatever light spilled between the trees from the distant traffic. The rain continued to fall, streaking the night like the scratches on an old reel of celluloid. A sort of natural deterioration.

JK

PART TWO

Conversations

'The theatre is not our home'
A conversation about space, stage and audience

Claudia, Joe, Nick, Romeo

Joe: You've just completed an episode at Laban in London and now you are planning for the tenth episode of *Tragedia Endogonidia* in Marseille. We hear that there are two spaces in Marseille you'll be using and that you're doing a diptych. Perhaps we could open this conversation by talking about different sorts of theatre spaces and how you construct a specific relation in the space between the show and the audience. We imagine that this is an important thing for you.

Romeo: Particularly for the continuation of *Tragedia Endogonidia*. In this project, the relation between the space and the city is very important, and the theatre we perform in is like a metonym of the particular city we are visiting, so the relation to the space is fundamental. In every instance, there's a sort of animalistic response to the space as volume; it's not an architectonic space but a volume, a cavity, like the volume of a sculpture. I mean that facing any space you can have an animal, infantile reaction to its volume; it becomes very clear and evident how this volume can speak.

With the theatre at Laban in London, it was about proximity and intimacy, a soft volume, like a cascade, like a liquid falling towards the stage from the auditorium, although not in the opposite direction. The stage itself was like a big sack. A second sensation has to do with the location of the volume in the city, in this case outside the city, close to a canal and two churches, St Paul's church and St Paul's cathedral. There is a line, a history, involving the ships, the history of the empire and the poverty of the area, an accumulation of memory. These, though, are intellectual considerations. The first impression is not intellectual but physical, such as whether there is a feeling of danger or not. At Laban, I didn't have a feeling of danger, or of strong exposure. In Marseille, though, there are two spaces: the Municipal Theatre, an old Italianate theatre (very badly restored) and a second space, the Théâtre des Bernardines, an old church planted right in the centre, like a cylinder, a monolith. The first is a space where the relation to the public is very hard and violent because it is obliged to offer up 'spectacle'; everything is prepared in such a way that something *has* to happen. There is coercion; there is a relationship of violence in this waiting for the 'spectacle'.

Nick: This is violence to the body of the audience or the 'body of the spectacle'?

Romeo: The spectacle, I believe.

Nick: So the waiting of the audience is an act of violence . . .

Romeo: Yes, the layout of the auditorium, with the different levels one above another, is belligerent, like in the Roman circus. There is no possibility of passage or circulation between the audience and the stage, there's a clear separation. It's a space that belongs completely to the city, a civic space; while the second space, Les Bernardines, still has a very strong ecclesiastical spirit and its volume is that of a true and proper sculpture with a vertical development, in a material and not a spiritual sense. This is the impression I get. It's a very interesting space because you feel you could inhabit it, like living inside a statue, like in Hugo's *Les Miserables* where a character lives inside the statue of an elephant, as if in a house.

Joe: In London, it was a case of working in a newly built theatre. The Marseille theatres, on the other hand, are old spaces, with much to remember. Does the space have a memory? Can we find this memory?

Romeo: For me the space has to be 'empty'. Even if I know that many things have happened there, I have to believe that the space is empty of memory. It would be too demanding for me to retrieve the memories of that place. For the spectator it is a different matter.

Nick: So when you begin to make a work for a specific theatre, let's say for a stereotypical space like the Teatro Valle in Rome, another Italianate theatre with a particular story and culture, is it perhaps necessary to have a certain amnesia with regard to this history?

Romeo: Amnesia is necessary in certain cases. When it comes to spaces with a historical and non-conventional aspect, like the Bernardines, you have to consider them afresh, in all their strangeness, every time. In the case of the Italianate theatre the space is so highly codified that amnesia is not necessary. It is true that in Rome the identity of the theatre came out when attention was drawn to the painting of Harlequin on the ceiling, the ghost in the fresco, which makes the Rome episode a different case, but until this moment the space of Rome was inhabited anonymously.

Claudia: The anonymity of the Italianate theatre shouldn't be confused with neutrality. What Romeo says about anonymity is true, but from the start there is already that stratified convention of audience boxes in circles one above the other, which is the convention of people coming together in a space dedicated to spectacle, and Romeo plays on this. I'm thinking of the Rome episode in which this relation is very marked, to the point of saying at the end of the work 'Don't look', an anti-theatrical motto par excellence in a place where the theatre is always trying to say 'Look'. And so, while it is true that there is this amnesia, the Italianate space itself is not neutral. It is a natural environment for the human animal. Entering a theatre means entering the environment of the spectacle.

Romeo: Also, the Italianate theatre is a very authoritative space. Its shape contains a power, which comes from rhetoric. When a child enters a theatre he is struck dumb because he senses the power of the structure.

Joe: What does this rhetorical authority of the theatre consist of? What is it supposed to do?

Nick: And for whom?

Romeo: It would mean going over again the stages of the relation between rhetoric and theatre. This particular theatre shape derives more from Rome than Greece; the auditorium of the Italianate theatre derives from the Roman circus. The first circuses were circular, and then they became semi-circular. If you cut the Colosseum in half, you get exactly the same shape as you find in the Italianate type of theatre. And so what remains is this idea of the fatally bisected circus, this circle around which the power of the word can be put to use. The Italianate theatre serves the word, not the image. In fact, this was the difficulty we faced. Our work is 'antibiotic' with regard to the Italianate theatre space, it's like a foreign body assaulting it. It can't be anything else but an assault on the rhetorical structure of this shape, and that's what the Italianate theatre is, first of all: a shape, a half-circle. It's not about choosing to be a foreign body, it's a necessity. In a theatre like this, if you are working beyond the word, or without the word, you are lost. There is a negative relation, which creates a gap. In general, for us, the stage is not a base. Every time you have to reconnect the structure to what's going on around. You need to take a step back, every time, so as to reconfigure the structure, not just the architectonic structure of the space, but the ontological structure, the structure that contains everything you're doing. In our experience, you can't cohabit with such a space without thinking about this.

Claudia: I'm still interested in this question of what the rhetorical authority of the theatre consists in and who it functions for. It's true that with respect to the Italianate space, and so with respect to the rhetorical authority that inspires it, our work functions in an antibiotic way. But that also means that we are involved in rhetoric, that we ourselves engage rhetoric, although there would still be the question *for what* and *for whom*?

Romeo: It's not really possible to say for what. In some ways, it's a necessary question, but impossible. As regards for whom, perhaps for the spectators, but perhaps also for the gods or for extraterrestrials. Really, we don't know who we do it for.

Joe: In relation to these ideas of the space as a volume and also some sort of power or authority, I have an image of the stage as a large mouth, with the actors and everything else inside this mouth, the mouth of a large animal that consumes and disgorges the figures.

Romeo: It's a beautiful image. I find it beautiful because often there is this threat behind the stage, which can be infernal at times – as if the memory of the place, which is where its power resides, were in a position to devour at once spectator, city and community. This is why you need to inhabit this animal.

Joe: An example, of sound. In several episodes when a figure on stage touches an object, we hear one of Scott's sounds. For example, in the London episode, when Francesca Proia touches the Greek mask which is hanging on a pillar. At such a moment, it seems, just a little, as if what one hears is the spirit of the theatre. Another sort of example would be the appearance of the leviathan, the Chinese dragon, at the end of the Paris episode. Until this point, the stage has been governed by the police, but now another sort of authority takes over. And who is it? Well, it's the beast, which then arrives on the scene. It's like the theatre contains a sleeping beast. You disturb the beast by touching the mask, and then something happens.

Romeo: The image of the sleeping beast is, again, a beautiful image. There is a telluric relation with the sleeping animal, capable of provoking an earthquake, because this animal is packed with energy, like a nuclear core. It's not a poetic energy, or a textual or political energy, but a physical energy provoked, not by the spirit but by *spirits*, by the phantoms that gather and thicken on every stage.

On the material level, as in Paris with the image of the dragon, you see an actual 'leviathan'. The sounds produce a more subtle sensation, but it is the same sort of sensation in every case. I believe, though, that the beast of the stage is transformed from one shape to another; it's not the same beast. In the Paris image, it is the beast of the

State with the policemen as its representatives. At certain times, as with the Greek mask in London, there is a 'bestiality', a bestial entity, which passes through the image, which is what happens with the grin of that mask. It's the grin you find in tragedy, a kind of mockery or practical joke, an ironic sneer at life, which, for me, is a more infernal beast than the one in Paris. Not least when Francesca picks up the mask and places it on her backside so that the mouth becomes an anus.

What matters, though, is breaking with the reality principle, interrupting the real. This is the important thing for the theatre. If it's about going into a hell mouth, it's about going into the hell of the real, not a metaphysical inferno. The 'infernal' belongs to the real. And this is possible, with an experience of form. You might find a ready-made form, or you may have to reconstruct the form. Nor is it a question of a particular artist's style. It's more like an explosion, something that detonates across every dimension and touches everyone, the young, the old, without distinction. The form is inalienable, like something stopped in time. In this sense, it's about 'reawakening' the form. Maybe the true beast of the stage is the form.

Joe: What is the relation between the universal aspect of this form and the specific material, the material present on the stage?

Romeo: The material, the surface, that is chosen each time is the 'conductor' of the form, it is not yet the form itself. On no occasion is it possible to say, 'the form is this'. Nor is the form the symbol. It's even more primitive, if that's possible. Form is something I can share with an animal. This is impossible with a symbol, but with the form it is possible. The combination of light and gold, this is a form. Or marble. Hunger, thirst, these are forms. Darkness is a form, or hardness. The circle, the cube, these are forms. They are things that make up part of our life, every day.

Claudia: I've recently been reading *The Future of the Classical* by the Renaissance specialist Salvatore Settis,[1] who speaks of the classical idea of universal forms, which are supposed to provoke the same basic reactions in whoever encounters them. A peculiarity of European cultural history, according to this book, is that of 'rhythmic form', which is what links European and classical culture. The classical itself is a 'rhythmic form' that returns, in however hybrid a state. Aby Warburg[2] would say that, with respect to European culture, it's to do with a rediscovery and not a recurrence, although in European cultural history there are forms that recur. This is the 'rhythmic

---

1 Salvatore Settis, *The Future of the Classical*, Cambridge: Polity Press, 2006.
2 Art historian Aby Warburg devoted much of his life to the exploration of the reappearance of images of pagan antiquity in the art of the European Renaissance. For the influence of Warburg's work on Societas Raffaello Sanzio, see the passage in Nicholas Ridout's essay 'Make Believe' in J. Kelleher and N. Ridout (eds) *Contemporary Theatres in Europe*, London and New York: Routledge, 2006, pp. 179–82.

form'. It was right to recall this in relation to Romeo's plan for *Tragedia Endogonidia*, which touches one of the recurrent forms of our culture, that of tragedy. Then, perhaps, we might want to ask, why the necessity to recuperate this form, because tragedy also is a recurrent form.

Romeo: And the recurrence of a form even older than tragedy itself. The *tragic* is a form.

Nick: The tragedy is the instance of the tragic form . . . Returning to the question of materiality, in your reply to Joe, you spoke about gold, marble and so on as surfaces. In this, there is a problem for the theatre; when I am in the audience, and I see, for example, the golden room, I ask myself: is the gold *only* superficial? The same goes for the marble in Brussels.

Romeo: It's the ancient mechanism of the theatre. As long as we use these means, everything is false, everything is corrupt. With mankind, it is necessary to deceive him. This was the principle of Gorgias, the paradox of rhetoric, that he who deceives is wiser than he who is not deceived, that it is better to be a deceiver than a non-deceiver.[3] It is necessary, then, to construct a deceit that declares, 'Watch out, I am false.' There is neither sincerity nor truth in the material.

Joe: There are moments in the episodes when someone seems to be putting this to the test. There is the old man in Brussels, or the figure of de Gaulle in the Paris episode, who touches the stage wall, as if testing the material. But also as if testing the history of things, or testing the reality of this present moment in time. And it's as if, in this, the figures share the uncertainty and curiosity of the spectators, who often want to go up to the stage after the show and touch the objects.

Romeo: This is a nice idea, but for me this gesture is about the extreme solitude of mankind in front of things. This is only my personal opinion, but when someone touches the wall like that, it gives me a sensation of sidereal solitude. I am alone in the universe. I touch it because it is strange, not because I am able to feel it.

Joe: In *The Open*, Giorgio Agamben writes about different sorts of solitude. There is the animal's solitude and the human's.[4] The animal's solitude is not of the world but of its environment. The human solitude is of the world. Is the figure who touches the wall like that a 'human' creature?

Romeo: On stage, I think, both aspects are involved, because at a certain level the actor is also playing the role of the animal. The actor is man and animal at the same time,

---

3 See, for example, Plato's anti-rhetorical *Gorgias*, especially the opening exchanges between Gorgias and Socrates.

4 Agamben's argument is derived from Heidegger. Giorgio Agamben, *The Open: Man and Animal*, trans. Kevin Attell, Stanford, Calif.: Stanford University Press, 2004, pp. 49–50.

because it is clear that the stage is the actor's environment and not his world. There is an animal level to what goes on that passes through a haptic relation, a relation to surface, and that reveals the scenography as an environment.

Claudia: On the other hand, when there is a figure on stage that interrogates its existence, its being there, for example, in the scene where Jesus stands before the Sphinx in the Paris episode, the actual animal that appears on stage at the same time – a horse – is put in a position where it is unable to see, given that it is shown in perspective. We see the profile of the horse – and only the hindquarters at that. But the same goes for the man. Jesus is also shown in profile, so Jesus is put in the same position as the animal.

Joe: But also, when the figure of Jesus comes on stage at first, he looks out at us, the spectators. It's not a simple communication, but, even so, we are there, at that moment, for him.

Romeo: It's true, very often there is a gaze, which I believe is an empty gaze, of the actor in front of the spectators. There is always someone who looks. In the Brussels episode, it's the baby. In Zagreb, when we performed the episode there, it was beautiful.[5] The baby was magical, she had the ability to suspend time. The show stopped. As if there was no more show. Everything was suspended. Who is that? Who are we? It was like looking into a fire. It was like being bewitched. Nothing happening. Everything floating. And it is clear that the baby is not an actor, it's clear. Maybe it's us who are playing a character for her.[6]

Nick: Perhaps it's not quite the same thing, but this reminds me of the cats in the London episode and also, perhaps, the dogs in *Genesi*.[7] When the cats begin to explore the environment, and in the process they arrive at the glass at the front of the stage or else they exit the stage altogether, there is a process – for us in the audience – of a certain revelation of the nature of the environment in which the animals are placed.

Romeo: It is our form of consciousness of the stage. The cat is a projection of the capacity to surprise the spirit of the stage, which, in this case, has to do with the ways out of the stage. Cats can always find the ways out. And so the spectator, by way of the cat, finds their way out. A cat doesn't stick, it doesn't walk, it slides; it doesn't have gravity. So, yes, every animal brings back to the spectator a consciousness of the material.

---

5 *BR.#04* was one of several episodes subsequently presented in cities other than those in which they were originated. Performances in Zagreb were presented on 22–23 June 2004.
6 See pp. 95–6 for another reading of the infant 'actor'.
7 The dogs appear in Act III, 'Abel and Cain', of Societas Raffaello Sanzio's *Genesi*, 1999.

Nick: I want to ask something else about the relation with the audience. It's about an intensified audience awareness of the nature of the stage. There are moments at the end of a show where the problem of the relation with the public is revealed, for example, in *Genesi* with the clapping of a headless robot. The act finishes, the robot claps, rubble falls on its head, and it's as if it's saying 'Don't look at me', 'You must not have a relation with this', 'Don't applaud' . . . In the Strasbourg episode, though, it's even more difficult because the episode ends with a tank, and it's very difficult to applaud a tank. There seems to be this embarrassment in the relation between the public and the stage, which is a normal condition of the theatre. You talked earlier about the potential belligerence of the audience. Is this problem of relation something you focus on deliberately, or is it just something that happens?

Claudia: The relation with the audience is always thought about, but never with a final intention. In other words, the relationship with the audience has always been part of the theatre, for the reason that this relationship *is* the theatre. There is, however, no design upon the audience, nor is an audience envisioned. When the work is being created, the audience don't exist. Whoever creates is already, herself, astounded by what she creates, which is why there is no pedagogic intention, or intent to provoke. The relationship is always already there.

Romeo: Perhaps it comes out of the character of our actual political condition, that of the permanent spectator. All of us are permanent spectators. This is a new condition for the human community.

Joe: There are also, though, particular spectators, or particular images of the spectator that you include in the work. There is the audience of rabbits in the Berlin episode, obviously. But I'm thinking also of the mechanical bow in the early episodes that fires arrows into the golden room, like a spectator firing back at the stage with their gaze.

Romeo: Sure, the relation between the stage and the audience will often take on a more material form. And so the image of the arrow can, perhaps, be an image of the penetration of the audience into the show. And also the rabbits, of course, but also a few other little things. A particular relationship is transformed into material that is capable of assuming a form; but it's not a precise thing, it's something that comes about. For me, as it happens, the arrow is not an image of the spectator's gaze, but something else. In this sense, the base of the image is a prism in which it is possible to divide and multiply a single ray in different directions. For you, it is one thing; for me, another.

Claudia: The relation with the audience, or the spectators, is fundamental for our theatre. However, it's a slippery argument because it could be taken in exactly that finalistic sense. It is, though, rather a structural, ontological argument. As Romeo said, this relationship emerges in different ways, in different directions. For example, the actor who looks at the spectator reveals to the spectator his own gesture, a form of mirroring that also creates a profound equivocation and puts in doubt the spectator's proper role. Once again, this doubt is not functional, but ontological, with respect to our being actors or spectators of this life. The crossbow that shoots darts into the stage can be understood in terms of something Romeo said some years ago about the actor as a masochistic figure with respect to the theatre. The actor is purposely put in place to receive, like arrows, the gazes of the spectators. In this sense, perhaps unconsciously, Romeo has taken something from this image, because he has often spoken of the gaze of the spectator transfixing the actor, whose condition is to suffer and endure. The actor is a pathetic figure.

Romeo: Pathetic in the sense of passion; passion in the sense of non action, to suffer the action.

Nick: I also have a particular interest in the end of the show, the moment when the actors return to the stage to take their bows. As Claudia said, in the moment when the actor looks at the spectators, there is something equivocal in the relation. But, for me, this equivocation happens because normally the relation is so clear: he is 'King Lear' and I am 'Nicholas Ridout'. The extreme case is this moment after the end of the show, because it is very difficult, from my point of view, to tell who is who. And it seems to me that *this* is theatre, this moment of extreme equivocation. At the end of your shows, this problem is often made explicit. Perhaps it is not, as Claudia said, a final intention but something that happens because the theatre tries to hide this problem.

Claudia: The end of the Brussels episode is framed by those titles rolling down the screen, like the titles of a film, but that say nothing.

Nick: This gesture of the titles, or credits that say nothing, like some other gestures of your theatre, is one of those moments in which Socìetas Raffaello Sanzio appear to be making out that it wasn't them who made the show; indeed, as if someone else might have made it.

Romeo: That's right, and it's a beautiful idea. It would be perfect. My desire is for the audience to think that the show was conceived by extraterrestrials, from a world in which other rules apply. This is why the symbol of *Tragedia* is the greeting from the space probe, as if the whole project were someone else's response . . .

Joe: Why this idea?

Romeo: Because the theatre is not our home. It is someone else's home.

Nick: In the London episode, Socìetas Raffaello Sanzio are on the stage, but in the role of the 'Raffaello Sanzio Cleaning Co'. As if the extraterrestrials had employed you to make this work. You are the ambassadors of the extraterrestrials. In a certain sense, this is the normal situation of the theatre. There is always an overlapping of levels of representation.

Joe: Another point on this. If, as a theatre-maker, I have a responsibility, a responsibility to the forms or, let's say, a responsibility to the instructions of the extraterrestrials, there is a possibility that I will succeed in my task. By the same account, there is a possibility that I might fail. In your theatre, everything seems so precise, so intended, but I wonder if this precision harbours also a possibility of failure, or uncertainty. When Jesus Christ breaks into the theatre in Paris and then stands there on the stage, looking out at the audience, it is as if to say, simply, 'I am here'. But, at the same time, there is a quality to his being there which seems to say something else, such as, 'I would like to be here, but I am not sure how to be here exactly'. Similarly, when Charles de Gaulle arrives and touches the walls . . .

Romeo: The first impression is the certainty of the object, which is closed in on itself. But, at the same time, as Joe correctly said, there is radical doubt, abyssal doubt. Certainly, this is an image of Jesus. There he is, you know it is Jesus. But, at the same time, you can't be sure that you know who Jesus is. Where did he come from? Why is he here? Why is he looking at me?

Nick: And perhaps the most certain image, and the most doubtful image, is when Jesus Christ or Charles de Gaulle seem most certain. If I am Romeo in *Romeo and Juliet*, there is neither certainty nor doubt. They are who they are. When, however, it is Mussolini on stage before us, things don't seem so clear-cut.

Romeo: Yes, because Mussolini and de Gaulle are icons of history, and Jesus Christ is *the* icon, the icon par excellence. The figure of Jesus Christ is also the history, the body, of Western art. It is a super-icon, just as de Gaulle is for the French, or Mussolini for Italians. All of these figures play on the same terrain, the historical figure's the same as a figure like Jesus. And it's true that their certainty is the motor of doubt, precisely because they are in the wrong place, at the wrong time. And this sense of something gone wrong, something strange, indeed, derives from the certainty of their images, from their punctuality, their being just so. Doubt, though, is something that can't be communicated. You can't say to the actor, 'Watch out, here there is supposed to be doubt'. On the contrary, all of the company work on exactness, only on exactness; but we all know that only through exactness is it possible to open the door of doubt. Doubt has something of the unknown about it. Only through a formula of the figure is it possible to open the doubt.

A conversation about dramaturgy, contd.

Chiara, Claudia, Joe, Nick, Romeo

Romeo: There are, I think, two kinds of dramaturgy. But first we need to know what we mean by the word 'dramaturgy'. In other contexts, it has a very precise meaning. It refers to writing, to the text. The dramaturg is the person who writes the text. In our case, dramaturgy is something different: dramaturgy, in essence, is an economy of figures and time, and of rhythm.

This is why there are two types of dramaturgy. The first, which is entirely mental, and which comes first, before rehearsals, is the dramaturgy of design, and is thus a dramaturgy of the figures. The second is the dramaturgy of rhythm, of the pulsation of time, and it can only happen in the rehearsal phase, during the rehearsals, with the actors, with the objects, the contradictions of the actors, the contradictions that come from dealing with the weight of things, with the weight of objects. The second dramaturgy defines the ideal figure of the first dramaturgy and gives it extension in time and space. This, I think, is the general scheme of it, put briefly. So, you can see clearly how these two dramaturgies, that work by opposition to one another, function. The first dramaturgy is entirely mental and free from the constraints of materiality, but thinks it; while the second moves only in the material. In the first phase, you have to meet and deal with ghosts, with images that don't exist, with a world that doesn't exist.

The initial idea is always very big, very broad. In fact, it's always *too* big. The demand imposed by the second, material dramaturgy is to carve the stone, to make the figure possible, to translate it into the world of reality, to make it concrete, an object. In this sense, it is a chemical precipitation. This second dramaturgy, the working dramaturgy, has the task of finding the pulse of this body, the task of giving it breath, of giving life to this otherwise entirely imaginary figure, and for that it must form a kind of housing, a temporal and rhythmical structure whose dynamics are composed of volumes and cavities. Rhythm is one of the foundations of biology, there is no life without rhythm: in the second dramaturgy, rhythm functions in rather the same way. It is a transparent language applied to figures already written or given by the first dramaturgy.

Chiara: There is an intuitive dramaturgy which stands above everything. I don't know whether the word 'intuition' is right, but what identifies a place is an air, an atmosphere, and that is something that one intuits at the level of inspiration. It is an inspiration, then.

I think atmosphere is the radical dramaturgy, and, at root, it is about knowing where you are, in what atmosphere. The question of which atmosphere is the problem of light and the problem of sound which can (by means of either their absence or their presence) create this type of atmosphere. So, above everything, there is an inspired dramaturgy, of place, of where you are.

Then, on the basis of this dramaturgy, figures start to flourish, figures which are free and pose no technical problem. Thus, from the start, it is a mistake to consider the figures in terms of technical problems. You need to have total freedom and so forget about how you might realise them. In this total freedom, it is possible to wander at large, giving rein to an unlimited 360-degree dramaturgy. You can feel the possibility, always inspired, the possibility of realisation itself. You feel the possibility that you might be able to use any kind of form or technique. You are absolutely not preoccupied with the limits that constitute the theatre, its technical limitations.

Once I'm looking at the figures, reading them, what I don't get from outside is this sense of total possibility. So this is another inspiration, I think. The inspiration of possibility; to be able to concretise anything at all. The first sensation comes back, the sensation of the place, the atmosphere, the air, and the density of the air, and the figures start to enter this place, or, perhaps, they are born right there and then, because there's no unique approach to the work, it's not that whatever marks out or defines the figures born in the space is all at once perfectly adapted to the characteristics of the place. This process also liberates you from the fear of throwing ideas away, so it can become a kind of nursery, if one may use such a word, for other shows.

Romeo: Let's take as an example the Rome episode. There's the idea of working with a chimpanzee, with priests and with Mussolini. These were the three elements. The task of the working dramaturgy is to say that we have these elements and that we know intuitively that these three elements have a certain exactness: the chimpanzee, the priests, Mussolini – it's perfect, it works, because these three things relate to one another.

So the working dramaturgy has to reckon with the fact that the first scene is the scene with the chimpanzee, because the chimpanzee has an opening power, it opens the field. But the working dramaturgy also has to understand that the scene with the chimpanzee has to be the first scene, for the simple and practical reason that in the second scene the possibility of its entrance no longer exists. There is a practical, physical sense to this in that when the curtain opens, the chimpanzee can be there in the scene because there is something there for it to eat, but in the middle of a show it is not possible to do that. You can't bring a chimpanzee on stage after the first scene. So here all the contradictions of materiality replace the considerations of the first dramaturgy.

Another example of working dramaturgy is making one figure reverberate against another. To make the image of Mussolini reverberate with the chimpanzee, something else needs to take place between them because otherwise they would be too close. So there is a scene, which, in this case, was the scene of the priests, the priests playing basketball, because there is a friction between the two scenes. This, in turn, creates a circulation of images, in which Mussolini returns later and the ape returns too in the form of the image of the ape-mask. So they connect up. It is the circulation of a figure.

Chiara: Each show inaugurates a language, a language that is also defined by its own technical requirements. The problem of the ape is simply a technical problem but one which inaugurates the language of the show.

The most vertiginous dramaturgy is in the moments of passage from one scene into another. It's easy to manage the dramaturgy of a scene when it is in one place, but in *Tragedia Endogonidia*, the main difficulty lies in the passage from one scene to another, and it is in that moment that the dramaturgy comes undone, because it's in the gaps. It's a bit like in music when you pass from one note to another by means of another note, the half-tones; in that moment, there is a montage in music.

That is the moment of maximum crisis, because if the arrangement fails in the moment of crisis, in the moment of passage, the technique of theatre is revealed, the shabbiness of putting one thing or another on stage, in just the same way as it feels shabby when the curtain is opened on the stage and the first thing that comes into your mind is ah, that's it, in that blackout they put a table on the stage.

So, dramaturgy is really at work in the moments of crisis, in the passage between figures, and this arises most forcefully in *Tragedia Endogonidia* because there is no narrative connection by which any figure might be connected to any other, and, furthermore, any kind of narrative figure is, in a certain sense, an enemy (to use a word that is far too strong). And so the work of dramaturgy in Rome was to deal with the fact that the relationship between the chimpanzee and Mussolini was too clear, that there was a strong relationship between the name, Mussolini, and what happened (the narrativity of the name), and thus to work against the narrativity of this name. I had to do so, therefore, with a montage that was always anti-narrative. So, every show has within it a dramaturgical language that inaugurates it, a language that is made up of little scraps but also of major moments of conception.

Romeo: Rather than render a figure communicable, one searches, not to hide it, but to complicate it, because the task of this dramaturgy – and of all possible dramaturgies, really – is to break or close down communication. There is no communication, no direct communication that works for everyone. And that is why there are figures which are separated. We often use the curtain to close it down, and every time we do, the curtain has to have a very strong motivation. The curtain is a very strong character which intervenes very often. Every time it intervenes, it has to have its motive, its personal motive, but the spectator recognises the necessity of this closing, that exceeds, that must exceed, its merely practical function. The curtain is not an instrument but a character, and it closes when it wants to.

Chiara: The curtain has this elementary idea of closure. The curtain is very simple – it closes – an elementary gesture.

Romeo: It closes, or it opens. What is the real function of the curtain? To close or to open?

Chiara: Sometimes, we use sound to underline or to open the gaze of the theatre without closing the curtain. For example, when the little girl in Bergen lifted her head and looked at the audience, we used the same sound as we had used alongside the curtain in Brussels, as though it were the theatre making it, as though it were something objective, something extraneous to the figure, because the curtain belongs to the audience. In fact, when the curtain closes, you feel the need to bring the house lights up, to see the audience, to let it be understood that there is an interruption, but an interruption that is held in suspension because there is this current that passes from the curtain, to the sound and to the audience.

This incandescent light, used with the white curtain between the scenes of the Brussels episode, makes it possible to see the faces of the people in the auditorium and, thus, see this non-community, this community that cannot be called a community, of individuals. It is in this individuality that there is also the theatre as objective presence, and often in the theatre as a figure in itself, as in the case of the little hominoid who applauded in *Genesi*. It's a strange mechanism but one in which the theatre looks like itself. There are little short-circuits because you feel not just an inspired dramaturgy, so it's not just the figure that you expect when the curtain opens . . . although we are waiting for this image which is in the process of establishing itself, although we are awaiting this image which might say to us, 'It is I', but we are also awaiting an opening of the curtain on the theatre, in a universal sense, in an objective sense.

Romeo: But not in a tautological sense. It's not a matter of a tautology of a theatre that reflects on itself, a Brechtian technique.

Chiara: In fact, the moment in which the techniques of the theatre are unmasked, according to a logic of dramaturgy that accepts the disclosure of the technique of theatre, that is the moment that also achieves the maximum emotion. I'll give you an example. The bottle of blood in Brussels which is unscrewed and poured onto the ground is a plastic bottle with coloured liquid in it. It's theatre, theatrical technique, and the theatre offers it as such. It's not making a tautological gesture. At the moment in which you unmask according to the optic of montage and rhythm, of dramaturgy, the theatre, in the shape of that bottle of blood, takes the measure of the situation, and the beating builds on this blood, the blood expands, the blows given by the sound create a violence, and, thus, this 'blood' becomes blood. And so you collaborate with the theatre too, which, like the curtain, carries with it a sound which is almost like an eye that closes, a physical eye that closes. These are elements of the theatre which are not available to the cold and Brechtian mode because that epic mode has nothing to do with them. Because it is always a dramaturgy of the emotions. It is a dramaturgy that works on the nerves.

Claudia: I would like to add a little to what Chiara said, because for me it is very important and also very complicated.

Chiara: Extremely complicated.

Claudia: I think I want to take the risk of speaking formulaically, because it might entertain us a little. So the theatre is the show of reality, the spectacle of truth.

Romeo: Of truth?

Claudia: Of truth. Wait now. The spectacle of reality and the spectacle of truth. Therefore, it has come about in our historical reality, it has come to pass that the spectacle has become a system of communication, because communication today has become the principal vehicle for political consensus, for example – and, thus, the spectacle, as Debord teaches us when he says that this is the society of the spectacle.

And so the society of the spectacle has become the society of the second truth, which is no longer the truth, but a second truth. So, our work finds itself in a condition that has got the better of it. The society of the spectacle has got the better of it. And so the theatre, which was the spectacle of reality, now, in a certain sense, is the reality of the spectacle, shows the spectacle, becomes the reality of the spectacle, and returns to make the first truth heard again. This is what Chiara was talking about before, about the bottle and the fake blood. Now – making an exit from the formula because this will not really be a Brechtian speech – there really is a profound change, because the profound reality of representation, what is it? The profound reality of representation is to achieve truth, and, in this context, achieving truth requires a withdrawal from the spectacle, I don't know how to say this, a moving against, a moving in opposition to its own laws, moving one way as your horse moves another.

Romeo: Yes, but if you make it clear that the bottle is evidently a piece of reality, that shows that you renounce the mechanism of the spectacle, no? With theatrical illusion . . . it doesn't work like that in the cinema. Mel Gibson hides the bottle.

Claudia: But exactly!

Romeo: For the paradox of this choice is that we made the bottle visible, but then the scene proceeded all the same to become very violent and to try to leap up against the reality of the blood. If you use real blood on stage, it is necessarily false.

Claudia: Certainly! Certainly! Certainly!

Chiara: Something else comes to mind. Since the bottle enters into direct relation with the audience, because the audience recognise it, it is a very clear message for the audience, look at me opening the bottle, emptying it onto the ground. So, by means of this bottle, I communicate information to the audience. This information has the clarity of immediate communication between the person thinking the thought and the audience who see this thought. What happens? What happens is the audience follows this path of information. At a certain point, it feels the need to say, during the beating, enough, I don't want to see any more, it upsets me; enough, it's too much. Something happens that moves above and beyond logic, beyond thought, beyond that immediate communication that makes us all peaceful and tranquil and replaces it with an emotional aspect. An emotional aspect takes over. Emotional, rather than sentimental, in the sense that an emotion comes that makes you say, it's too much, enough, it's upsetting. From the first blow, you feel pain in your back, the first blow gives you a sensation of your own bones breaking. What's happening? Where is the idea in this scene? The idea is not in the original communication which was the opening of the bottle, but neither is it in the literal representation of a beating, so where is the idea? It is in the fact that the public, at the end of all this, says, have mercy, the theatre has taken me in. In the sense that there is this optic of the theatre and my body, my mind has not been able to react to this image with the same cool and lucidity with which I said look, let us open the bottle, let's empty it on the floor. I am sliding, I've fallen into representation, but not by a logical route which was the logic of opening the bottle. I have crashed emotionally into a representation that has neither narrative nor logical context.

A conversation about pretence and illusion

Chiara, Joe, Nick, Romeo

Joe: Many groups making experimental theatre today tend to avoid or critique illusion and pretence, but you make great use of it: for example, in the case of the presentation of Carlo Giuliani as a copy,[1] as a literal representation, or in the appearances of de Gaulle and Mussolini.

Romeo: In the examples you've given, like Carlo Giuliani, these are characters who possess a name, a surname and a very precise and specific historical identity, and it is precisely for that reason that the form in which they appear must be absolutely credible and absolutely faithful to the original. The case of Carlo Giuliani is a little different to those of Mussolini and de Gaulle, who represent two icons, as it were, of

---

[1] Carlo Giuliani was killed at the G8 demonstration in Genoa in 2001. A widely circulated press photograph of the dead, young demonstrator, rendered seemingly anonymous by his ski-mask was recreated as a three-dimensional image in the first episode of *Tragedia Endogonidia*. See Joe Kelleher's essay 'An organism on the run'.

the State, they are state icons. It's clear in this case that they constitute a trap set in order to capture or divert the flow of the show, to direct the flow of sensations in a specific direction, into a funnel, or a historical vortex. But to do that, to make a real trap like that, requires mimicry, camouflage. And, therefore, to assume as fully as possible the appearance of the original is to participate in its evident theatricalisation, in the obviousness of there being a costume, the obviousness of its being a piece of theatre. Thus, the basic mechanism of the theatre is taken up, and taken up completely. That's why every effort is made to produce an exact replica, just as in the waxworks at Madame Tussauds. What actually happens is that the actors put on latex masks, constructed for us by a sculptor. So they are not simply actors who take on the roles of Mussolini or de Gaulle, they are people who are, as it were, sculpted with this particular face: they are doubles. When these characters enter, precisely because they are made so precisely, because they are so faithful in their appearance, there is a moment of bewilderment. Bewilderment is a displacement. For example, when either of them, Mussolini or de Gaulle, enters the space, they are lost. Mussolini is a white figure on a white ground, as if lost in a cloud, and de Gaulle seems to be saying, 'What's going on here?', as if he had really been taken straight out of historical reality and dropped onto a stage where just a moment ago there had been a Chinese dragon.

The case of Carlo Giuliani is different because it is really a photograph, it's a fixed image which derives from the photo and which has become a contemporary icon representing anonymity. And Carlo Giuliani is not nobody. He is one of us. He is the name of the case. And, in this case, we worked on the photograph, extracted from the newspaper, removed from all the chattering. The background of the image was rubbed out and substituted with the gold of the icon. So the image is identical: there is the body, the fire extinguisher, and the reproduction is absolutely faithful, right down to the roll of scotch tape, the physique of the actor.

Chiara: Looked at from another point of view, these figures are like keys because they are insufficient unto themselves. Taken at face value, these keys are insufficient. Taking Mussolini and putting him on stage, taking Carlo Giuliani and putting him on stage – these are good inspirations, but no more. The excess in the face of such figures calls for its completion in other figures. What would Carlo Giuliani be without Radu's song? The song comes after, the song of the policeman, because the heart, the nucleus, of the idea of Carlo Giuliani is actually a movement. When the singer turns around, we see the red stripe down his trousers. To see Carlo Giuliani in a golden room is, I think, for us, insufficient, too literal. It is not a work of literality or of faithful reproduction for its own sake, but it serves a purpose; it is necessary so that something else can be released, which will come to complete the figure.

Romeo: For me the tragedy is the tragedy of the policeman, not the tragedy of Carlo Giuliani.

Chiara: For me, the key, the heart of this situation, is the fact that the policeman turns around.

Romeo: Radu sings with a feminine voice, this is like a funeral song, a song of tragedy, and when Radu turns and we can see the red stripe, immediately it is like a blaze of fire, and the pretence is right here, because it's a costume. When he turns with the red stripe, we can understand that he is the policeman who has killed Carlo Giuliani and that the beauty of his song is the weapon that has killed Carlo Giuliani. Violence is also a costume.

Nick: I have another question about pretence. You remember when I wrote about the beginning of the Rome episode and how for several minutes I wasn't sure if the ape was real or not.[2] In the case of Radu, the quality of the sound of his voice made me doubt whether it was him singing or not. It seemed to me to be a trap. Very often in your theatre, you present things as they are and then put that fact into doubt.

Romeo: Like the tank, for example, and the child. It's true, because very often the theatre, the experience of theatre, needs some kind of literalness, some excessive form of reality. This excess of reality threatens reality itself. And it is a reality that exceeds itself. The pretence lies precisely, I think, in this, that the world that it creates is another world with other rules. It's often a very artificial world, a world of conception, and it is, I think, interesting therefore, in investigating pretence, to turn our attention to the theatrical machines of the Jesuits, for example: towards the mechanism, the theatre as apparatus, as organism. But it is not a problem of technology, it actually means thinking of theatre as a kind of organism. And it is the pretence of giving access to another reality by means of simulacrum and resemblance to the real that is often taken literally, and it is for this reason that it exceeds itself.

Chiara: The figure of Jesus in the Paris episode is a literal figure too. The body of Jesus was chosen just as the nameless bodies of the policemen who roamed the stage. Each of these bodies was carefully chosen. It was important that the bodies should have the typologies of classic policemen. One thing which perhaps belongs to the the *mise-en-scène* phase is the detail, the detailed analysis that constitutes the passkey to a perception of reality in its every pore – as seen under a microscope. The fact that this reality is conceived in the most specific detail, the fact, that is, of its capacity for the most faithful reproduction, this is the key, the doorway through which this figure can enter and take part in a world which, in its turn, lets the figure be seen anew, which

---

2 See the essay 'Monkey business', p. 135.

reinvents it. This figure releases a new experience of itself, which allows me to make a leap; I don't make leaps as a result of any logical process; it's about finding myself automatically in another world, which makes me think with pleasure about the way that *Tragedia Endogonidia* is completely opposed to literality or story. The second part of the Berlin episode was devoted to a totally fantastical world: furry people, yetis, a scene of fur, a world with its own laws, which was full of work, which fed itself, which kept itself warm, where there was an organisation, a little community of people with rules, and a story. And, yet, it was still a strong moment of what we have been calling our pretence. The pretence of being able to gain immediate access to another world without passing through the real.

This gets us back to the terms of our discussion yesterday[3] because each episode has its own language . . . but this language of the figure is often at odds with it, finds itself at odds with the reality of the detail. It might be a historical detail. It might be a detail of form, a detail of sound, a sound that follows the movement. For example, the skin-woman has a sound that follows her movements in detail, and the figure expands a little as a result. The detail is important, as is its precision: the more physical the detail, the more it follows and enters into the figure or settles in the figure's ambit, the easier it is to find it in another reality, one with its own language, its own laws, and, thus, it is possible also to oscillate between one historical epoch and another. The tablets of the law do not belong as a concept to everyday laws today. We have a very strong conception of everyday laws, and I think that with every day that passes, this thinking about the law grows – at a very popular level, the level of the people – because laws are looked at more closely the more controlling they are. But the idea of the Mosaic laws fits perfectly with the police of our time, in this country, recognisable by their physique and typology. Thus, there is no longer any need for a logical coherence in this reality, because it is sustained by detail. I can pass across the reality of this figure by means of a detail that is beyond the real, beyond logic, because there is a logicity of the detail.

Joe: In the Bergen episode, when the child sits and watches the film, she seems to be looking into another world, or it is as though she were one of the prisoners in Plato's cave and that the message from 'another world' is, in fact, an image. We watch Eva's back as she is watching the film.[4] There is something about this that links the film itself to pretence.

---

3 See 'A conversation about dramaturgy', pp. 214–16.
4 Eva Castellucci is the youngest of Chiara and Romeo's six children. Agata, Cosma, Demetrio, Eva, Sebastiano and Teodora Castellucci have all appeared as performers in the company's shows, including episodes of *Tragedia Endogonidia*.

Romeo: It is all about the geometry of the gaze. Looking at someone who is looking at something creates the effect of looking at your own back, seeing your own back in the back of the child. The film itself is a film of the open brain (of course, it is also the film of ghosts, the ghosts of Norway, of Ibsen), and I think that the pretence here consists in the fact that there is a kind of promise in this film, a promise that there might be an image that is more true than that of the show. If I had to condense this show, I would reduce it to the stains, the Rorschach blots of the film. It is the concentration, and what works for me are the specular turbulences and the image, the materialisation, the concretisation of sensation, of emotion, the nervous flickerings of the cerebellum. That is the truest image.

Joe: Thinking about those stains, I remember an image from Lacan. He writes about a small shellfish that adapts to its environment by camouflaging itself, literally by taking on the appearance of a stain, and Lacan talks about mimicry itself as a sort of stain upon vision.[5] He asks then about the function of this little organism's mimicry and says perhaps there are good reasons for it – self-protection, survival and so on – but says too that he's unsure about all these reasons. Perhaps there is no 'reason' for camouflage, because there is something in pretence itself, a function of pretending, which is not about making an illusion for others. Usually we think of camouflage being for others, but perhaps it's not.

Chiara: I don't know about you, Romeo, but for me, in this moment, also in relation to the Crescita at Santarcangelo and thinking about Marseille which is coming up, this is a question that I like. This, I think, is a form of mimicry that is, then, very particular. Our theatre is full of signs – I don't know if 'signs' is the right word, of figures, then – and with care for the detail, the figure flourishes, in the sense that there is an excess of figure in the detail. In this excess of the experience of vision, we have a whole host of perceptions. At a certain point, and this is really a question of montage, of dramaturgy, it is as if everything had vanished, as if everything had been annihilated and the concentration is fixed on a single hand, the attention rests on a hand moving or on a face that makes movements, like any of Francesca's movements in the London episode. As if everything else were suspended and it became important that Francesca should do just this. The concentration on a gesture was of the utmost importance, and here it was on *this* gesture. Here it's as if, by means of naturalness, the apparent insignificance of a gesture, although prolonged, this gesture could give access to a metaphysics, to another world – as if producing a moment of pure and complete

---

5 See Jacques Lacan, *The Four Fundamental Concepts of Psycho-Analysis*, trans. Alan Sheridan, Harmondsworth: Penguin, 1994, pp. 98–100.

suspension, not in the actual cutting of a sound or anything like that, no, it is everything, for you see nothing other than this hand which completes a gesture and the repetitiousness of this hand that follows it. You enter, or rather you find yourself in, a state, a metaphysical state. For me, this is also the power of theatre. It is to return to this power.

Nick: I'm thinking again about the start of today's conversation, when Joe made the observation that it is very normal in English-speaking theatre to think that all the artists and theatre groups who make experimental work, who are trying to make new theatre, are ideologically opposed to illusion. Not English-speaking theatre as such, but the idea in the English-speaking theatre that in order to be experimental it is necessary to be against illusion, and that the theatre is always engaged in a struggle against the system of representation. What seems interesting to us is the way in which your theatre has a different relation to illusion, that it is a theatre that is interested in illusion. The battle against illusion may be something ideological, because there is a mode of making theatre, or cinema, or literature, which always says, 'I can show you that everything is an illusion'. It's perhaps the Brechtian, demystificatory mode.

Romeo: Yes, but it is also a Calvinist mode.

Nick: Yes, it's a *via negativa*.

Romeo: Yes, it comes from a self-discipline which arrives at a presumed honesty. No? This is the way things are. However, we come from a Catholic culture, from the Baroque, from oil painting, and so for us illusion and artifice are only ways of getting to the object, not the object itself. Calvinism, meanwhile, falls into the object.

Nick: The distinction, perhaps, between a critical path and a negative path as regards the image is the use of the image and of artifice as an affirmative practice.

Romeo: Affirmative, yes, but it derives algebraically from a double negative and, like the double negative, becomes a positive. In this affirmation of the image, there is a double negation, there is a taking of the image behind its back, not frontally as it is used in advertising. There is always an image that you don't know what it is, it is the shadow of the image.

As for language, I think we use language in a homoeopathic way, taking on a language because it is essentially an extraneous element, an element that attaches itself to us at the moment we take it on, taking us into language. For we enter language the moment we have to accept that it does not originate within us. It is not that we are against the word, that's not how it is. It is a matter of using words exactly like objects, on the same plane, and then, taking on things and taking on words, not because we believe in these things or in these words, but because they have been taken on, as I say in a homoeopathic way, like toxin. So it's inevitable, working in this way, making use of all the elements of creation, of the world, words and things, that you will put a great illusion on stage. The illusionist doesn't believe in what he is doing, he knows perfectly well that there is a rabbit hidden in his hat, he knows this because he is creating an illusion, a third reality. So his is a metaphysics of the skin, an absolutely superficial metaphysics. Our theatre is very superficial, for it is at the surface that may be found, in a radical sense, everything that determines our presence in the world. We are an extended surface, superimposed on the surface of the world, so we are reclaiming the surface, in a sense, rather than conducting research into truth. There is no research into truth because this is the wrong place for it. The theatre is the very last place for a research into truth. Look for truth in the mountains, not at the theatre.

A conversation about composition

Chiara, Claudia, Joe, Nick, Romeo, Scott

This conversation took place the morning after a performance in July 2005 in Cesena of *The Cryonic Chants: Songs and Objective Poems, Taken from an Impassive Animal*, a concerto created by Scott Gibbons and Chiara Guidi, involving live musical composition by Scott and vocal performances by Chiara, Claudia and Monica Demuru. Key elements of *The Cryonic Chants* include a stark black-and-white visual design and the incorporation of a rhythmically edited video of a goat (the 'Poet' of *A.#02*, the second episode of *Tragedia Endogonidia*) grazing upon a white carpet marked up with letters of the Western alphabet.

Nick: The Italian word *emotività* says something that the corresponding words in English, emotionality and affectivity, don't. Its meaning is somewhere between emotion and motion or movement. Last night, Chiara, after the concert, you talked about the importance of intuition and emotion in the making of a work, rather than logic. It's also, though, important surely that this emotion, this intuition, this non-rationality, is not a gratuitous, aleatory thing but a rigorous element of the composition. There is a very strong relation in your work between 'emotivity' and the rigour of a composition. Could we talk a bit about how composition is guided by intuition?

Chiara: I believe that it is movement that stirs up emotion. A movement goes towards the construction of a space and a time, and it is this that makes the relation between emotion and movement so strong. We sense something moving within a space, and this movement creates a particular sense of time. During the montage stage of the work, it is this quality really that connotes a place and determines the movement of materials within it, enabling the possible trajectories of the materials inside the space to be seen. What gets produced isn't, then, just a scene, it's a physical place, a mental space, very precisely structured with clear boundaries. Material is moved in this space and, as it gets moved, a time is born, because this movement has a number, a specific quantity. This is its rigour. The rigour is born from the fixing of a number, and this number is rhythm. And so, yes, there is a strong relation between movement and *emotività*, but also a strong relation between this emotivity and space and time.

I believe that once the space is fixed, once the space is decided, the montage can take effect inside this space. In this instance, the space is the goat's carpet. The goat moves around touching the letters. The idea is engaged, and then the goat, which has helped me get inside the space, is forgotten. The space now goes in all sorts of directions, which enables the drawing out of a design, the design of the melodic structure, the compositional structure. Perhaps I am putting into effect another world. Scott, when he composes, brings everything down to earth, while I follow an order. If I begin with a short beat, I then have to add two long ones, and then I negate the two long beats with two short ones. It's a logical, methodical way of constructing according to what is given in a film. With this method, I can inhabit a space that I have perceived intuitively, constructing a time, because time is constructed through montage. This is what I mean when I say emotion is strongly linked to the choice of the space in which the montage functions and how it is that the movement of the montage gives birth to a time.

Nick: You also spoke last night, with respect to the montage of *The Cryonic Chants*, about specific vocal movements, the movement from 'g' to 'a' to 'g', or the choice of 'mnv' over 'mnfa', little distinctions that are absolutely necessary if a decision is to be true, even if such decisions are not rationalised according to a logic of the world.

Chiara: I don't know. It's difficult to prepare for this sort of material, because it has to do with the basically arbitrary nature of any choice, something which, for me, is unnameable, because the artistic process is obscure. Not everything can be explained. There is an originary intuition which is impossible to explain in terms of an artistic process. Eventually, however, this arbitrariness becomes authoritative, it becomes a still point in the world, which has to be dealt with. The act of creation throws something into a space or into a time that becomes authoritative.

Claudia: Its authority derives from the fact that it is generative, that it has the capacity to generate. Yesterday evening we talked also about chance. The word *caso* (chance, event, fate) has the same Latin root as *causa* (cause). Just as Chiara was saying, a chance event turns into causation. It's true, though, that it's very difficult to explain the distinction between a logical process and an analogical process that lies outside of logic, as difficult as trying to explain as a rule what happens in poetry. Poetry is this bringing things together, this indivisible and indiscernible joining, between chance and calculation, between chance and causation, so that it is impossible to tell where one thing finishes and another begins.

Chiara: But on the artistic level, there is a very practical effect, which surprises me every time. You say to yourself that this element is right and that element is not right, but the difference between right and not right is only clear to me, or to him, or to her. For someone else, there is no discernible difference between this and that, whereas for us there is an abyss. Indeed, getting this wrong is not just an error as far as our process goes, it is a scandal, an absolute scandal. This sort of problem often comes up for me, for example, with the voice, when I am leading others who are performing alongside me. You need to be patient because sometimes, due to this very precise intuitive trajectory, a slight difference in vocal timbre that strikes me as an error is inexplicable to the other people.

Scott: I'm not sure if I'm understanding the nuance, maybe it's not even a nuance, between intuition and practicality, because there's a very real practicality, not only an intuition, involved. Because it is possible to observe and sense and really to know, 'Oh OK, it's wrong'. The process is not all in the mind; it's in the body as well.

Nick: If this choice, this intuition, which is personal but also objective, is linked in a certain sense to the objectivity and reality of one's body, it's not possible for someone else to understand exactly the experience of being me in this body. There is a relation between this intuition and the objective fact that I am this body, so my experience of this sound, my choice that this sound is right, is a relation between my corporeality and this sound?

Chiara: Yes, but there's another aspect. The thing which you choose, there and then, you don't choose it because it pleases you. It's not about the pleasure you take in your choice. It's about measure, and that is something very different. There is no psychological involvement, or anything personal at all. In the initial phase, the choice is detached from your own body. I don't choose this thing because it belongs to me. I don't choose this thing because it is part of some ideal aesthetic 'me'. It is an extension of my body, but without my having agreed with myself, and it is only later that I register the structure. And this is important, because it isn't that I have this thing and I say this thing is beautiful, this thing is ugly. Rather, it is something that comes about organically, and although something might be rejected, it's not on the basis of a decision between the beautiful and the ugly but a sort of organic extension of an intuition. And yes, in the next moment, the aesthetic concept of beautiful-and-ugly is born. The aesthetic is born in the very next moment. But, initially, there is no aesthetic process. It is active, immediate, but not logical.

Claudia: Perhaps, then, it would be interesting also to say something about the performers that are there on stage with Chiara, because she is the one in charge. As Chiara said before, she understands when something is wrong or when a thing is not what it should be, even if only slightly. And the others – us, the ones performing with her – maybe we don't understand why, but if things go well, we enter into a resonance with her, a harmony, which is always objective. Certainly, it's happened for me many times, as a performer, that Chiara will tell us the next day to do something in a different way than she told us the day before. And we say 'But why? The day before you said to do it like that'. Yes, but now it is like this. And, therefore, we are always trying to find a way of talking about proportion and measure and harmony. That, basically, is how it is for the performers. We have to keep listening to this talk, and the conversation is always active, it is never simply a matter of notating pentagrams.

Joe: The first time that I saw you both give a performance of this sort, another performance based upon the movements of the goat, was in the Avignon episode of *Tragedia*, during the speech of the ambassadresses. I'm thinking now about the movements of ambassadors as such. Ambassadors are people who go to this or that country and then return home. They make a journey in a way that is analogous to the making of a composition. As an ambassador, I see and I hear things; I see this and that, the beautiful and the ugly, perhaps. All of which becomes something I have seen in another country. And now I come back, I come back to the stage, and whatever is being communicated is communicated through the word of the ambassadors who tell us how it is in another country.

Romeo: Although, actually, the country of the goat, the country of an animal, is not so much another country as another world. It's important also because everything is made possible through a choice, and this choice of opening the door so that an animal may enter and then leaving it be, is, I think, a revolutionary gesture. A small revolutionary gesture, perhaps. A very small revolutionary gesture. But, in a certain sense, this project could, in the last analysis, be a way of returning an animal to the stage. Maybe the history of Western theatre could be seen this way, that the goat is what has been missing since the beginning. The goat has left the building. And so the ambassadors bring this message: the goat has turned back.

Chiara: Watch out!

Romeo: Perhaps it's not a revolution against this thing or that thing, but against yourself. In the sense, perhaps, that it negates your foundations. Opening the door to an animal negates, at a stroke, any proportion, it negates your system of logic, your system of writing. Suddenly, in the face of this revolution, these things break up, they decompose. It's not a revolution against, it is a revolution *in*. It carries the most extreme consequences. In this sense, it is right to highlight the fact that the performers are ambassadors.

Joe: There is also a question of the face. At the end of *Cryonic Chants*, we see the face of the goat on the video, looking at us. And, at the beginning, there are the faces of these women, the ambassadresses. I'm thinking, too, of the alphabet video in the Cesena and Avignon episodes of *Tragedia Endogonidia*, which begins with letters, followed by Rorschach blots that start to look a little like faces. I've recently been reading Davide Stimilli's book *The Face of Immortality*,[1] about physiognomy as an idea of literary criticism, and I'm interested in this movement between sounds and faces and letters in your work, although I understand this movement as a circulation rather than a transformation of these things.

Chiara: I also understand something else from this: that physiognomy, the weight of physiognomy, which is legible in a human face, becomes legible in the animal and becomes legible also in the sound for which it is an emotional path. There is a physiognomy which involves a direct emotional language. Through this structure, you can see the physiognomy of the letters, the character of the individual letter and the character of the sound. The physiognomy remains; it isn't transformed at all. It doesn't transform, but, rather, it reveals. It is an emotional physiognomy. My intention in *The Cryonic Chants* has to do with a microscopic acoustic that enables you to enter, through the physiognomy of sound, the physiognomy of the letter, into the opening of the mouth, the vocal cords, to enter into the character of the work. And, for me, it takes on a timbre, but it doesn't transform.

Romeo: For me, the image of the alphabet also has to be seen though the eyes of the goat. As the goat walks, each letter becomes stained; it is no longer something that means. For me, this is an image of the materiality of language, but material reduced to shit, reduced to something which has fallen. The letters are actually under the feet of the animal, like shit in a cowshed. There may be a possibility of shaping it in some way, one may still want to make something of it. However, the word, the language,

---

[1] Davide Stimilli, *The Face of Immortality: Physiognomy and Criticism*, New York: State University of New York Press, 2005.

has become material, or, rather, a cynical image, or, rather, again, a nihilistic image, a way of observing the image of the alphabet as something ejected, something shot out.

Chiara: It is important, though, to understand that the alphabet isn't transformed *into* a stain but rather *is* the stain. There is no work of transformation, because that would be banal, wouldn't it, to transform reality into music? So banal. Reality involves a seeing. It's the same thing when one talks about 'un-sensing the support' . . .

Romeo: . . . Derrida's phrase, *a propos* of Artaud, '*forcener le support*', to unsense, to madden the support.[2] Again, it involves extreme consequences. The support, in this instance, is language, the alphabet, which, ultimately, is a series of stains. For me, this idea of language, of alphabet, is a threat for the human community, because language is the only thing capable of holding the community together. If you touch it at a soft point, the language panics, because we have nothing.

Nick: Only the stain.

Romeo: Only the stain, if we hold to this vertiginous image of nihilism.

Joe: Perhaps this relates to the way black and white functions in your work, like a digital system, or like a language system which has been deconstructed into these basic oppositions. Why is the black and white important?

Romeo: Because it is the maximum drama in the least possible information, but a drama which, in this case, becomes an optimum means of liberating the process. It is pure vibration, like a fibrillation or like Scott's puntiform sounds.

Scott: Maybe it's interesting to mention that when we first began talking about doing a musical project from *Tragedia*, this concerto, the first two considerations were the text from the goat and the black and white stripes. These were the two points of departure for the entire concert, and the black and white lines, for me, were the first sound. The first sound is inaudible, and yet the first sound is also very strong, although it is not immediately apparent. You see the room, OK, black and white lines, and then it enters into your body and has a strong yet subtle effect. And this was the point of departure.

Romeo: For me, the language of the women vocalists is also interesting in the way it is like a false language. It sounds like a language of this world, but it also sounds false. I find this fact very powerful.

Chiara: Although the fact that the goat delivers the letters means they are dead. They are dead letters. They say nothing. You try to read them, and all you get is 'g', 'g', 'g'.

---

2 Jacques Derrida, 'To Unsense the Subjectile', in Jacques Derrida and Paule Thévenin, *The Secret Art of Antonin Artaud*, trans. Mary Ann Caws, Cambridge, Mass.: MIT Press, 1998.

Romeo: In the last analysis, it's also like that with Italian, or English. Think of being before a child, or before an animal. Languages don't have different sounds, there is only ever a noise, just as with an alphabet there are stains.

Chiara: What comes out is, actually, a fractured language.

Romeo: This is what comes out next. It is succeeded by a cultural system. The important thing is to use this material, this language, *as* material, like a fallen material. The rest is invention. Perhaps the material can be rearranged into a verisimilitude of language, but it is not a true language.

Chiara: For me, the idea here is like it was in an earlier piece, *Uovo di Bocca*, where there was an invention of a language on top of another language.[3] In *Uovo di Bocca*, it was a case of constructing a rhythm derived from Claudia's words, a rhythm that gives you the possibility of comprehending this text even in a country where a completely different language is spoken. For me, the wager today for the theatre, the way of invention for today's theatre, is about not going to the text anymore in a dead way, through the dead tongue of the theatrical text, but giving the text in a rhythmic manner. A return to the originary rhythmic structure. When the mouth is opened, what follows is the score, the long–short–short, the metre. There is an invention of metre.

Romeo: The metre, then, returning to black and white.

Chiara: It is an originary metre.

Romeo: Although, in reality, this language is made up of greys, not black and white. For me, black and white is the structure upon which this thing leans, upon which it is founded.

Chiara: Yes, it's a chromaticism of voice.

Romeo: Yes, black and white is not language.

Scott: Maybe, when Chiara recites the language, it is in a particular shade of grey, although for me it wasn't grey, even less black and white. It became a colour.

Chiara: Black and white is boom-boom. You read it in the way a goat reads, as a rhythm.

Nick: I was thinking of how in the revelation of a sound there might be an inaudible sound which already has an effect upon the body, so that even those things you can't hear have a physical effect upon the listener. Do you think that the emotional work

---

3 A video recording of Societas Raffaello Sanzio's performance of *Uovo di Bocca*, given at the Conway Hall in London in April 2003 as part of the symposium *Civic Centre: Reclaiming the Right to Performance*, appears on the DVD curated by Gianna Bouchard that accompanies the *On Civility* issue of *Performance Research* 9(4), 2004, ed. Alan Read.

that sound does upon an audience is dependent, for example, on the retention of those inaudible things? So that if, in fact, somehow you digitally cleaned up some sound so that all of those things vanished, if you took those out . . .

Scott: I do like to use sounds taken from the camera, from a video camera, which have a lot of ambient noise. And also, with many of the recordings we made, there is a lot of noise from the boards. We used some very old mixing boards with a lot of noise on them. These have a very different effect, though, and it just makes the whole thing sound more human, more organic, more dangerous, if it's not so polished.

Chiara: The notion of the inaudible is, I think, very important, because there is also the work of hiding the idea. You reach a moment where the sound becomes so saturated it disappears. But not because it leaves nothing, but because it leaves something dense, open and indivisible.

Scott: There's one other thing I could mention about cleaning up sounds, although it might be too practical for this conversation. When you asked the question, I was thinking about the concerto. For *Tragedia*, it's completely different, because in *Tragedia* there's this interplay between the audience and the scene, and as soon as you introduce noise, as soon as you introduce a recording, it pushes the spectator away from the scene. It immediately becomes a 'scene'. And, OK, I'm not into the scene, I'm remembering that I have me here in my seat, I'm remembering that I am a spectator, so it becomes useful and also dangerous. But the problems become different depending on the circumstances. If I sit and watch an episode of *Tragedia*, I very often find myself being pulled into a scene and being pushed out of a scene, playing the role of spectator and also playing the role not of a spectator but more of a fly on the wall, an observer of some things that are happening. Whereas, for a concert, it's very clear. You have performers and an audience. It's another thing altogether, and it's not theatre. It's impossible to have the audience on the stage in the scene with you.

Probably too practical?

A conversation about rehearsal

Chiara, Claudia, Joe, Nick, Romeo

Romeo: The rehearsal phase is only a moment of checking things out, which we experience as a moment of resistance between an idea and its reality. In this sense, the fewer rehearsals there are, the better it is. As a principle, we don't depend on the rehearsal phase for the growth of the work. Rehearsal is closer to what a sculptor does, a *via negativa*. Generally, the work doesn't grow but rather diminishes. Usually, when we are planning work, we need to take a step back, because eveything is separate but also tangled. The ideas grow like brambles, and so there is no rehearsal-room improvisation; rather, there has to be a separating out of all the elements. First, there are the ideas, then there is a written plan of these ideas, a mental montage, and then a checking out in rehearsal, followed by a second montage and a final verification before the audience. This is a skeletal outline of the usual process. The first phase involves gathering ideas by making notes, like a river gathering the channels that feed into it, the widest gathering possible, carrying everything along. There will be elements of reality, elements of the mind or of an imagined reality, all converging towards a point: this transcription of ideas into notes, which is work that goes on every day. After the gathering work, the next phase is reading these notebooks, in the general context of the work, so that the strongest points can emerge, like nodes, like stones, like buds, the hardest and most obstinate. And then the ideas are organised through these nodes, arranged in a structure like a tracking of the constellations. On the basis of what is read and transcribed in the notebook, these nodes expand into a structure from which it is possible to understand the character of a work. There is an encounter, a period in which the character of the work can be recognised, even if it is a very vague recognition, more of a mental than an intellectual process. When a plan does emerge, you find iconographic correspondences which can lead to a universe of sounds, as well as literary or pictorial, physical or historical – indeed, all sorts of possible inflections. This, in brief, is the phase before the moment of verification that happens in rehearsal. Before we go into rehearsal, the work must, in a certain sense, be already finished. There has to be this type of illusion, and you can't afford to treat it as an illusion, because when you think about the work's structure, you think immediately about all the possible weaknesses, the possible failures, and your work becomes all about the prevention of errors, which are inevitable anyway and a matter of chance.

From this plan, the threads of a reality are drawn out, the demands you are looking to intuit, to perceive, of a show that is becoming something like an entity, a mute, wordless spirit which you have to interpret, not like a psychoanalyst but like a psychiatrist, to understand the brain structure of that new entity. You have to follow to the point of inertia wherever the plan takes you, such as whether there needs to be a person, whether there needs to be actors, and what these actors have to be like, or else to the emotional tonality or the colour or the type of sounds, that is to say, all of the traces, the suggestions that are going to be reinterpreted on stage by the performers. It's strange because the plan becomes impersonal, like something you have discovered rather than invented. A written plan follows, with the entrances and the exits, the costumes, all in detail, and then finally the first day of rehearsals begins so that every part of the plan can be tested out. In a few cases, there is an immediate correspondence with the ideas, and so the rehearsal phase is quick. At other moments, it falls to pieces, it becomes difficult to find a way; in some cases, certain little ideas become like tumorous excrescences, they become immense. It is possible for this or that small detail, there in the plan, to grow beyond all measure.

Nick: For example?

Romeo: For example, in Strasbourg the idea of projecting an image, of establishing a link with *Psycho*, became a very significant element but was supposed to be a very quick detail. But also the black soldier-women: there was only supposed to be a few passages in silence, and instead it became completely mute and silent in which there was only the walking around.

Joe: What did you mean when you talked about resistance between ideas and reality?

Romeo: Resistance, perhaps, in its second meaning, the 'electrical' meaning, but also in the sense of combat. It is something that resists through two different tensions, because there is the need to go ahead with the ideas from which so much comes, the requirement to not betray the idea, and also the inevitable clash with reality. In short, it's the world of conception against that of reality. In the middle, there are the rehearsals . . .

Nick: There isn't resistance between the idea and the materiality?

Romeo: Yes, there is the material, the rehearsals are an encounter with material *tout court*. By material, I mean the actors' bodies, the voice, even the words which are material in their turn. I'm not referring to the irrationality of material against the sublime of the idea, it's not about that. It's the confrontation of two worlds that can't help colliding.

Chiara: It's the reality of the idea, or rather the physicality of the idea, not so much its reality. In the sense that the clash with reality is the clash with the physical reality of that idea. It's not a clash with the real, with what happens, but with the reality of that idea. Actually, it would be important to understand the different nature of the ideas, because every idea establishes a method of work, a stragegy. As a matttter of fact, we've often talked about strategies. They are ideas that are hidden in their extreme simplicity and complexity, just because they are so simple. They hide, and as they are realised, they bear already within themselves a reality, a physicality. For example, having Jesus confront a sphinx is clear enough; but this clarity leads you to risk a time which is the time of immobility, by adding seconds and annulling the action, almost filling it over again with stasis. On the other hand, there are other sorts of ideas that are very clear on paper, but the moment you go to realise them they become banal. For example, the women in the Strasbourg episode have to move about in the space and do the sort of habitual actions you do when living in a camp, like digging or preparing something to eat. When the moment came to begin rehearsing, everything was very ugly because the actual reality of the Comandini was no help in any of this. It would have been different if we could have started rehearsing immediately on the mound of earth, because it was the earth that created the physicality of the idea. This is why I say it is very important to understand the difference between the individual ideas and to always put the idea in relation to its place. Because rehearsing means perceiving the physicality of that idea but also knowing that there will always be a place that awaits it. For example, the marble room. One option was to rehearse here in Cesena with a baby, to perceive its strength, its powerlessness, which, in its turn, becomes its strength. However, to see it, finally, in a marble room: what happens? What happens is that immediately this place, the marble, becomes a hospice, a room of torture. It is the room that begins to shift. The problem of rehearsal is always linked for us to a capacity of transferring the little that gets seen there into the true physicality of the idea, which includes its environment, its sound and, in turn, its time. The rehearsals we do here in Cesena are quick, because we know that they only enable so much: it will be important to see things again in the actual space. This is why those weeks we have in the cities before the debuts are so important. For example, the figure of Jesus, a very emblematic figure, therefore a very difficult figure to bring on stage. But immediately, the first time we rehearsed a car falling, I was sure that later the presence of Jesus with the fallen car behind would be like a leap in which the figure of Jesus might begin to have a body, thanks to the car.

Romeo: It is an extreme example of trusting a scene which we can't get to know during the rehearsal phase. The cars only fell during the show.

Chiara: Throughout the days of the rehearsals, we were at loggerheads over the figure of Jesus: where should he enter from? Already the mere fact of having him enter was a problem. He couldn't come in like the policemen: the same entrance for Jesus? There was a conflict: we called Claudia who had stayed behind in Cesena. But the moment the car fell, it was easier to understand where to make him enter from. It is difficult to touch upon this argument because it means touching upon the dark zones of creation, you can't really explain it. Among other things, every idea calls for a particular method and a rehearsal technique. However, it is also true that even as we are searching for a method, this method is a method of opening but also of contradiction. Everything is very under control, but we are still waiting to be surprised by something we haven't thought about, that might appear in what we can see. And this also changes the act of montage. There are also figures that grow, thanks to the rehearsals, in the sense that there are points that we haven't foreseen. You try to foresee everything and imagine everything; however, there are moments in rehearsal which are closed to us, and we say, 'Let's do it, let's see'.

Romeo: Even so, there isn't any improvisation, nor is it a creative phase. The rehearsals serve to remove or reduce or amplify a figure that is present in the plan. It is impossible for a new figure to enter during the rehearsal phase. As for the actors, it could be said that the actors, along with all the other elements that make up the show, such as the objects or the lights, are like *objets trouvés*, in the sense that they already have an objective reality that coincides with the idea of which they will be made the bearers and which they wear like a glove. There is no actor training, the actors are already ready, they already have one foot inside the form. And many examples could be given. All children have an objective presence; there is nothing to rehearse, the most radical instance of this idea being the baby in Brussels. The same thing could be said of the chimpanzee in Rome, or any of the animals in the work: they don't have a task or function, so there is nothing to rehearse. They don't have to be tamed, because they are what they are. In a certain sense, this is true of all the actors, for instance Claudio Borghi, who moves in that particular way, who has that face, who turns his head in a manner that only he is able to do. The work has to do with pushing forward or following a movement of inertia, towards the form. This work is already running through the plan, like a furrow. Again, in the case of the Strasbourg actresses, we had to work hard because temperamentally they had this great expressive power which contradicted the plan. With their movements, it was difficult, like trying to steer – trying to steer a vehicle – an idea of melancholy on an African earth.

Chiara: To find the right tempo for the way they walked, for their reactions, was first a work of accumulation and then of slowing down.

Romeo: We also worked on the concept of pause. At moments, the action freezes, it doesn't flow, but at these times it is also much easier to find the actors' relation with the earth. All of the work is there . . . It was beautiful to discover, and in this case it did happen during rehearsal, to discover how this relation might be much stronger than we imagined.

Claudia: I'd like to divide this talk about the actors into two parts. What Romeo says about starting from what the actor is actually like, about the actor being this irreplaceable stone, is fundamental. Nevertheless, I'd like to highlight something Romeo didn't say but which I see as a spectator of his and Chiara's work. There is an enormous amount of work on gesture which, as Romeo says, does seem to depend almost entirely on what the actor is like, how he naturally moves, the particular way his profile stands out. There is, I repeat, an enormous amount of work on gesture which begins in the sort of minimal movements that are almost impossible to see in the theatre. The tiniest gestures have the capacity to radiate on stage, a movement of the finger-joint, the smallest eye-contact even, even the slightest meeting of gazes can radiate and multiply, so that this little gesture becomes *the* gesture, the centre, upon which attention is concentrated, the ultimate attention being the eye of the spectator.

My work is different to this work on gestures. It is more mechanical because I receive from Romeo and Chiara some information about what is needed mechanically, at the level of articulating a certain movement. But I don't work on the emotional tonality. They work on the emotional tonality, which is something subtler. I work on something more gross, on articulation. Gesture, though, introduces that ineffability of sensation and also the conception of emotion, which only the relations internal to the work are able to produce.

Chiara: I believe that the information that the actors have received during these years, about how to perform certain actions, have been very precise. I'm thinking of the movements of the young women in Berlin, when they come out from under the bed and perform their choreographies: information at the level of the performer's interpretation, instructions about attitude. Because the movement, in turn, gets filled up with colour, with tension, with electricity, with expression. Among the instructions given to the actors the most important is, in the very next moment, to forget, to hide the instruction, not to show what the gesture expresses, but to hide it, to live it in a more intimate manner.

Romeo: The most serious danger is demonstration and intentionality.

Chiara: In the face of demonstration and intentionality, the eye of the audience, the eye of the single spectator, sees the technical, practical work and is incapable of being moved. Because the spectator knows how to read, she knows how to recognise intention. You have to be able to hide intention. This hiding is a rule that governs all the rehearsals, it is the arm that guides us through the sort of resistance we were talking about earlier. Because, often, you resist hiding the idea, trying to make it enigmatic, so as not to give the idea a singular reading.

Romeo: In certain cases, I might even say always, the general conception of speaking and movement begins in stasis, it begins with the statue. The general principle, if a general principle exists, is that of moving as little as possible. Every movement comes up against its own zero, comes up against the capacity, the possibility, of not being. And this is the most interesting thing, something that gets its incentive from the deepest necessity, the necessity to push on. Just raising an arm, why do you do it? It's not an intellectual response but a necessity, and this is why there is this general tone of coldness. It doesn't come from some vitalistic principle of energy, from the expenditure of energy, there is no such thing. The same goes for the words, the use of the voice. Here, too, there is always a zero, a sustained silence at the base of everything. To move carries consequences.

Chiara: Opening the mouth carries consequences if there is no architecture around the words. In certain cases, absolutely, move as little as possible, so that the work might be packed with the forces of restraint. The actor's task isn't to express but to restrain, to hold back. In this sense, there aren't any movements without tension. There is a coming and going, which generates a very strong friction, an interior friction that is expressed through the skin. The task is to create a weight or volume and then radically reduce this volume, to let go, in a way that is coherent with the idea and, above all, with the gaze of the audience, who don't know where you are coming from. That is, it should be coherent with a point of vision, but the most open one possible. This can only be enforced, though, if there really is a volume there in the first place. Two or three times with the Strasbourg women, we thought about using African songs and typically African gestures. We rehearsed with these gestures for a while, and this was necessary work for bringing this group of people together. But then, at a certain moment, body and earth entered into such an adhesion that all of the African business became too much, and the day before the first night we got rid of everything that had anything ethnic about it. The songs, the gestures, we squeezed the work dry of them. But only because we needed to get to a root, to a minimum unity. Rehearsal is the possibility of giving the idea a body, but in its minimum possible unity.

Nick: It's often said that the rehearsal process doesn't finish with the first public performance of the show, and this is because rehearsal is a process of verification, as you've said, and because the true theatrical situation is one that includes the audience. It seems to me that this is a familiar idea and something that is said by many people who make theatre, but I have the feeling that for you this experience of verification with the audience is much more important than it might be for other theatrical groups. I have the feeling that from one evening to another, during a run, the show changes a lot. How does this happen during a show? How do you get the sort of knowledge from an evening's performance that enables you, perhaps, to make big changes?

Chiara: We follow our noses, it's not a totally rational process.

Romeo: It's like an untuned instrument.

Chiara: The craftsman comes to my mind. It's a problem of craftsmanship. It's like when the potter notices a fault in the clay. If he is experienced, he manages to save the vase. If he's not experienced, he throws it away.

Romeo: It is a problem of form and also, if you will, of rhetoric. If we change things on the day, even if these changes are contradictory, it's because, in the end, it's the work that interests us, not its truth. There is no truth. The only truth we have to offer is a form, a surface tension, a body, an epidermis, which must be more or less tense, like the mathematical structure of a musical instrument.

Chiara: Often, in these situations, it's a function of time, of rhythm. For example, it often happens at the preview that the show is twenty minutes too long and needs to be cut, which means you can remove more and make it more enigmatic.

Romeo: The time of the show is the bio-rhythm of the spectator, they are two things which must be made just so. You understand it also from the reaction of the audience, the way they move in their seats.

Chiara: Not that you watch the audience during the show, it's something you sense. That's what I mean by following our noses. I'm thinking of hunting dogs that sniff out the shortest way to the quarry. It's a question of technique. To work in the theatre, with all its traps, you need to have technique, and you also need to hide your technique, feeling all the time, at your back, the spectators' experience, the spectators' perception. Not that at the end of the show you go and interview the spectators. That's not how you understand. You understand by staying quiet. Indeed, the less that is said after a show the better. There are, though, real moments of something falling into place. It is the moment in which the show comes home to roost, against you, attaching itself to you. It is the moment of final combat, the moment of revolutionary change. You finally see the show in front of an audience as it devours itself, in the sense that you see things you can't recognise, things that don't fit any aesthetic, and so the show goes against you. You realise you still haven't tamed it. It's not a systematic process; it tends to happen in miniature. It's like testing a racing car and then counting the nuts and bolts, it's identical. It's very craftsmanlike, very practical. It's the most practical phase but also the moment of the greatest clash with the work. It's the moment of difficulty. But it was always like this. There are those moments where everything is out of control, and then, suddenly, everything clears up, thanks to some drastic realisation after the performance. These are moments of great surprise; in certain situations, they are almost unexpected.

Nick: Has the frequency of this experience changed over the past two years, with so many episodes of *Tragedia Endogonidia*?

Romeo: Yes, it has changed, because the devising time has become shorter and the process, in part, has become a process of response. One thing finishes and then the next step is, in some way, a response to what preceded it, either in the sense of a continuation or a contrast, a counterpoint. Such a short rehearsal period also means that sometimes the intelligence is replaced by the nerves: having so little time obliges you to make quick reactions, unpremeditated, which can result in a major loss of control, but also, if we want, something more unconscious, braver.

Chiara: One thing I've come to understand during these years is that if, from the first moments of rehearsals, you set about making radical choices about what to put on stage, and if there is integrity in the way you seek to realise the idea, if the procedure is solid, then, when you arrive at the end at a point of crisis, you will still be able to depend upon your material. If, though, you begin with the wrong actor, and you find yourself at the end in a crisis situation, the issue you failed to resolve at the beginning becomes an enormous problem, a chasm. It is very important that every step you make, from the first day of rehearsal until the last preview, be radical, faithful and retain its integrity with respect to the idea. Never betray the idea. Because, if you betray the idea, either through an actor or an animal who is not perfectly adapted to express the situation, or through scenography which reveals parts in which you can't recognise yourself, this defect will hold you back across the entire arc of the process, to the point where at the preview everything collapses upon you. That unresolved issue becomes a chasm in which, truly, all hope is lost. Everything that you do should, instead, be firm and rooted, even at the cost of causing a crisis for the organisation or the technical apparatus. We often have to insist upon an idea, not because of a lack of good will, but because of the way that often the ideas force the material. We ask something of the material, and, hence, we ask the people who work with the material, the technicians or the producers, to ask something of the material, to force the material, in turn. To make a car fall onto the stage, the material is forced. And if, right from the beginning, you aren't radical in what you want, confidence is lost. If, though, even if in the end the preview goes badly, you have faith and a conviction that it is impossible to stop that car falling, it will be impossible to stop. You need to proceed with this sort of attitude, and you will manage to arrive at the first night. If, though, you have left behind any doubts or defects, it's not possible to arrive at the first night. This is why it is possible, from one day to the next, to change everything, precisely because there are no unresolved problems behind your back.

Romeo: Although the plan, the system, which is what must be safeguarded, is a system superior to myself. It is a found system whose subjectivity must be respected. It has nothing to do with some superstitious idea about the artist's fantasy or imagination. When you recognise the strength of a structure, and you are in a position to restore it, just as you uncovered it, then your responsibilities fall back on the structure. Your only responsibility is to get as close as possible, without moderation, to go along the shortest path, moving the smallest possible number of muscles, doing the least possible, so as to give access to this structure which is being uncovered.

A conversation about gesture

Chiara, Claudia, Joe, Nick, Romeo

Nick: I'd like to ask about working on gesture. I remember, for example, the gesture of an old man, in *C.#11*, who did something extraordinary, a certain way of looking upwards and pointing with his finger, a very particular gesture. This man is, I know, not a professional actor, and maybe the unfamiliarity for him of being on stage plays a part here. It seems to me, though, that in order to find such gestures it might be necessary to open the work process to a species of chance. Is it possible to work towards moments like this, when, by definition, it is impossible to know what is going to happen?

Romeo: There isn't the sort of construction of gesture you might get in dance. Our attitude is very different. I believe that these gestures and postures have their origin more in a strange form of amnesia. In other words, they are not gestures that reconstruct something. Often, gestures follow a path that anyone can recognise, because gestures are forms first of all and, as such, are universal. This is the sort of gesture that is revealed in the actor you cited. It is clear and exact. His gestures have the exactness of formulas, to the extent that every spectator can recognise themselves in such gestures, not because they have studied them at school or in art books, but because the gesture imposes itself, like a form. For example, pointing at the sky. A man points at a star, and it is clear what he is doing. These are gestures which an animal can understand too. They are the same sorts of gestures which plants assume towards the light, towards the cold. It's a matter of understanding the origin of gesture, except we have lost this understanding through amnesia, we don't know it anymore. Agamben speaks about Western mankind's loss of experience.[1] Maybe this is another argument, although there are many points worth developing to do with this substantial loss of experience on the part of Western man. Even so, these gestures have a significance here. Western theatre is founded on an amnesia, on an absence, on something lacking. We don't know why we make theatre, we don't have any idea. The foundation is lost, we have lost our memory. This is the terrain on which gestures bloom. There isn't an intentional construction.

Chiara: In the case of *C.#11*, the fundamental thing was the dialogue, in the sense that there was a fair amount of dialogue in this episode, and the dialogue came first. The work on gesture was the last thing we rehearsed, and often the dialogue got cut and replaced with a gesture. Which is how, little by little, the actor came to be known.

Romeo: In *C.#11*, there was a contrast, a reaction even, going on between speech and gesture. The speech was almost naturalistic, notwithstanding the pauses. There were a lot of pauses, long pauses; pauses lower the temperature immediately. The reference, though, was to the naturalism of the cinema. The cinema influenced this show a great deal. In terms of the tension between speech and gesture, however, while the speeches were conducted in the banal language of film dialogue or cartoons, the gesturality was the sacred gesturality of saints in altarpieces. In this sense, the work on speech and gesture were going in opposing directions.

Chiara: With the music heading in a third direction, a recognisable and melodic piece of music rather than a column of sound, which followed a fixed trajectory and remained playing throughout. So there was speech and gesture, with the fixed trajectory of this song opening underneath.

Claudia: The gesture is an element that, like the word, only interests us as a thing in itself, an objective given, to the extent that it is taken on by a particular actor. For example, the gestures of high iconography derived from altarpieces in *C.#11* have a flavour and a tonality when they get applied to certain people, as was said earlier, rather than to a professional dancer. Gesture should be thought of as a dynamic

---

1 See, for example, Giorgio Agamben, 'Kommerell, or On Gesture', in *Potentialities: Collected Essays in Philsophy*, trans. Daniel Heller-Roazen, Stanford, Calif.: Stanford University Press, 1999. See also Agamben's *Infancy and History: On the Destruction of Experience*, trans. Liz Heron, London and New York: Verso, 2007.

element, which creates potential, and not as an objective code. Hence, I know that this gesture means such and such, and as such I use it so that everyone more or less can recognise what's going on. The gesture – along with the history of that gesture – only functions on stage, though, if it comes primed with the capacity to be reborn; it only works when it gets reactivated. It's a bit like the words: you can have a text that works well, a text that seems to function well enough, but which in the theatre, because it is a dead letter, fails to dominate the stage, which is the maximum point of verification for words as well as gestures. In the same way, gestures, in and of themselves, say nothing. Or rather, they say a lot; they have their story to tell, if it can be activated.

Romeo: The problem is that they say too much in some cases.

Claudia: They say, yes, but in a way that is already common knowledge. On stage, however, for there to be a word, for there to be a gesture, for these to be the first things admitted to the stage, they must be capable of enabling something to be born, so that an ultra-codified gesture such as this can be reactivated, due to that person or that actor. And, first, due to Romeo applying this gesture to that actor.

Nick: We know something about the work of painters' models because these gestures are familiar to us from painting, but I wonder if in the process of Renaissance pictorial composition there is this sort of work with models.

Romeo: In terms of the use of models in Renaissance painting, Caravaggio is an extraordinary example. To continue Agamben's reasoning, in that age there was a certain sort of experience and so it was possible to work with models. In our case, there are no models anymore, unless these are the models that emerge in the collective memory. For example, this gesture you mentioned, Nick, can indicate many things. When it's a dad showing the stars to his own son, it is a common gesture, a gesture of protection that goes back to the pharoahs. For Caravaggio, his models represented reality, but these models don't represent reality anymore. They represent a completely interior universe, something hidden, made up mainly of floating images.

Joe: In a painting by Caravaggio of *The Meal on the Road to Emmaus*, there is an old woman, a serving woman, who stands behind the other figures, a little bit apart. She looks out at us and, unlike the others, she looks like a contemporary person. She seems to have a knowledge that the others don't, about the scene that is taking place and also about us, the spectators. In terms of your work in the theatre with actors and gestures, I'm thinking of similar instances, for example, the 'soldiers of the conception' in Bergen, who perform their gestures and then laugh. This laughter seems like some sort of left-over knowledge, again to do with the scene and how it might appear to the spectators. You spoke about amnesia, but in order for there to be amnesia, there needs to have been knowledge, a knowledge which is still somehow there, left over.

Romeo: It is through amnesia, in my opinion, that the spectator is captured inside the show because there is a mirror effect. To this extent, amnesia becomes a form of knowledge, into which we are born. However, it is not an acquired knowledge. To my mind, it is a knowledge of forms.

Chiara: I'd like to bring into sharper focus the discussion of the model in the Renaissance. Romeo said that there is no experience any more, and so we don't have models any more. I believe that there are certain themes in the history of mankind. Maybe it is banal to put it like this, but there are certain things, which are just like models, and which exist always, like love, like imagination. There is still the model, even if it doesn't have this Renaissance optic. What has changed in history is simply the way of conceiving the model, but it's not true that there is no model because there is no experience.

Romeo: I'm thinking of the model as someone who stands there and makes a gesture for you.

Chiara: That's because you have a model in your memory, you're referring to an image.

Romeo: It's the model of a model; it's not a direct model.

Chiara: Look at Giacometti, who chooses that model because he had a particular facial connotation, or because they got on well, or because he was a friend or because they had this type of understanding. You, on your part, have a very precise model in mind when you choose the face of the actresses to perform in Strasbourg, or when you choose someone to perform Jesus.

Romeo: That is the form of Jesus, it's not the model. It's very different. The model, in the way Caravaggio understood it, is a very precise human figure, whereas the actor who plays Jesus is not there to be himself; he is there to support the weight of another.

Claudia: I believe that both positions could be true. I agree with Chiara that Romeo and Chiara's work is soaked in models. But perhaps to understand it better, we could use the phrase 'rhythmic form', because it's not so much a matter of form *tout court*, but of form as it is repeated in history, which is why it is called model, certainly in our history. I wouldn't say that a way of working is legitimated by *being* Italian; even so, I imagine that for non-Italians our work does come across *as* Italian, because it is completely immersed in this condition, which is a condition so rich in models. It's a slippery argument because it could appear to be saying that in as far as it is Italian, our theatre is conditioned from birth to produce a theatre in reference to these models. But if I mention Italianness, it is because throughout our history, within this existential fragment we've been living here in Italy, it is clear that these gestural models have always been in the air we breathe, models that, as Romeo says, are not to be taken up as scholarly citations or as the raw repetition of that gesture, that historical figure, that costume, that posture, that composition, that picture. They are never citations, because what counts in the model, in my opinion, is breathing life back into the material. For us, the model is like a stone, it is like an object, and to that extent an object no different to a plant or a man or any other thing. But it is an object that, as it gets touched, as it gets taken on, is reborn. Not, I repeat, like a recognisable citation, but because the gesture is born anew. As such, to my mind, I don't want to say it's universal, but it has the capacity, as something expanded and pregnant, of appearing, living and dominating, simply because it manages to come outside, because it manages to revive. One wouldn't say, though, as Romeo does, that the work is free from models, but rather swarming with models.

Romeo: We need to say what we mean by this word. It is an ambiguous word, and, between us, we are talking about three different things. A conversation of this sort can only begin with the definition of models.

Claudia: Then it is right to go down into the definition of a model.

Chiara: For me, the model is this: once the idea is clearly established, what are the elements that will give a body to this idea? It's about going in search of a body, animal, vegetable or mineral, which would be able to stay faithful to this idea, and so not be false, and so not be a hypocritical choice. The model is that which comes closest. There are novels that are false, there are languages that when you hear them, they are false.

Claudia: It's too aleatory to speak of authenticity, it's too much dependent on chance.

Romeo: This is another conception of model. To my mind, if you have a model, it means you have a very clear object you want to represent. The moment the representation is finished, the model is done with, it goes away, it leaves the stage, the model is not seen again.

Nick: Not in the theatre, because it seems to me that the theatre is complex in a particular way. I mean that the actor can be at the same time model and actor, model and picture. The fact that this man is, means perhaps that there was a model or that this man has become a model. In the process of discovery of the rehearsals, this role of model is arrived at, and the incarnation of this model is performed by the same man that was the model for it.

Chiara: I also believe that the model is something that loses its boundaries, its outline, because in the theatre you forget to look at this man; you look at his gesture, and you might look at how the fabric of his costume falls, you might see the objects around him, although you don't analyse any of that. You've seen the gesture, you haven't seen the actor. You aren't asking yourself what the actor's name is; the gesture has struck you. It's the same in certain pictures of female nudes, the sensuality isn't born from the body itself but from the surrounding objects, from the way the fabric falls. In this sense, the outline of the model needs to be hidden.

Romeo: You were talking, Claudia, about Italianness.

Claudia: I know it is a bit of an irritating topic.

Romeo: But it's something we often have to come back to.

Chiara: Especially when we take a show abroad.

Romeo: In some cases, it is more obvious, in others less so. It's a problem of surface tensions, the tensions in the surface of classical representation: the positions, the proportions, the geometries. Any of our shows can be analysed according to the parameters of classical representation. This is what is Italian about us. Perhaps it's anachronistic . . .

Claudia: You're referring to composition from the pictorial point of view.

Romeo: It's not just a question of picture, it also involves sculpture, architecture. In any case the conception of volume, of space.

Claudia: It's certainly not the Italian theatrical tradition.

Romeo: Certainly not, the Italian theatrical tradition ends with the Roman *atellanae*. Italian tradition tends to mean Pirandello, but these are conceptual problems we are talking about. We are not part of that tradition, we are closer to the theatrical problems of the Jesuit theatre.

Claudia: If we speak about 'rhythmic forms' instead of models, we might think about it in terms of going to Seoul to show *Genesi*, where there are people who don't know the book of Genesis, although we take it for granted as something that belongs to us. We take on certain forms, those of Adam, Cain and Eve, for example. All of them are models in our little European world, whether it's Middle Eastern or Western, as they are in South America, although not in India or Asia, where these models are less known. How is it, then, that *Genesi* was understood? Because the work that was done, and which makes sense to us, is a theatre that makes visible and tangible the rhythmic forms that precede these same models. They are rhythmic forms of behaviour, of gesturality, which arrive before these models and which humanity is able to comprehend.

Romeo: Then the use of the word 'model' is mistaken? The word 'model' falls into crisis in other cultural systems like Seoul's. *Genesi* was understood because there is a structure at work. The extraordinary power of a structure is that the contents don't matter. A structure, as the structuralists showed, is universal and interchangeable. A structure makes provision for the things that will occupy the places within it. The place remains invariable; that which is inside it is the variable. In this sense, if the structure of *Genesi* was understood, it was because it is a transcultural structure. It has nothing to do with the culture; hence, it has nothing to do with models.

Claudia: But it does have to do with rhythmic form.

Romeo: All forms are rhythmic, because all forms return.

Claudia: There are some forms that don't return.

Romeo: In any case, what is revealed is also a form of strength, of energy. And this, in its turn, can become a form. We were talking about gestures, and I wanted to say something else about the kind of reference that derives from iconography. There is a typical example in which the gesture is completely banal, it doesn't follow any construction, but it adapts itself in a hyperreal way to reality: it fits. An example is the second *crescita* in Avignon, in which there are some workmen doing their work. They use some tools, they eat and so on, and for the entire length of the piece the emotional dynamic falls. It keeps falling until one actor pauses, a pause so long that little by little the spectators are also able to enter this flow of time, which becomes more and more mixed up with reality. At a certain point, this actor, Claudio, gets up and goes into this white cube, throws a bucket of black paint against the walls and goes away. And so, all the gestures that had been conceived up to that point are overturned. And so gesture gets reinterpreted, unemotionally. And this is a typical conception of gesture. What it means is that the gesture doesn't reflect an immediate reality but is left until the end. A few gestures have a very long dynamic; for example, in the case of Avignon, it needed twenty minutes to carry to completion this gesture that is in fact *one* gesture, rather than lots of little gestures. In that case, it meant going back outside to put together a gesture which can be redeemed, reclaimed.

In other instances, the gestures depend upon a parasitic relation to clichés, to different spheres of activity, different domains of knowledges. For example, the gestures of the Soldiers of the Conception resemble the steps of majorettes. Another order, other universes. The work of Francesca Proia in Berlin involves certain gestures of the porn star. Other gestures derive from the circus, for example, or from languages put together in an incoherent way, or like a Eucharistic wafer. This wafer becomes an ulterior thing; it points to an ulteriority, which is to say something that doesn't belong to this world. It inaugurates the world of the stage. The reality of the show is another reality.

Joe: Is the actor responsible to this other reality? Is the gesture, in other words, a gesture on behalf of others? I'm thinking, for example, of the large group of people, about forty of them, which we see outside the theatre in Strasbourg through the glass wall at the back of the stage. They may be film extras, they may be tourists; anyway, their gestures seem to be the gestures of some 'other' group. Whoever they are, in their gestures they respresent others, maybe others who can't be here, who don't exist anymore.

Romeo: It's true those people there are silhouettes, shadows. Between us and them there is the glass. This glass is capable not only of separating but also of presenting.

Chiara: What do you mean by the word 'responsibility'?

Romeo: The responsibility of bringing a gesture before you. As a theatre-maker, as an actor, I take responsibility for doing something in front of you.

Joe: For me, responsibility might have to do with an object. I say to the other person, or someone says to me, hold this for me please, for a few moments. And I must stay here with this object. I don't know why I must, but I have said yes, so I stay here for these few moments. This is a responsibility, although it doesn't, as with the actor's reponsibility, necessarily have anything of intentionality about it.

Romeo: When we talk about responsibility, I think of the extreme case of Duchamp, who takes responsibility for saying that the bottle-opener is a sculpture. That is a gesture heavy with responsibility, full of consequences. Responsibility is a moral responsibility, in my opinion, with respect to the forms that the artist has or doesn't have. But when we speak of the responsibility of the actor, this is a more primitive responsibility. It has to do with having the courage to go before someone and be false, to declare a thing, and to declare oneself in a position to sustain the type of rhetoric on which representation is founded. Representation is a plethora, an unnecessary superabundance. The strength of the actor or of an artist is to render this thing necessary, even while it is obvious to everyone that it is not necessary to life, that it is not essential.

A conversation about the future

Chiara, Joe, Nick, Romeo

Chiara: Something has opened up for us with *Tragedia Endogonidia*, a new way of working, a new relation to technique which is likely to be modified in future, but which also, to some extent, determines that future. It involves, for example, a preoccupation with montage over narrative structure, and the openings this gives us into other arts such as cinema and music. This, perhaps, is the focus for the future.

Romeo: It's true, *Tragedia Endogonidia* has opened onto a way of working around an emptiness, or from a zero point: a work of total creation, without the rhetorical assurance of a text or the sort of pre-existing literary or theatrical structures that we used in pieces like *Amleto, Giulio Cesare* or *Genesi*. It's like being in a state of drift, without being able to make out any reference points, given that the idea of tragedy is itself founded upon a loss of memory, upon an idea of ruin, of incompleteness. There is something missing, an emptiness. None of us knows what a tragedy is. Even after all the important books that have been written about it, something of tragedy is still missing. This state of drift will probably continue into the future. Even so, it is not certain that the future work will not involve narration.

Narration also has a structure that can be assimilated. To my mind, the last episode, *C.#11*, has a narrative.

Chiara: However, it's also true that the idea of *Tragedia Endogonidia* was to do with a self-reproducing system, like an organism. And this isn't just a theoretical idea removed from any practical process. In fact, *C.#11* was, perhaps, the moment of greatest friction with this system. Right from the start, though, each show would be a reference point for the show that was being made next. It really was the case that inside the initial core there was the possibility of generating other forms, and with total freedom as regards theatrical language. Communication was not the issue. This freedom to found a new language every time was perhaps the strongest aspect of *Tragedia Endogonidia*, as it will be in the future. To be able to move any which way, with no concern other than a concern for formal coherence, although even then all forms are possible.

Romeo: What Chiara says about the organism is right. It was a process that developed irrespective of any preconceived plan. There wasn't time to plan. The development of *Tragedia* was like the growth of an organism, like an endocrinal potential. It was, and remains, a system of ramification, a system that expands in space, like a tree.

Chiara: And so, in future, it might well arrive at narrative, but it might just as well not. What was established was the system, and this is much more important than the individual episodes. In fact, in future, it could be possible to do without the titles made up of numbers and initials but retain the subtitle, 'from *Tragedia Endogonidia*', because it is the system that interests us: a concept of theatre that goes back to *Tragedia Endogonidia*, a way of seeing, a way of existing . . .

Romeo: . . . a way of seeing that, even so, is not our 'expressive' invention. There is still the problem of really taking on the word 'tragedy', of getting to the bottom of it as an invincible form not just of theatre but also of the Western system of representation. As we know, so many things derive from the tragic system of representation that in a certain sense, tragedy is an obligatory choice. It is a way of knowing how to see. It's not about making tragic things but seeing in a tragic way. Because all human spectacles have a tragic basis, whether we are talking about television, comedy, circuses . . .

Nick: If the tragic is an element of all Western representation, is this to do with the fact of a problem, a tension, a complex relation, between the world and the image?

Romeo: Yes, I think so. There is a basic formation that involves a problem, a tension. To be situated in front of an image means being situated before a *detached* image, something removed from its context, its background. Because this is what an image is. The Western experience of the image is of something cut out from the general context, so that the context no longer exists; it is lost, probably from the moment the gods died. This is a hypothesis, but maybe, even so, a way of bearing witness to the negative foundation of images in the West. An image can't be a positive affirmation anymore; it can't be a link between the Heavens and the Earth anymore as it is in the East. This is what characterises the Western image. Also, the Western image is condemned to progress; it has to keep going forwards, on and on and on. This is a source of distress. What matters is not so much researching the new, but researching how to be new in front of the image, how to be surprised, how to find the proper origin of the image. These are, though, in every way, hypotheses.

Joe: Might this link back to the question of narrative? I'm thinking again of the narrative element in the last episode of *Tragedia*. For me, it is true that over the eleven episodes as a whole there is no narrative; the sequence is not an epic. Even so, within each episode, there is always the possibility of narration; indeed, it is inevitable. For example, in a non-narrative episode like Brussels, there is a figure, then darkness, then another figure, then darkness and so on. We see a baby on stage, and it is just that: a baby. However, it is also possible that the old man we see in a later scene can be understood, by the spectator, as the baby at a later stage of life. The work of the spectator, then, is the work of making narration. I think that if we say that in all Western representations there is something tragic, then for me this tragic element has to do with narrative. It could be that the tragic aspect of the spectacle, for the spectators, is in that narrative possibility, its perpetual beginning. It is impossible to live in the world without this process of narration. Through these narrations, we conceive our futures. And this is what happens in the theatre, a projection into the future, a way of 'narrativism'.

Chiara: Narration, however, is only born where there is an experience. I believe that the theatre, being amongst the most powerful of the arts in as much as it manages to be 'real' – or rather, in as much as it substitutes for reality – is responsible for enabling an experience. If there is an experience, then I can leave the theatre and tell about what I saw. And, because narration is not only about the connections between the various figures, this first telling is also a theoretical process. All that I can actually tell, though, is, 'in a marble room there was a baby'. The wager of these episodes is that they may have a narrative, but that narrative is reinvented on the basis of experience, because otherwise we fall into a consolatory way of speaking: 'I liked this show because I understood it'. Instead, the wager of every episode is that, irrespective of having understood the montage, I manage to tell what I saw, which means I am able to perceive an emotion.

For example, what are the connections between the cars that fall onto the stage in the Paris episode and the figure of Jesus who stands upon the stage as the cars are falling? Of course, it is all rather disagreeable. It is too much, and it might even seem forced. On paper, you have doubts at the theoretical level. But when you see it, it is the emotion that restores the narrative to you, because that narrative involves you singularly, it looks at you. At this point, it leaps over any 'universal' narrative laws. And this is the point, in any of the episodes, where a language might be founded: the language of experience. And we make that first telling possible when, in the process of constructing the work, we say to ourselves, 'What, as a spectator, do I see?'

If the figure is clear and crystalline, then I can tell what I see, I mean, as long as it is crystalline in its enigma. If, instead, it is contorted, confused and overcharged with meaning, weighed down with the theoretical thought leaning over it, you won't be able to tell a thing.

Romeo: Especially if it is surreal. The grave danger is surrealism; the automatism of surrealism is the worst thing. There is a great difference between a surreal image and an enigmatic image. In the enigma, there is always a system, like a bomb that needs defusing, although there is a logic to it. The surreal image is an automatic image, a decoration for the spirit; its shock is a pseudo-shock. To go back, then, to what Chiara said about emotion: it may be that at the narrative level a few elements don't work, but when the meeting with reality happens in rehearsal, you find yourself in front of an objective presence, as unquestionable as the mass of three automobiles hitting the ground. It is a presence, a display of force and weight and mass that is beyond discussion. The same goes for the indifference of an animal: it has an objective weight, there is nothing to discuss. Or the scene in the Brussels episode of the old man on his knees; this also has an objective presence, as does the baby. Everything becomes invincible to the extent that it is innocent, objective.

Chiara: May I ask you something? What is it that makes the fall of the three automobiles not just a spectacle but a dramatic thing? In the theatre, to have three cars falling onto the stage, this is something spectacular, demonstrative. Except, in reality, it is dramatic. When they hit the ground, I am almost moved. So what is the process by which the most extraordinary thing in each show can come across not as 'spectacle' but as drama? I'm thinking that this is the wager of the individual ideas, because taken in themselves, none of the individual ideas are anything more than that: 'good ideas'.

Romeo: I think it has to do with what we were saying earlier. They are objective presences, and that's because they are physically there in front of you. I remember the wind and the noise of the cars as they fell, the physical sound.

Chiara: But take, for example, the wind that blows into the auditorium in C.#11. It is something spectacular, but even so, it is dramatic . . .

Romeo: . . . because it involves the whole of the spectator's body. There are these objective presences, but then there is also the combination of these objective presences. The three cars work because at the same time there is a woman on stage squeezing her breast, unable to produce any milk. There is also the silent figure of Jesus. There is a pause, and in the pause, the cars fall onto the stage, during Jesus's silence. It is a sacred image, like a contemporary altarpiece.

Chiara: A silence that is also created by the orchestra that has gone away.

Romeo: It's like a sequence, inside of which there is also the fall of the cars.

Chiara: Every element of the narrative is put in its place, contained and, so, protected. Your experience, then, is drawn into a very specific, particular ambit.

Nick: So that when the cars fall, these are the dramatic points, within the specific context, that outline a rhythmic logic: points in space and time.

Romeo: It's also pure drama, a representation of drama as a clash between two realities.

Chiara: It is drama in its briefest and most intense form possible. Maybe it is worked out at a rational level, but it happens to you at an emotional level. Actually, the practical work is very often about preparing the place in which to gather the figures. If objects were accumulated on stage in the preceding action, these objects have to be removed so that this other figure can be inserted. Having other objects there at the same time is distracting. The figure must arrive in an absolutely controlled place, there shouldn't be any flaws. Every little detail becomes part of the language of that figure, which is why the place has to be protected. This is the overlap with the logic of classical representation, with iconographic and pictorial representation. In the theatre, there is movement, but for the figure to be seen, it must be isolated in an image, a fixed image like a photo; but you can only isolate the image if the context is clean, which is why for us the theatre is often not just about movement but also stasis.

Romeo: This is also because the brain of the spectator is like a cine-camera, it is selective.

Chiara: At certain moments, we look at the theatre like a photo, or like a picture. If anything of the preceding action remains, just a rag, a scrap of fabric, it has to be got rid of; otherwise, it ruins the figure that comes next. It's a concept of theatre as harmonic construction, in all its parts, in a moment of stasis. It has to be absolutely perfect, in tune with the idea.

Joe: The idea of the theatrical image as a picture or photograph reminds me of an earlier conversation we had about models and actors. The key distinction there, I suppose, would be that the artist's model is not in the same space as the image anymore, whereas the theatrical actor still is – as, too, are the spectators, who are present 'here and now'. I'm thinking too about Georges Didi-Huberman's analysis of the photographs of 'hysterical' women collected at the Salpêtrière hospital in Paris at the end of the nineteenth century.[1] Didi-Huberman reads these images, in part, in terms of

---

[1] Georges Didi-Huberman, *Invention of Hysteria: Charcot and the Photographic Iconography of the Salpêtrière*, trans. Alisa Hartz, London: MIT Press, 2003.

performance, little hysterical dramas around which it seems possible to construct a narration or a diagnosis. One thing that the writer suggests, however, is that the photographer always appears to arrive late. There is a sense of something 'out of phase' between the image and the life that it appears to bear witness to. In the photographic images, there is something sentimental, nostalgic even. If, then, on stage (which would include the stage of these women's 'live' performances at Professor Charcot's Tuesday Lectures), there is something tragic in the images instead, it has to do, perhaps, with this 'here and now'. It could be that we are unable to process the moment as it happens, for example, as we watch the figure of Jesus standing there on the stage. But, even so, something happens. And it happens right now.

Romeo: The fact of being 'in flight' renders the image tragic. You are there but you can't stop it.

Joe: It is a question, perhaps, of the event of the image. I'm thinking of someone who sees, say, an episode of *Tragedia* in their own city – sees it, and then it goes. It is an experience of an encounter with something which is, nevertheless, constantly changing. Does this experience, this event, mitigate against conserving the episodes as pieces of repertoire? Is there something in this work that demands that it happens just the one time?

Romeo: Yes, it's like being before a fire that burns and then passes away. Not being in the repertoire, they can't be brought back into the memory. Their presence is more flagrant. It's not possible for another group, one day, to put on the Paris episode.

Chiara: I think that this is a logical error. When the work has taken place, it becomes a 'classic' of its age. Which means it is possible to remake these shows. Some better than others, but they don't decay. Conceptually, at least, I believe it could be possible.

Romeo: I don't believe it. It would be like trying to remake a performance.

Nick: But there is the possibility for one spectator to have several encounters with the same show?

Chiara: The same spectator can see the show ten times, yes. I think, though, we shouldn't confuse the theoretical problem with the practical aspect. We are having a theoretical, and therefore utopian, conversation. In the theoretical and utopian conversation, I say: for me, in today's theatre, it is absurd to take a piece of Shakespeare and put it on the stage. It is absurd. If the text is the fulcrum of the production, it is not possible to invent upon this text and stay true to the text at the same time. It's something that doesn't make any sense anymore; it's nostalgic, like lyric opera. Of course, I am talking theoretically; I am taking up a position.

Right now, the problem has shifted, which means no one in the contemporary theatre is writing dramatic texts any longer, so much as they are concerned with founding a new dramaturgy. There are new dramaturgical forms that are developing new concepts in relation to the theatrical tradition, and we need to take note of them. New dramaturgies are being written, in the sense that there are some very interesting shows being made. I see these shows, I take note of them, and what I derive from them is a dramaturgy: a text. And that text is a new idea of theatre, a new way of writing. If, then, I hear that text after some years, and it still sounds urgent, if it survives the years, then I can put it on stage because it is a dramaturgy in action. This is the theory. In practice, it is another matter.

Nick: To me, this seems to be something that is already going on in the dramaturgy of Beckett and might be the reason why the Beckett estate are so demanding when it comes to productions of his plays. Beckett is a terminal point for dramatic writing; but, from another direction, he is a point of departure.

Chiara: The contemporary theatre doesn't have a lot of time for writing, though, and in Beckett there was a lot of writing.

Romeo: A writing which always alludes more and more to silence.

Chiara: Certainly, although that's how it points towards another phase.

Romeo: To my mind, we still live in the sphere of Beckett. He is a sort of point, or lever, around which everything has shifted. There are artists who attempt to break away by trying to affirm something. Beckett is Copernicus, a Copernican revolution.

Chiara: I think that at the moment something else is going on, although I'm not certain.

Romeo: Beckett's work can't be avoided. You can't pretend that he doesn't exist, although there is a part of the theatre which carries on as if Beckett had never existed.

Chiara: Thinking of the future, and trying not to simplify the thought too much as I put it into words, there is one sort of tension that has to do with working without the consolation of a text; but there is another which involves doing without the consolation of a theoretical apparatus. At the moment, a lot of experimental theatre only seems able to step on stage if it has a strong theoretical apparatus to justify it. Theatre, right now, is divided between those who still use words in a traditional manner, with an anachronistic vision of theatre, whether they are dramatic texts or texts taken from literature; and, on the other hand, an abstract theatre, safe in itself only so far as it has a theoretical apparatus behind it.

Nick: I think that I know some of the theatres you are talking about, but could you say a bit more about the type of theoretical apparatuses that you mean?

Chiara: *Tragedia Endogonidia* for one. It is a theoretical apparatus that has to be explained every time a show is put on. I have to explain that it is an episode, that it has a strange title and so on. It's too much.

Romeo: Although *Tragedia* can also be seen by someone who knows absolutely nothing of this. The first level of involvement is cortical, in my opinion: it takes place in the cerebral cortex. You are there as a sentient being before an event.

Chiara: It needs to be even more radical, the theory needs to disappear totally, to the point where you forget you are in a theatre.

Nick: In which case, it may be necessary to eliminate the word 'tragedy'. I'm not sure that the theoretical apparatus of *Tragedia Endogonidia* is consolatory and self-justifying, but if it's a case of solving the problem in a radical way, it may be necessary to eliminate the word 'tragedy', which is already a theoretical apparatus.

Joe: It seems to me that there are different sorts of theoretical apparatus. There is one sort of theory, a written theory, the theory we get from theoretical authors. However, if we go back to our conversations about rehearsals and the sorts of decisions that get made in relation to actors and materials, decisions, for example, about the rhythm of the work, this seems to be a different sort of theory, which has to do with a spectator's way of seeing, not an author's; a theory that has to do with intuition.

Chiara: I agree with this, but I was talking about something else, about theatre-makers who use theoretical preoccupations to justify their work. There are many contemporary groups making work based upon literary authors, unknown authors, as if this is sufficient justification.

Romeo: In this sense, dance is more exposed, more open to disaster.

Chiara: For example, one of the strongest things I have seen recently is the work of Habillé d'Eau, whose work is immediately self-revealing, simply by virtue of their deciding to be on stage in that particular way.[2]

Romeo: Again, it's like standing in front of a fire. You can't take your eyes off it because it is there, a presence.

Chiara: There's nothing you need beyond the pleasure of being there. It confirms your own decision about going to the theatre. And, when you leave the theatre, there is a superstructure that continues to grow, and that burns you, like a fire, and whose logic is this: you burn me, and I cannot *not* burn. This fire cannot be calmed, as if it had touched something outside of my reason, outside of my conception. There is no consolation of any sort. I have understood nothing, except that this is the situation in which I find myself. This, I believe, is the future of the theatre.

Romeo: For me, the future of the theatre is that of the spectator. Perhaps this project, *Tragedia*, was an attempt to go in this direction. In all probability, it is an incomplete attempt, and only a step, towards this dimension of the art of the spectator, and no longer of the artist.

Chiara: Towards where the drama of the spectator happens, because the spectator lives a drama. It burns you, and you don't want to burn, but you are burned anyway, it burns you inside. A drama is in operation, the drama of the spectator.

---

2 Habillé d'Eau are a company founded in Italy in 2002 by Silvia Rampelli.

PART THREE

Disjecta Membra

Entries from a notebook of Romeo Castellucci

- A burns victim immediately after the accident. Many areas of his body are now without skin, areas of exposed flesh have been seared by the flames, and his face is completely disfigured. He is alone in the middle of the stage, lying on a hospital stretcher. He speaks under his breath. It is a kind of delirious monologue. With some difficulty, we are able to make out that it is a speech about light.
- Bearded children in a white room.
- A metal thread that leads from the mouth of a man to the ear of a little girl. The man whispers something. The thread starts to heat up, to smoke and finally glow incandescent red.
- An actor has to breathe nitrogen dioxide.
- The Wizard of Oz. Oz to Ur of the Chaldees. Oz to Ur. The Wizard of Ur. The Wizard of Ur goes to Oz with ice crampons and 1920s mountaineering equipment.
- Fight symbols with symbols. To have done with symbols. To have done with culture in general.
- A girl, her back to us, in a far corner, beats furiously on a big drum. She stops and only then do we hear her crying.
- A 'Shakespeare barbecue'. What would that mean?

- The golden knees of an adolescent.
- A girl sings, on her feet in the middle of a room where the floor is covered with chlorine; she sings a sad song under her breath.
- A black flag swinging through the space succeeds in 'extinguishing' the lights on the stage by capturing the light within its folds. One light after another goes out until they are all extinguished. Darkness.
- Actors clothed and completely covered in black rubber with aqualungs and breathing tubes. A flautist, dressed identically. Fetishism of speech. The sound of breathing.
- The time of an action is determined by the time it takes to boil an egg.
- Beating a pile of soft pink blankets with a baseball bat. The destructive fury of interpretation.
- A pistol shot that gives life.
- Someone constantly hungry for oxygen. They breathe quickly, deeply. All the time.
- A beginning that is off the rails, comic, textual, narrative, with costumes.
- Burning some Chanel No. 5 on an incandescent sword. Perfume steam. An adolescent libation. Chanel No. 5 in place of the Holy Spirit.
- Using not a 'text' but a system of phrases. The greatness of the system. The greatness of structure. The greatness of structuralism.
- And then Tocqueville. 'Democracy in America' as a possible title. But it should have nothing in its argument that has anything to do with the theses of the book in question.
- Furs, pubic hairs, sugar.
- Flashes of red light. With each flash of light there is a dry noise, like an electrical detonation.
- Manure and folklore. Popular dance in a tradition that has never existed. Precision in the costumes, in the details.
- Two light boxes either side of the stage. 'L' and 'R', white and red, respectively. They light up alternately in time with an electrical sound. Left and Right as two characters. The Scylla and Charybdis of the stage. 'Left' and 'Right' as the demons of the stage space. Tweedledum and Tweedledee.
- The theatre I respect is antibiotic. I hide myself behind theatre to escape biography, biographies. The horror of biography.
- Aesthetics v. Ethics. I always, always hide behind Aesthetics.
- A blind dog and a white laser beam. Alone on the stage.
- A red neon slowly dipped into a tank of black oil. In and out. Many times.
- A geometry of smoke in front of a dark red wall.
- A girl's 'Easter'. She punches the lamb and bitter herbs with steel-coated fists.
- A television which explodes. Twice.

- The tremendous power of the banality of this age; the even stronger banality of prayer.
- In the dark, a large black horse is bathed in milk.
- A rigid black face. A man who is looking for something or someone; and a little boy hiding beneath a bush, so that we can only see his knees.
- Repeatedly punching a hard, wet leather cushion.
- A bed from the 1940s, red sheets and pillows. A white horse enters the child's bedroom and eats hay from the bed, as if it were a manger.
- A suite of gym machines that 'come to life' and function on their own. High amplification. The microphones pick up and make a din of the pneumatic and hydraulic mechanisms that move the parts of the machinery.
- Smoke that rises up in front of a dark red wall.
- A snack eaten in solitude.
- Trying to disappear in front of the audience; not moving a muscle, not taking a step.
- Someone naked, their skin coloured silver, in the half-darkness of a black room. The floor is covered in straw.
- The entire action takes place behind a great black window. Night blue.
- A big countdown display at the back of the stage. On stage, there is just a chimpanzee. The countdown starts at twenty minutes. And at zero?
- Kneeling with one knee on a little fish. Looking at oneself over one's shoulder.
- Men wearing black rubber with black rubber masks. They carry out abstract and codified ceremonies around the naked body of a very small and very white man – a very old man? a little boy? – are they carrying out a circumcision? They place across his chest a black sash on which 'Yamaha' is written in white. No one speaks. Everyone breathes.
- The light comes on. A diorama faithfully representing a primitive landscape: two 'Neanderthals', one male and one female (represented hyper-realistically), have sex with each other. No pretence. Once the sexual encounter is over, the male gets up. End of performance.
- Taking turns to play at being crucified. Laughing.
- A completely black cartoon speech bubble descends onto an actor wearing ancient underpants.
- A mucus red stage. Pink light. Brown walls.
- In a shiny black room. A young woman elegantly dressed in black with a red flag that doesn't move, amidst twelve big black horses who tremble.
- A deer, free on the stage, which looks blurred behind a semi-transparent PVC curtain. The idea of dawn. The idea of fog. A panorama appears to be a long way away.
- Right to left. Left to right. In shoes. In words.

- Wiping up sweat with a handkerchief taken from a trouser pocket. The end.
- After completing a series of pirouettes in the empty space, a ballerina leaves the stage. Darkness. Light. There now appears on stage a tangle of curved slender iron tubes that visually represent the ballerina's pirouettes and that fill the entire space. The metal coils prevent anyone from entering.
- A bean plant grows out of the arse of an old man who is searching on all fours for something he has lost.
- Throwing dice. From the dice throws, the letters of the actress's own name are obtained. She writes them one by one on the back wall with a silver spray can.
- And then the Soldiers of the Conception.
- An infinite series of black curtains (forty or fifty) which open one after another (they have pieces of white material sewn onto them, in different shapes), until they reach the back of the stage. At the end, the brick wall of the theatre can be seen. The end.
- Washing a leather armchair really well. Washing it with water and soap, with scrubbing brushes and sponges. Washing it thoroughly, with commitment and determination.
- A machine on stage that breathes and that smokes 5,000 cigarettes at the same time. It is laid on the ground. The whole of the centre of the stage is filled. It's a sort of big spiny carpet. For each cigarette, there is a nozzle and a little tube. The waves of smoke are synchronised with each other. Then the synchronisation breaks down and something new is created. Different geometrical patterns. When the cigarettes are finished: the end. Darkness.
- A black wooden wall between the audience and the stage. A white frame opens a gap through which the performance can be seen. With each scene, the frame changes. Note: it is not the scene that changes, it is just the hole in the wood, taking the form of a star, a circle, a pentagon, a moon, animals, people.
- A big white painting comes on stage on two slender legs. In reality, this is an actor who is carrying the painting like an enormous shield which hides him completely from view. The actor is walking on two very thin stilts, like insect legs. The impression is that of seeing a giant abstract walking on two spindly legs. At a given moment, the actor falls to the ground to reveal his presence, naked. Here, on the ground, he speaks and weeps.
- A stick-man, like pipe-cleaners, comes on stage, completely out of context with respect to what has come before. The stick-man is grasping a pistol and shoots. It's a big and completely abstract puppet, made out of wood alone. At the end of this, like an arm, a pistol appears, which fires for real. The stick-man is furious.
- A white neo-classical wall in front of which dirty actions unfold.
- Work on time. Time alone.

- The laments of Oliver Hardy as the cries of humanity confronted by the end of the life of the species.
- A show with the title *Americana*. A show without a subject.
- A man with a black face that is oozing something. An enormous quantity of viscous scum. A lament is heard, coming from the man, who stays on his feet all the time.
- Working around the idea of vision purified of everything. Light. Atmosphere. Vibration of luminous fasces.
- The trumpeting of elephants.
- No eros. No INRI.
- A big black cloth falls unexpectedly to fill the whole frame of the stage, spontaneously cutting through the representation. Written on it in white: STORY. There is just time to read it. Then darkness.
- A trilogy the first part of which is completely without humans.
- A little boy arrives by boat.
- A resin and silicone mould that awaits and presupposes a gesture: always.
- An army of little miniaturised men who silently invade the stage and take it over.
- A series of *prie dieus* from the future.
- Redon's *Armour* with slender spines.
- Unexpectedly, at the back of the stage, a character from Beatrix Potter crosses furtively.
- A tank of 'x' with prussic acid and grass.
- Black and golden stones which roll around the stage, remote-controlled.
- Fifty or 100 white mice free on a red floor. 'Pink noise'.
- A white, deep-pile carpet spreads over the stage. In some areas, glass shapes press down upon it.
- A white man with white eyes, white gloves and black knee-pads plays a perfectly silent white grand piano – the strings don't sound – to the dismay of a number of white rabbits. There's a white top hat somewhere. Only the sound of his fingers on the silent keyboard of the piano can be heard.
- A big circular hole in the back wall through which we see the image – reflected by a mirror placed at an angle – of a pane of glass suspended above it on which a man, for example, is walking. The feet of the man are seen from below. Or the belly of an animal.
- We catch sight of a little boy with an abnormal erection. His ejaculation invades the stage to coincide with the arrival on stage of a submarine.
- An albino man sitting on the floor hitting a little pile of sugar with a stick.
- Straight black vertical lines that shoot up from the bottom of the stage to the top at different speeds. They fill the entire visual field.

- A Leda frantic for a swan. They are not seen. The 'sound' of their coupling.
- A seat with a structure that tilts. To the right. To the left.
- A low glass structure which replicates Pavlov's labyrinth, with a cat and a bell, a bowl of food and stuff like that.
- Stitching and embroidery on the metal frame that protects the head of a microphone.
- Blood in the golden chamber. An empty, silent chamber; electrolysis of blood. Powder of blood.
- A whole series of little characters with white eyes who busy themselves with the lights, the tips of their fingers covered in little black hoods.
- A stout, pallid person dangling flippers. Presumably naked. Whitened by chlorine. Head thrown back.
- A man puts on a pair of shoes overflowing with brown blood.
- Writing carved into panels. It only becomes visible when a dark liquid is poured over it.
- An operating theatre in surgical green, equipped with medical instruments. A group of apes freely occupy the space.
- A mechanical bow shoots arrows into the wall of a golden room.
- Breaking bones mechanically. A mechanical press squeezes slowly down on the skull of a cow. The only sound on stage. A professional contortionist carries out exercises in bodily dislocation.
- A real rifle range for air rifles. Those who shoot are wearing red leather with white stripes. Close-fitting costumes.
- An old woman seen from the back; only the hairs on her neck move.
- Fruit bats let loose in a Second Empire room.
- An object (like a dead light-bulb) slides down a track that cuts diagonally across the stage, repeatedly knocking to the ground the hat of a man who ostentatiously puts it back on. Fifteen minutes.
- A whole series of cretinous and depressing gags. In the end it becomes a scene of sadness.
- 'Red' applause? What would that mean?
- A curtain made of real hair.
- Wrought iron baroque railings in which a black actor is trapped. He can neither move forward nor backward however hard he tries. (*The Nigger of the Narcissus* by Joseph Conrad.)
- Moses with the tablets of the law made out of frozen milk.
- An inanimate man tied to the back of a door.
- Two lovers embrace. Then they look out into the auditorium, at the audience, for a long time. With immense sadness.

- All the actors have moustaches.
- A street at night. The 1940s. Seen from above. A man with a hat is walking along it (he is tied with an invisible thread so that the steps he takes are on what, in reality, is a vertical support). A tram passes.
- A series of professional mourners from the Balkans. They weep all the time.
- A black wall of shining steel, reflective, as large as the back of the stage. Little by little, slowly, it curls in on itself with the sound of metal buckling.

Theatography

Cenno. An apartment at 40 via Michelangelo Buonarroti, Rome, November 1980.
Diade incontro a Monade. Teatro La Piramide, Rome, April 1981.
Persia-Mondo 1 a 1. Accademia di Belle Arti, Bologna, June 1981.
Popolo zuppo. Teatro La Soffitta, Bololgna, May 1982.
I fuoriclasse della bontà. Teatro Bonci, Cesena, March 1983.
Oratoria No. 1: Rimpatria Artistica. Lavatoio Contumaciale, Rome, March 1983.
Oratoria No. 2: Raptus. Spazio Zero, Rome, February 1984.
Oratoria No. 3: Interferon. Galleria Nazionale d'Arte Moderna, Rome, September 1984.
Kaputt Necropolis. Cantieri Navali, Venice Biennale, October 1984.
Glory Glory, alleluja. 'Theatre in the Piazza' festival, Santarcangelo, July 1985.
Santa Sofia: Teatro Khmer. Teatro Bonci, Cesena, January 1986.
Oratoria No. 4: Tohu Wa Bohu (Apparenze pre-mondiali). Teatro delle Moline, Bologna, March 1984.
I Miserabili. Teatro Petrella, Longiano, February 1987.
Oratoria No. 5: Sono consapevole dell'odio che tu nutria per me. Acquasparta Terme, September 1987.
Alla bellezza tanto antica. Teatro Petrella, Longiano, February 1988.
Il gran reame dell'adolescenza. Trilogy of *La cripta degli adolescenti, L'adolescente sulla torre d'avorio,* and *Oratoria No. 5.* 'Theatre in the Piazza' festival, Santarcangelo, July 1988.
La Discesa di Inanna. Teatro Alfieri, Montemarciano, March 1989.
Gilgamesh. Instituto Vannicola, San Benedetto del Tronto, February 1990.
Iside e Osiride. Teatro Petrella, Longiano, December 1990.
Ahura Mazda. Laboratori Meccanici Comandini, Cesena, September 1991.

Amleto. La veemente esteriorità della morte di un mollusco. Laboratori Meccanici Comandini, Cesena, January 1992.

Le favole di Esopo. Laboratori Meccanici Comandini, Cesena, April 1992.

Masoch: I trionfi del teatro come Potenza passiva, colpa e sconfitta. Teatro Comandini, Cesena, January 1993.

Hänsel e Gretel. Teatro Comandini, Cesena, April 1993.

Lucifero: Quanto più una parola è vecchia tanto più va a fondo. Teatro dell'Officina, Polverigi, July 1993.

Oratoria No. 6: con evidenza per coloro che intendono. Teatro dell'Officina, Polverigi, July 1993.

Persona. Cocoricò discotheque, Riccione, 31 December 1993–1 January 1994.

Festa Plebea, with *Oratoria No. 7: anche il peggiore può parlare, ma non deve farlo per me.* Teatro Comandini, Cesena, March 1994.

Le fatiche di Ercole. Teatro Comandini, Cesena, May 1994.

Orestea (una commedia organica?). Teatro Fabbricone, Prato, April 1995.

Buchettino. Teatro Comandini, Cesena, May 1995.

Pelle d'asino. Teatro Comandini, Cesena, April 1996.

Giulio Cesare. Teatro Fabbricone, Prato, March 1997.

Ophelia. Art Performing Festival, Toga (Japan), August 1997.

La prova di un altro mondo. Teatro Comandini, Cesena, April 1998.

Genesi: From the Museum of Sleep. TTA Theatre, Holland Festival, Amsterdam, May 1999.

Voyage au bout de la nuit. Villa Medici, Romaeuropa Festival, July 1999.

Uovo di bocca. Accademia Albertina, Turin, May 2000.

Il Combattimento. Luna Theatre, KunstenFestivaldesArts, Brussels, June 2000.

Tragedia Endogonidia, C.#01. Teatro Comandini, Cesena, January 2002.

Tragedia Endogonidia, A.#02. Baraque Chabran, Festival d'Avignon, Avignon, July 2002.

Tragedia Endogonidia, B.#03. Hebbel Theater, Berlin, January 2003.

Tragedia Endogonidia, BR.#04. La Raffinerie, KunstenFestivaldesArts, Brussels, May 2003.

Tragedia Endogonidia, BN.#05. Bergen International Festival, Bergen, May 2003.

Tragedia Endogonidia, P.#06. Odéon, Théâtre de l'Europe, Festival d'Automne, Paris, October 2003.

Tragedia Endogonidia, R.#07. Teatro Valle, Romaeuropa Festival, Rome, November 2003.

Tragedia Endogonidia, S.#08. Le Maillon, Strasbourg, February 2004.

Tragedia Endogonidia, L.#09. Laban, London International Festival of Theatre, London, May 2004.

Tragedia Endogonidia, M.#10. Théâtre du Gymnase and Théâtre des Bernardines, Marseille, September 2004.

Tragedia Endogonidia, C.#11. Teatro Comandini, Cesena, December 2004.

Cryonic Chants (with Scott Gibbons). Festa Elettronica-Romaeuropa Festival, Rome, 2004.

Hey Girl! Odéon, Théâtre de l'Europe, Festival d'Automne, Paris, November 2006.

Bibliography

Publications by Socìetas Raffaello Sanzio

Il teatro iconoclasta, Socìetas Raffaello Sanzio, Ravenna: Edizioni Essegi, 1989.
La Discesa di Inanna, Romeo Castellucci, Cesena: Edizioni Casa del Bello Estremo, 1989.
Gilgamesh, Romeo Castellucci, Cesena: Edizioni Casa del Bello Estremo, 1990.
La Mistica del Corpo, Claudia Castellucci, Cesena: Edizioni Casa del Bello Estremo, 1990.
Disputa sul natura del teatro, Giuseppe Bartolucci, Claudia Castellucci et al., Cesena: Edizioni Casa del Bello Estremo, 1990.
Disputa sull'atto di creazione, Marco Belpoliti, Claudia Castellucci et al., Cesena: Edizioni Casa del Bello Estremo, 1991.
Amleto: La veemente esteriorità della morte di un mollusco, Romeo Castellucci, Vienna: Wiener FestWochen, 1992.
Il teatro della Socìetas Raffaello Sanzio: Dal teatro iconoclasta alla super-icona, Claudia and Romeo Castellucci, Milan: Ubulibri, 1992.
Masoch: I trionfi del teatro come Potenza passiva, colpa e sconfitta, Romeo Castellucci, Cesena: Edizioni Casa del Bello Estremo, 1995.
Orestea (una commedia organica?), Romeo Castellucci, Cesena: Edizioni Casa del Bello Estremo, 1995.
Diario della Scuola sperimentale di teatro infantile. Anno I/Anno II, Chiara Guidi, Cesena: Edizioni Casa del Bello Estremo, 1996/7.

Giulio Cesare, Romeo Castellucci, Cesena: Edizioni Casa del Bello Estremo, 1997.
Genesi: From the Museum of Sleep, Romeo Castellucci, Cesena: Edizioni Casa del Bello Estremo, 1999.
Voyage au bout de la nuit, Chiara Guidi, Cesena: Edizioni Casa del Bello Estremo, 1999.
Uovo di bocca, Claudia Castellucci, Turin: Bollati Boringhieri, 2000.
Rhetorica: Mene Tekel Peres. Catalogue for Romeo Castellucci's exhibition. Rome: Edizioni Aldo Miguel Grompone, 2000.
Epopea della polvere: Il teatro della Socìetas Raffaello Sanzio 1992–1999, Claudia and Romeo Castellucci, Chiara Guidi, Milan: Ubulibri, 2001.
Les Pèlerins de la matière: Théorie et praxis du theatre, Claudia and Romeo Castellucci, Besançon: Les Solitaires Intempestifs, 2001.
To Carthage then I Came. Catalogue for Romeo Castellucci's exhibition. Claudia Castellucci, Joe Kelleher and Nicholas Ridout, Arles: Actes Sud, 2002.
Idioma Clima Crono: Quaderni della Tragedia Endogonidia, nine volumes, Céline Astrié, Joe Kelleher, Nicholas Ridout et al., Cesena: Culture 2000 of European Union, 2002–4.
Epitaph, Socìetas Raffaello Sanzio and Romeo Castellucci, Milan: Ubulibri, 2003.
Hey Girl!, Romeo Castellucci and Socìetas Raffaello Sanzio. Photographs by Francesco Raffaelli. Cesena, 2006. Book of images to accompany premiere at Odéon: Théâtre de L'Europe with the Paris Festival d'Automne, 2006.

Other books

Giannachi, Gabriella and Nick Kaye, *Staging the Post-Avant-Garde: Italian Experimental Performance after 1970*, Bern: Peter Lang, 2002.
Ridout, Nicholas, *Stage Fright, Animals and Other Theatrical Problems*, Cambridge: Cambridge University Press, 2006.
Tackels, Bruno, *Les Castelluccis*, Besançon: Les Solitaires Intempestifs, 2005.

Articles in English

Castellucci, Romeo, 'The Animal Being on Stage', trans. Carolina Melis, Valentina Valentini and Ric Allsopp, *Performance Research* 5 (2), *On Animals*, ed. Alan Read, 2000, pp. 23–8.
Castellucci, Romeo, 'The Universal: The Simplest Place Possible', interview with Bonnie Marranca and Valentina Valentini, trans. Jane House, *Performing Arts Journal 77*, 2004, pp. 16–25.
Causey, Matthew, 'Stealing from God: The Crisis of Creation in Socìetas Raffaello Sanzio's *Genesi* and Eduardo Kac's *Genesis*', *Theatre Research International* 26, 2001, pp. 199–208.
Escolme, Bridget, 'Performing Human: The Socìetas Raffaello Sanzio', in *Talking to the Audience: Shakespeare, Performance, Self*, London and New York: Routledge, 2005, pp. 126–47.

Fenton, Rose de Wend and Lucy Neal, 'Genesi: From the Museum of Sleep', in *The Turning World: Stories from the London International Festival of Theatre*, London: Calouste Gulbenkian Foundation, 2005, pp. 162–7.

Kear, Adrian, 'The Memory of Promise: Theatre and the Ethic of the Future', in Judie Christie, Richard Gough and Daniel Watt (eds), *A Performance Cosmology*, London and New York: Routledge, 2006, pp. 148–51.

Kelleher, Joe, 'Ethics of Voice: In Conversation with Claudia Castellucci and Chiara Guidi', *Performance Research* 9 (4), *On Civility*, ed. Alan Read, 2004, pp. 111–15.

Kelleher, Joe, 'The Suffering of Images', in Adrian Heathfield (ed.), *Live: Art, Performance and the Contemporary*, London: Tate Books, 2004, pp. 190–5.

Kelleher, Joe, 'Falling Out of the World: In Rome with Freud, a Friend, Moses and Socìetas Raffaello Sanzio', *Performance Research* 12 (2), *On the Road*, ed. Paul Rae and Martin Welton, 2007, pp. 35–41.

Ridout, Nicholas, 'Animal Labour in the Theatrical Economy', *Theatre Research International* 29, 2004, pp. 57–65.

Ridout, Nicholas, 'Tragedy at Home: Socìetas Raffaello Sanzio at Laban', *Performing Arts Journal* 81, 2005, pp. 83–92.

Ridout, Nicholas, 'Make-believe: Socìetas Raffaello Sanzio Do Theatre', in Joe Kelleher and Nicholas Ridout (eds), *Contemporary Theatres in Europe: A Critical Companion*, London and New York: Routledge, 2006, pp. 175–87.

Theater, special issue on SRS, with articles by Romeo Castellucci, Joe Kelleher, Nicholas Ridout and Daniel Sack, ed. Tom Sellar, 37 (3), 2007.

Video

Socìetas Raffaello Sanzio, *Tragedia Endogonidia*, by Romeo Castellucci, Video memory by Cristiano Carloni and Stefano Franceschetti. Music by Scott Gibbons. Rarovideo, 2007.

Related titles from Routledge

Contemporary Theatres in Europe
A Critical Companion

Edited by Joe Kelleher and Nicholas Ridout

Through specific examples, case studies and essays by specialist writers, academics and a new generation of theatre researchers, this collection of specially commissioned essays looks at current theatre practices across Europe.

From *Théâtre du Soleil* to *Societas Raffaello Sanzio*, the authors reconsider the possibilities of theatre practice, its relation to history and location and its place in Europe at the turn of the twenty-first century.

Contemporary Theatres in Europe examines a wide range of topics including:

- mainstream European theatre;
- experimental performance;
- music theatre;
- theatre for children;
- dance theatre.

Tailor-made for students, offering clear examples of different ways of thinking and writing about performance, this is a richly detailed introduction which brings key themes to life for all students of European theatre.

Hb: 978–0–415–32939–2
Pb: 978–0–415–32940–8

Available at all good bookshops.
For ordering and further information please visit:
www.routledge.com.

Forthcoming from Routledge

The Wooster Group Work Book

Edited by Andrew Quick

Described by Ben Brantley in the *New York Times* as 'America's most inspired company,' the Wooster Group has consistently challenged audiences and critics alike with their extraordinary performance works, many of which are now recognised as 'classics' of the contemporary stage.

The Wooster Group Work Book accesses, often for the first time, the company's rehearsal methods and source materials, as well as the creative thinking and reflections of director Elizabeth LeCompte and her main artistic collaborators. Focusing on six performance pieces, Frank Dell's *The Temptation of St. Antony* (1987), *Brace Up!* (1990), *Fish Story* (1994), *House/Lights* (1999) and *To You, the Birdie! (Phèdre)* (2002), this new volume gathers together an astonishing range of archival material to produce a vivid and personal account of how the company makes its work.

This book's intricate layering of journal extracts, actors' notes, stage designs, drawings, performance texts, rehearsal transcriptions, stage managers' logs and stunning photographs traces a unique documentary path across the practice of the Wooster Group, one that will be an indispensable resource for all those with an interest in contemporary performance and its impact on contemporary culture.

Highly accessible to the student, scholar, theatre-goer and practitioner, and including three contextualising essays by Andrew Quick, this book offers a series of remarkable insights into the working practices of one of the world's leading performance companies.

Hb: 978–0–415–35333–5
Pb: 978–0–415–35334–2

Available at all good bookshops.
For ordering and further information please visit:
www.routledge.com.

Related titles from Routledge

Bobby Baker
Redeeming Features of Daily Life

Edited by Michèle Barrett and Bobby Baker

The first full-length book by and about one of the most important performance artists working today, this collection brings together a 'best of' selection of the myriad articles written about Baker's work by various writers and academics including Marina Warner and Griselda Pollock with a narrative about her work by Baker herself in conjunction with renowned feminist critic and writer Michèle Barrett.

Although Baker is wildly funny, there is always a darker, more painful and rebellious side to her work, including themes such as mental illness, of which she has recently 'come out' as a sufferer. Her style is tragicomic, and her oeuvre has been described (by Marina Warner) as the 'theatre of embarrassment'.

Including a unique collection of photos of Baker's work right from when she first started out to the present day, this will be a valuable resource in itself for students, teachers and practitioners.

Hb: 978–0–415–44410–1
Pb: 978–0–415–44411–8

Available at all good bookshops.
For ordering and further information please visit:
www.routledge.com.

Related titles from Routledge

Small Acts of Repair
Performance, Ecology and Goat Island

Edited by Stephen Bottoms and Matthew Goulish

'Small acts of repair. Calming the hands in a troubled world. Restoring damage to renewed use.'

How do you repair?

What is the meeting place of ecology and performance?

What does the impossible look like?

Goat Island are one of the world's leading contemporary performance ensembles. Their intimate, low-tech, intensely physical performances represent a unique hybrid of strategies and techniques drawn from live art, experimental theatre and postmodern dance. *Small Acts of Repair: Performance, Ecology and Goat Island*, is the first book to document and critique the company's performances, processes, politics, aesthetics and philosophies. It reflects on the company's work through the critical lens of ecology – an emerging and urgent concern in performance studies and elsewhere.

This collage text combines and juxtaposes writing by company members and arts commentators, to look in detail at Goat Island's distinctive collaborative processes and the reception of their work in performance. The book includes a section of practical workshop exercises and thoughts on teaching drawn from the company's extensive experience, providing an invaluable classroom resource.

By documenting the creative processes of this extraordinary company, this book will make an important contribution to the critical debates surrounding contemporary performance practices. In so doing, it pays compelling tribute to committed art-making, creativity, collaboration and the nature of the possible.

Hb: 978–0–415–36514–7
Pb: 978–0–415–36515–4

Available at all good bookshops.
For ordering and further information please visit:
www.routledge.com.